THE CRIMINAL BODY

THE CRIMINAL BODY

Lombroso and the Anatomy of Deviance

David G. Horn

Routledge
NEW YORK AND LONDON

Published in 2003 by
Routledge
29 West 35th Street
New York, NY 10001
www.routledge-ny.com

Published in Great Britain by
Routledge
11 New Fetter Lane
London EC4P 4EE
www.routledge.co.uk

10   9   8   7   6   5   4   3   2   1

Library of Congress Cataloging-in-Publication Data

Horn, David G., 1958–
    The criminal body : Lombroso and the anatomy of deviance / David G. Horn.
        p. cm.
Includes bibliographical references.
    ISBN 0-415-94728-6 (alk. paper)—ISBN 0-415-94729-4 (pbk. : alk. paper)
    1. Lombroso, Cesare, 1835–1909.   2. Criminal anthropology—History.
3. Criminal anthropology—Italy—History.   4. Forensic
anthropology—Italy—History.
I. Title.
    HV6035.H67   2003
    364.2′4—dc21   2003008814

For Simon and Graham

Table of Contents

List of Illustrations

Acknowledgments

I have benefited from the suggestions and critical readings of colleagues in a wide variety of disciplines over the last several years; I can only hope that I have been wise enough to heed their advice. Portions of the book were presented at conferences and workshops on "Pain and Suffering in Human History" (Los Angeles, 1998), on "The Criminal and His Scientists" (Florence, 1998), on "Revolution and the Poetics of Identity" (Tel Aviv, 1999), on "Michel Foucault et la médecine" (Caen, 1999), and on "The Italian City" (London, 2000). I am grateful to the organizers for their invitations, and for the responses of Philippe Artières, Peter Becker, Luc Berlivet, Jane Caplan, Frédéric Chauvaud, Daniel Defert, Elisabeth Domansky, Greg Eghigian, Gabriel Finkelstein, John Foot, Peter Fritzsche, Mary Gibson, Jan Goldstein, Igal Halfin, David Hoffmann, Peter Holquist, David Hoyt, Pierre Lascoumes, David Millet, Marcia Meldrun, Laurent Mucchielli, Ted Porter, Nicole Rafter, Francisco Vazquez Garcia, and Richard Wetzell. Ivan Crozier, Otniel Dror, Chris Forth, Jonathan Xavier Inda, Peter Redfield, Jenny Terry, Jackie Urla, and two anonymous readers provided insightful readings of sections of the manuscript.

I am grateful, too, for the patient support of my colleagues in the Department of Comparative Studies—Eric Allman, Philip Armstrong, Katey Borland, Luz Calvo, Xiaomei Chen, Gene Holland,

Abiola Irele, Nancy Jesser, Lindsay Jones, Tom Kasulis, Jill Lane, Rick Livingston, Margaret Lynd, Sylvia McDorman, Frank Proaño, Dan Reff, Brian Rotman, Barry Shank, Maurice Stevens, Thuy Linh Tu, Hugh Urban, Julia Watson, and Sabra Webber—and in the College of Humanities—especially Michael Hogan, Jacqueline Royster, and Chris Zacher. The research for this book was supported by a fellowship from the American Council of Learned Societies and by a Grant-in-Aid from the College of Humanities at The Ohio State University. Thanks to Ilene Kalish and Priti Gress for their interest in this project, and to Nikki Hirschman, Donna Capato, and Salwa Jabado for helping it through to completion.

Finally, thanks to Graham and Simon for being nothing like the children Lombroso imagined, and to Victoria, for her wisdom, humor, and inspiring example.

1

Bodies of Evidence

"The scandalous notion . . . of *dangerousness* means the individual must be considered by society at the level of his virtualities, and not at the level of his acts."
—Michel Foucault, "La vérité et les formes juridiques" (1973)

I. Introduction: Deviant Science

This volume traces, following a variety of genealogical threads, the history of our turning to the criminal body, and of the very idea that bodies can testify (or be made to testify) to legal and scientific truths. The book is focused on nineteenth-century Italy, the site of emergence of a family of discourses and techniques intended to qualify and quantify the bodies of dangerous persons: criminal anthropology, legal psychiatry, and forensic medicine. In each field, though with some important differences, the body was made an index of the interior states and dispositions of suspected individuals, a sign of the evolutionary status of groups, and a more or less reliable indicator of present and future risks to society. Bodies were measured, manipulated, shocked, sketched, photographed, and displayed in order that judges, penologists, educators, and social planners might be guided in the identification and treatment of individuals, and in the development of appropriate measures of social prophylaxis.

This book participates, a full century later, in a renewal of interest in the body-as-evidence, but seeks to problematize this fascination (in the academy, in the laboratory, and in courts of law) by writing its history. Neither a comprehensive account of Italian social sciences, nor a biographical study of their founders, it is organized around particular kinds of *worrying over, interrogation of,* and *faith in* the body. It aims, in this way, to make provisional sense of our continued efforts to generate truths from the surfaces and depths of bodies. At the same time, this book is intended as a contribution to historical and cultural studies of science. It works to situate sciences of deviance (and the practices and technologies these engendered) in particular historical and cultural contexts, and to read sciences now marked as illegitimate or pseudo-scientific in relation to those that have become canonical (evolutionary biology, physiology, biological anthropology, ethnography.) Only such a blurring or transgressing of comfortable boundaries makes it possible, for example, to locate criminal anthropology in relation to the emergence of new reading practices (penile plethysmography, facial thermography, PET scans, the "decoding" of the human genome) that seek to make human difference and dangerousness legible.

With rare exceptions, Italian criminal sciences have not figured in the origin stories anthropologists—even Italian anthropologists—have told about themselves.[1] This is not because the anthropology of the criminal body was, during the last half of the nineteenth century, on the margins of the "science of man." Indeed, the newly formed discursive field of general anthropology (one could not yet call it a discipline) did not have a well-defined core and periphery, but rather multiple centers for the production of knowledge about human identity and difference. Much of the publication of "anthropological" research went on in the acts and proceedings of local and regional scientific and medical societies. At the same time, anthropology aspired to be a totalizing science, and when the first Italian journal in the field began publication in Florence in 1871,[2] it was host to articles on folklore, archaeology, ethnology, philology, evolutionary biology, and criminology. If some of the authors of these articles no longer count as ancestors, it is because the discipline has, in Italy as elsewhere, fragmented over the last hundred years, and in the process has sought to distance itself from elements of its past.[3]

Criminal anthropology has not fared much better in the discipline of history of science, which has not found it worthy even of the attention given to alchemy, astrology, or phrenology. Instead, criminal anthropology has been limited to a supporting role in a cautionary tale about deviant or spurious science; it has been invoked either to make visible the differences between impure and pure ways of knowing, or else to reassure us of the ability of real science to police its borders or to straighten the path to truth. The most familiar account to English readers is no doubt Stephen Jay Gould's treatment in *The Mismeasure of Man*. Although Gould is at pains not "to contrast evil determinists who stray from the path of scientific objectivity with enlightened antideterminists who approach data with an open mind and therefore see truth," he is unable to resist taking a mocking distance from the work of the criminal anthropologists, labeling the discipline as "pseudoscience" and its arguments as "scientifically vacuous."[4] For others, the statistical criticism of Charles Goring (1870–1919) is seen to have struck a final, mortal blow to the scientific pretensions of criminal anthropology.[5]

Finally, within social history, the work of Italian anthropologists has been positioned as fundamentally at odds with ethnographic and sociological approaches to crime and other social phenomena, particularly as these developed in France. This binary was first established in debates between the "Italian" and "French" schools of criminology at the end of the nineteenth century—largely at a series of international conferences—but has been reinforced by the historiography of the 1970s and 1980s.[6] In the most whiggish tellings, the crude and reductive Italian anthropologists, obsessively and excessively focused on the deviant bodies of criminals, are roundly (and forever) defeated by the more subtle French sociologists, attentive to milieu and environment.[7]

Although comparisons between Italian and French criminologies have been productive, more recent historical work—occasioned perhaps by an erosion of our confidence that "nurture" did, in fact, triumph over "nature"—has revealed a variety of problems with this familiar and comforting story.[8] First, the binary opposition of the French and the Italians has worked to obscure differences and debates *within* both "schools," which were never as coherent as the term implies (in Italy anthropologists fought not only with classical jurists, as we will see below, but also with other scientists for the right to speak authoritatively about the bodies of criminals). To be sure, these labels had *rhetorical* force at the end of the nineteenth century. For the Italians, to affirm the existence of an "Italian school" (a name that was, for its self-proclaimed members, synonymous with the "scientific school," the "positive school," the "modern school," and the "new school") was to aspire for international recognition at a historical moment when the marginalization of the Italian sciences was acutely felt.[9] For the French, meanwhile, to set oneself against the "Italian school" was to link the fate of a broad range of heterogeneous claims made by Italian human scientists to the reputation of one man (Lombroso) and one theoretical construct (the born criminal).

The accounts of social historians have likewise tended to minimize or obscure assumptions and approaches *shared* by the French and the Italians, at a time when there was in fact considerable porosity of both disciplinary and national boundaries.[10] We have thus lost sight both of the French (and British and German) attention to the body of the criminal, as well as the sociological imagination at work in Italian anthropologies of criminals: the notions of social defense, the role of doctors and hygienists in surveys of health in urban areas, and the ethnographic work undertaken by criminal anthropologists in Italy and other parts of the world.[11]

Finally, the comparison has, in foregrounding tensions at the level of *theory*, downplayed the significance of criminological *practices*—experiments, instruments, techniques of collection and display, measures of prevention and social defense—that circulated throughout and beyond Europe.

II. Texts and Bodies

Although this book is focused on the books and journals of Cesare Lombroso (1835–1909), it does not purport to offer an intellectual biography. Instead, Lombroso stands in, sometimes awkwardly, for a whole discursive or epistemic formation.[12] The various editions of *L'uomo delinquente* [Criminal Man] and the journal *Archivio di psichiatria, antropologia criminale e scienze penali* [Archive of Psychiatry, Criminal Anthropology, and Penal Sciences][13] were, much like the bodies of criminals, dense transfer points and generative sites of intersection. If anyone ever doubted the messiness of science-in-the-making,[14] the bulky, unwieldy, editions of *L'uomo delinquente* are proof enough. On one hand, they appear to have grown by simple accretion rather than by incorporation; as we follow the expansion of this foundational text from one volume of 225 pages in 1876 to four volumes totaling almost 2,000 pages in 1896–1897, it is striking to see how little Lombroso revises.[15] The result is a heterogeneous text, full of contradictions, inconsistencies, and errors. The work is at once organized by an ambition to build a totalizing science of criminal man, animated by an insatiable hunger to know (to measure, to collect, to probe, to categorize) and held together by the naive hope that knowledge is additive or cumulative.

Lombroso's books are noteworthy less for their defensive armatures than for the porosity of their boundaries.[16] The texts, and along with them the pages of the journals and the proceedings of international conferences, are therefore wonderful places to explore the traffic in measurements, photographs and drawings, graphs and tables, arguments, and statements produced in the libraries and laboratories of scholars as diverse as Charles Darwin, Francis Galton, Camillo Golgi, Angelo Mosso, Bernard Perez, Giuseppe Pitrè, Moritz Schiff, Rudolf Virchow, Richard von Krafft-Ebing, Emil DuBois-Reymond, and Carl Ludwig. At the same time, Lombroso's own productions (data, photos, theories) travel outward to reappear in a wide range of texts in a variety of disciplines, in and beyond Western Europe. The point is not that all of these authors were allies of Lombroso or aligned with his theories. Instead, they may have shared with him nothing more than a fascination with the diagnostic or therapeutic possibilities of electricity, a faith in the reliable working of certain graphical recording devices or in the power of statistics to uncover social facts, or a commitment to the experimental method in physiology. They may have been linked to Lombroso by nothing other than an international trade in scientific instruments, handwriting samples, or parts of skeletons.

At times, it must appear that nothing held together the assembled materials but the covers of the volumes themselves. But, as Latour reminds us, and as we will have occasion to see, a considerable amount of work (and not only rhetorical) was involved in trying to make these texts cohere, to hold everything together under the umbrella of a new discipline, and to have it all count as science.[17] The work involved not only building networks among persons, laboratories, instruments, and bodies that could result in durable facts; it was also about resisting the efforts of others to sever these links, and in particular to remove from the network (from the physiology laboratory, from the anthropology journal) the criminal body. That work becomes visible if we read horizontally—out from the *Archivio* and *L'uomo delinquente* to other texts with which it is in some unstable communication—rather than vertically. Our concern will not be to establish priorities or to trace the chronological development of the discipline, but precisely to make visible the (often chaotic) circulation and (often unstable) linking together of knowledges, practices, and bodies.

Finally, we must remember that the bodies of criminals and of "honest" persons were not passive, not simply sites for the intersection of scientific discourses and practices. On one hand, although the criminal body may have been constituted as a text to be read, it was frequently imagined to resist the exegesis of both lay and professional readers, or to be only partially legible. On the other hand, especially in physiological research, the body was assumed to be actively involved in the production of anthropological knowledge; in particular, it was imagined to testify against itself. Indeed, much of the anthropologists' interest was in the ways the body might *give itself away*—by writing, by gestures, by movements—if the scientist only knew how to prompt it, or to get out of its way (Figure 1.1). We may be joined with the past by a certain kind of anxious faith in the body—in its potential to signal social dangers, and in its habit of testifying or confessing.

III. From Crimes to Criminals

Italian criminal anthropology positioned itself as a modern, scientific discourse and practice, with links not only to evolutionary theory, but also (and perhaps more important) to the emergence of the science of statistics, which had enabled both the "discovery" of social facts and the identification of populations as appropriate objects of scientific knowledge and government.[18] The production of "the criminal"—and, more specifically, the criminal body—as objects of knowledge in late-nineteenth-century human sciences was dependent on technologies of counting and calculation that had worked to reconfigure crime as a social and scientific problem: a patterned and predictable consequence of social life, rather than the sum total of individual acts threatening the sovereignty of law or the king. Just as "the knowledge of the calculus of the probability of human life" had given rise to societies of life insurance, Lombroso observed, "the knowledge of the perpetual

1. P. C., brigante della Basilicata, detenuto a Pesaro.   2. Ladro piemontese.

3. Incendiario cinedo di Pesaro,   4. Misdea.
sopranominato *la donna.*

TIPI DI DELINQUENTI ITALIANI.

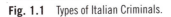

Fig. 1.1 Types of Italian Criminals.

succession, in given epochs, of homicides, thefts, suicides, etc." had begun to modify profoundly the "semi-barbarous" ideas of "juridical experts."[19] Crime had, in effect, become a "risk" that human scientists proposed to manage through knowledge of statistical laws and a new attention to the bodies typical of criminals.

Criminal anthropology's reliance on practices of quantification was, for Lombroso, one sign of the science's modernity. For some historians, he noted, the progress of modern civilization could be traced to the discovery and mastery of marvelous machines that had reduced temporal or spatial distances. For other, "more myopic," commentators, progress consisted of the triumph of certain principles: freedom of thought, nationalism, or universal suffrage. For Lombroso, what truly distinguished the modern era from all that had come before was the triumph of "the number" over the "vague opinions, prejudices, and vain theories" that had circulated from the folk to the learned community and back again. Among these was the conviction—shared by the masses and the greatest physiologists and psychologists—that there was an "immeasurable abyss" between the world of "life and intelligence" and the world of "brute materiality." But numbers, he observed in a volume on weather and mental illness, had been able to bridge the abyss, entering "with their marvelous power" even into the "mysterious world of life and the intellect."[20]

In a preface to his 1869 translation of the physiologist Jacob Moleschott's (1822–1893) volume on the "circulation of life," Lombroso celebrated the penetration of a quantifying materialism into even the moral sciences:

> Moral statistics, now rather aptly named social physics, demonstrated the succession, at determined days and months and hours, of marriages, births, deaths, suicides, murders—acts that many believed depended on the free will of man or on providential will; they revealed that there is in their unfolding a natural necessity, a complete regularity like the movement of the stars and the seasons and, in fact, dependent to a great extent on these.[21]

Numbers had shown crime to be "an unfortunate natural production, a form of disease, which demanded treatment and isolation rather than penalty and vendetta." Although it might have threatened human vanity to discover that the weather, for example, played a role in crime, genius, or madness, this knowledge offered, for the first time, a means "to prevent and treat" crime.[22]

For Lombroso, the second mark of the modernity of criminal anthropology was a new focus on the criminal imagined as a sick or monstrous person. Indeed the "positive school" of criminology sought to distinguish itself from its predecessor and rival, the "classical school," by this shift of objects: from the crime to the criminal and his or her environment.[23] The classical school, which most commentators traced back to the work of Cesare Beccaria (1738–1794), had operated at the intersection of legal code, criminal act, and penalty.[24] The juridical and moral problem at the center of Beccaria's liberal penal reform was to establish just (that is, uniform and nonarbitrary) punishments for specified offenses. As Lombroso's daughter and collaborator Gina Lombroso-Ferrero (1872–1944) put it, the classical school "aimed only at establishing sound judgments and fixed laws to guide capricious and often undiscerning judges in the application of penalties." All criminals were presumed to be "endowed with intelligence and feelings like normal individuals," and were imagined to "commit misdeeds consciously, being prompted thereto by their unrestrained desire for evil."[25] What varied instead was the gravity of the offense, and this in turn regulated the severity of sentences. If the personality of the criminal was left "in the background," this was because classical jurisprudence was concerned only with establishing the fact of a crime, the legal identity of the individual to be punished, and in unusual cases, with establishing his or her degree of legal responsibility—that is, his or her *capacity* freely to will the commission of the offense. This capacity could be diminished, for example, by being insane, drunk, a minor, or a deaf-mute.[26]

The new anthropological school centered instead on the two main poles of society (imagined as an object of prophylaxis and defense) and the criminal (imagined as a dangerous individual).[27] On the one hand, the positivists expressed a new concern with statistical regularities (including, as we will see in the next chapter, regular regional differences). Lawyer and positive sociologist Enrico Ferri (1856–1929) complained that the classical school had not been able to explain why there were 3,000 murders every year in Italy, and not 300 or 300,000: "No one, from Beccaria to [Francesco] Carrara, has ever thought of this problem,

Fig. 1.2 Head of a Criminal Epileptic.

and they could not have asked it, considering their point of departure and their method."[28] The goal of criminology, in contrast to classical penology, was to defend society against the "natural necessity" of crime.

On the other hand, the anthropologists argued it was necessary to take account of the social dangerousness of individual offenders. "It is not the criminal who wills," wrote Ferri. "In order to be a criminal it is rather necessary that the individual should find himself permanently or transitorily in such personal, physical and moral conditions, and live in such an environment, which becomes for him a chain of cause and effect, externally and internally, that disposes him toward crime."[29] Positive criminologists proposed replacing the classical school's typology of crimes, which Ferri termed a "juridical anatomy" of deeds,[30] with a typology of criminals and, as we will see, an anatomy of deviant and dangerous bodies grounded in scientific measurements (Figure 1.2). As Lombroso-Ferrero put it, "the 'modern' school maintains that the anti-social tendencies of criminals are the result of their physical and psychic organization, which differs essentially from that of normal individuals; and it aims at studying the morphology and various functional phenomena of the criminal with the object of curing, instead of punishing him." Criminal anthropology could, she proposed, be glossed as "the natural history of the criminal," because it embraced "his organic and psychic constitution and social life, just as anthropology [did] in the case of normal human beings and the different races."[31]

Criminal anthropologists sought to break classical theory's link between responsibility and practices of punishment or social defense. As one commentator remarked, the issue was not to learn whether an individual was culpable or responsible—these were "philosophical" questions—but "whether he is dangerous or not and to what degree."[32] Lombroso's collaborator Baron Raffaele Garofalo (1851–1934) argued that the social dangerousness (*temibilità*) of an individual might, in fact, be greatest when his or her legal responsibility (*imputabilità*) was least.[33] Indeed, for the first time, one could be a criminal (that is, a danger to society) without having committed a crime,[34] something that had been literally unthinkable for the classical school. This "social" construction of the problem of criminality implied a new regime of judicial and governmental practices that obeyed a double logic of diagnosis and prevention. Criminologists called for the elimination of juries, who would not be competent to weigh medical evidence or calculate social risks, and charged judges with making minute "anthropological" investigations.[35] The anthropological problem, as Garofalo put it, was to determine "in what manner and to what degree it is necessary for the health of society to limit the rights of delinquents."[36] Remedies and penalties, meanwhile, were to give way to practices of surveillance, preventive detention, and parole, and to proposals for making talented criminals "serviceable to civilization."[37] Vagabonds, Lombroso suggested, might be used to colonize wild and unhealthy regions; murderers might perform surgery or serve in the military; and swindlers might pursue police work or journalism.[38] These interventions depended in turn on estimations of the social risks posed by particular kinds of individuals; specific crimes figured merely as "indications" of dangerousness.[39] In the end, the Italian criminologists demanded nothing less than "a putting aside of legality—a true 'de-penalization' of crime."[40]

Attention to bodies, Lombroso argued, promised to deliver criminology from what he termed the idealism and "metaphysics" of the classical school. His anthropology shared with other nineteenth-century scientific (and political) projects the assumption that only the body could ground and locate difference.[41] In particular, a science of bodies promised to make intelligible the "dangerousness" that was the object of the new criminological discourse, but which threatened to remain invisible. Lombroso argued that the criminal was linked by his abnormal anatomy and physiology to the insane person and the epileptic, as well as to those other "others" who were constituted as the objects of the human sciences: apes, children, women, prehistoric humans, and contemporary "savages."

For Lombroso, the criminal was, in his body and conduct, an "atavism"—a reemergence of the historical and evolutionary pasts in the present. As we will see in Chapter 2, the pederast was tied by his unnatural desires to Periclean Athens as surely as the Italian murderer was tied by his violent, bloodthirsty acts to the Australian aborigine.[42] The slang of criminals was said to recall primitive languages,[43] the artwork of criminals to recall Australian handicrafts, and the hand-writing of criminals to recall pictography and hieroglyphics.[44] Finally, behaviors such as tattooing and "sexual excesses," and morphological features such as the slope of the forehead and the shape of the ears, linked criminals to lower forms of animal life, as well as to children and savages. Among the latter, criminal behavior would be identified as "natural," indeed "normal."[45]

IV. The Testifying Body

In the late nineteenth century, the body was, of course, a point of inter-section of multiple scientific, medical, and folk discourses. As we will see in Chapter 3, Lombroso occasionally drew on the sciences of phys-iognomy and phrenology, which had purported to find signs of interior intellectual and moral states on the body's surfaces, particularly at the level of the head and the face.[46] However, Lombroso rejected what he termed the "qualitative and deterministic"[47] readings of the phre-nologists in favor of physiological experiment, anatomo-pathological investigations, and anthropometry—the precise measurement of the dimensions and relations of parts of the body, a practice that had been joined to social statistics by Adolphe Quetelet (1796–1874).[48] Quantifying readings promised both to make known and manageable potential dangers, and to specify the social, historical and evolutionary place of the criminal body.

Lombroso's attitude toward anthropometry was, however, somewhat equivocal. Early in his criminological career, Lombroso "professed a firm faith in anthropometry, especially cranial anthropometry, as an ark of salvation from the metaphysical, à priori systems dear to all those engaged on [sic] the study of Man." But if he had once imagined that this practice of anatomical measurement could be "the backbone, the whole framework indeed, of the new human statue of which he was at the time attempting the creation," he later learned the vanity of this hope.[49] Lombroso had anticipated that measurements of dead and living bodies would reveal correlations between criminal dangerousness and such mundane features as body weight, height, proportions of the limbs, and cranial capacity. Many of his studies would, however, reveal only minute differences, useless for the identification of dangerous individuals.[50] But if Lombroso would, over the years, reduce his reliance on anthropometry (and especially on craniometry)—supplementing it with the study of anomalies and with physiological experiments—he continued to measure throughout his career, and to collect and tabulate the measurements of others.

The anthropometrical data reproduced in the pages of L'uomo delinquente are, if nothing else, traces of an obsessive poring over the criminal body. Although the first edition included, for example, measurements from 55 crania, the fifth edition reported the results of examinations of 689.[51] Lombroso and colleagues throughout Europe had measured or calculated the cranial capacity, the cerebral capacity, the circumference, the anterior and posterior semicircumferences, the anterior projections, arches and curves, the vertical index, the frontal index, the craniomandibular index, the width and height of the face, the nasal index, the mandibular diameter, the capacity of the occipital fora, the orbital capacity, the cephalospinal and cephalo-orbital indices, the facial angle, and the spinomalar distance (the distance from the anterior inferior nasal spina to the zygomatic tubercle on both sides of the face). Finally, they had classified the skulls based on the cephalic index (the ratio of the maximum width of the skull to the maximum length), dividing them into such categories as dolicocephalic, mesocephalic, brachycephalic, and ultrabrachycephalic.[52]

Another set of readings of these skulls sought to identify cranial *anomalies*. The most frequently found lesions were protruding supercilliary arches (46.7 percent) and anomalous development of the wisdom teeth (44.6 percent); the least frequent malformations included a low and narrow forehead (10 percent), trochocephaly (abnormally round head) (9.0 percent), and oxycephaly (pointed head) (4.5 percent). Most important, noted Lombroso, was the fact that 43 percent of the skulls had a "completely teratological aspect," uniting several atypical features in a single cranium, whereas only 21 percent had an isolated anomaly.[53] "Is it possible," Lombroso asked his readers, "that individuals who accumulate such enormous series of alterations have the same grade of intelligence and affectivity as men with perfectly normal crania?"[54]

Anthropologists also measured living criminals, as well as the bodies of the mentally ill, epileptics, prostitutes, and "normal" men, women, and children; by 1896, a total of 6,608 criminals (French, German, and Italian) were included in Lombroso's four volumes. Lombroso noted that there was inevitable imprecision in measuring the living, but he still found that the collected data were useful for confirming his conclusions.[55] Measurements and estimations of pathological anatomical structures on the head were not limited to the cranium, but included also the shape and relations of the ears, nose, eyes, and mouth. And though, as "the seat of all the greatest disturbances," the head "naturally manifest[ed] the greatest number of anomalies,"[56] studies were extended to the whole of the body. Anthropologists measured the height and weight, the reach of the arms, the circumference of the chest, the length of the fingers, and the width of the space between the toes (see below). They noted the presence or absence of beards, the prevalence of gray hair and baldness (both very rare among criminals, epileptics, and cretins, and linked to their "reduced emotional sensibility"), and cataloged a whole series of anomalies, including defects at the cellular level.

Lombroso acknowledged that some anomalous features of the criminal body were not inherited but due to patterns of behavior. He attributed the higher frequency of wrinkles on the faces of criminals, for example, to their habit of cynical laughter. Moreover, wrinkles of criminals tended to be confined to the nose and mouth, the most "material" and "least contemplative" regions of the face.[57] While the bulging eyeballs and the pallid faces of some criminals were, Lombroso speculated, effects of cerebral hyperemia, the thinness of the lips could be credited to the particular arrangement of the mouth during repeated expressions of hatred.[58] Repetitive facial expressions (i.e., the clenching of the jaw in anticipation of a violent physical effort or an act of revenge) accounted also for the larger mandibles of criminals: "It is easy to understand how the prolonged repetition of these contractions must cause the muscles and the bony parts to which they are attached to grow."[59] But Lombroso suggested many other anomalies could be accounted for only by atavistic regressions or the arrested development of the fetus. These included, for example, the presence of downy hair on the forehead, the exaggerated development of the frontal sinuses, or the absence of a beard—all of which helped to explain that "the Mongol or Lapp type reproduced almost exactly that of the Italian born criminal."[60]

Sometimes the typical features of criminal bodies might have appeared straightforwardly meaningful. For example, the criminals with the largest cranial circumference and capacity tended to be criminal bosses, counterfeiters, or famous con artists, whereas pickpockets tended to have long hands.[61] But what could have been the meaning of fact that the bizygomatic width was lowest in purse snatchers, or that murderers had long faces?[62] Indeed, Lombroso elaborated a whole series of "subspecies" of criminals with characteristic features: assassins with voluminous mandibles, widely spaced zygomae, black and thick hair, scanty beards, and pale faces; rapists with short hands, low median cephalic indices, narrow foreheads, blond hair, and anomalies of the genitals and nose; arsonists with low body weight, long extremities, and small and anomalous heads; con men with large mandibles and cheekbones, elevated weight, pale and frequently paretic faces.[63]

But although Lombroso and others proposed correlations between particular measurements and certain kinds of criminality, the connection was not usually imagined to be *causal*. Instead, the anomalies were the signs of something else (atavism, degeneration, social danger), and thus played a part in a medical *semiology*. Comparing the anomalies found in criminals to those found among cretins, Lombroso's daughter noted that:

In neither case have the anomalies an *intrinsic importance*, since they are neither the cause of the anti-social tendencies of the criminal nor of the mental deficiencies of the cretin. They are the *outward signs* of a mysterious and complicated process of degeneration, which in the case of the criminal evokes evil impulses that are largely of atavistic origin.[64]

Measurements and catalogs of anomalies served to locate the criminal body in relation to other bodies imagined as dangerous or underdeveloped, and to announce the danger of individuals to those qualified to read the text of the criminal body.

Further complicating these readings was the fact that only a small percentage of criminals, by Lombroso's count, bore the traces of the "criminal type." Although the criminal's body made visible and legible (in a relatively unambiguous, unmediated fashion) the degeneration of the *race*,[65] it was a sign of the *individual's* social dangerousness only in a statistical, probabilistic sense. Lombroso would eventually conclude that fewer than 40 percent of convicted male criminals had any physical anomalies, and still fewer bore the combination of factors (the "criminal type") that was considered a reliable predictor of dangerous conduct.[66] Indeed, the seemingly infinite possible combinations of signs of atavism and degeneration frustrated the effort to construct typologies and taxonomies, and Lombroso struggled in his writings to find the appropriate metaphor to capture the relation between physical difference and dangerousness. At times, Lombroso referred to anomalies as notes in a musical chord: the isolated anomaly had to be taken together with other physical and moral notes for the criminal type to take shape.[67] This musical metaphor was, in turn, linked to a modern notion of visibility. Lombroso compared patterns of atavism to impressionist paintings: "examined from up close, they seem shapeless, colored blotches, while at a distance they prove to be wonderful."[68] A wide (statistical) perspective was necessary for any image of the criminal to emerge.

V. Practices of Individuation: Signaletics and Semiology

Readers of Lombroso's texts were invited to make precisely such a move when they encountered photographs and drawings of criminals. The first edition of *L'uomo delinquente* included eighteen images (none of them photographs); by the fifth edition Lombroso had assembled enough graphical materials to publish a separate atlas. The goal of the atlas, Lombroso wrote, was to "offer the reader the means to verify, on his own, the truth of [his] assertions."[69] The atlas, he argued, was not only an integral part of the larger work, but "the most important" part. Because it included materials (photographs, graphs, maps, handwriting samples, sketches of tattoos) produced or collected by other scientists, there could be no accusation of an interested selection. Instead, Lombroso's critics would see that, despite their "sterile protests," the evidence for the existence of the criminal type was continually accumulating; the assembled images "spoke against [his opponents] more than any other kind of demonstration."[70] Of course, Lombroso acknowledged, some skeptics would *choose* not to see:

One hopes in vain to make the blind see colors, still less those who pretend to be blind in order not to see. It would be like deciphering music for a deaf person, who sees only black marks without significance.[71]

In the atlas and in the various editions of *La donna delinquente* [The Criminal Woman] even the lay reader was invited to scrutinize the assembled photographs (Figure 1.3). Although in some sense the pictures were constructed to "speak for themselves,"[72] and were presumed to tell the truth of male and female criminality, readers were addressed repeatedly and directly in the text. They were urged to observe particular numbered photographs and to note, for example, a "vile, repulsive air"; "oblique glances"; heavy jaws; rudimentary breasts; hair that was black and thick; and lips that were coarse, full, cracked, or sensual.[73] In short, readers were invited to read for themselves the criminal texts.[74] But if the reliance on photographs signals the importance of visual exegesis in Lombroso's anthropology, it is also important to remember that Lombroso deployed images in *particular ways* and invited *particular kinds* of readings. Although his texts reproduced police photographs—including mug shots from Germany, France, Russia, and the United States—he put these to new and very different uses.[75]

As Allan Sekula has noted, photographs were central to a variety of attempts to manage social dangers in the nineteenth century, from the nominalist "criminalistics" of Alphonse Bertillon (1853–1914), seeking

ALBUM DI DELINQUENTI TEDESCHI.

Fig. 1.3 Album of German Criminals.

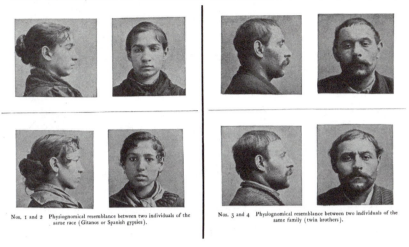

Plate 60 b **NON-IDENTITY OF INDIVIDUALS, WITH PHYSIOGNOMICAL RESEMBLANCE**

Nos. 1 and 2   Physiognomical resemblance between two individuals of the same race (Gitanos or Spanish gypsies).

Nos. 3 and 4   Physiognomical resemblance between two individuals of the same family (twin brothers).

Fig. 1.4   Non-Identity of Individuals, with Physiognomical Resemblance.

knowledge and mastery of individual criminals, to the realist criminology of Francis Galton (1822–1911), seeking knowledge and mastery of the "criminal type."[76] Lombroso's project differed in crucial respects from both of these. Many of the photographs Lombroso reproduced had been collected as part of an effort, usually credited to Bertillon, to document individual offenders.[77] This medicolegal project was essentially liberal or classical: the goal was to fix the legal or civil identity of suspected and convicted criminals, and to link specific individuals with specific infractions of the law. Bertillon's project, which he named "signaletics," aimed at a system of classification that would avoid mistaken prosecutions and that would assure the identification and appropriate punishment of recidivists.[78]

By the end of the nineteenth century, many would find fault with Bertillon's reliance on the photograph as a means of identification. For example, Italian criminologists Giovanni Gasti and Umberto Ellero documented the "multiple and grave errors" that photography could cause concerning "individual somatic characteristics." They concluded that police services could not rely on photography alone: "even a photograph executed with the rigor of the Bertillon method is not sufficient for record-keeping and identification if it is not accompanied by a scrupulous and exact description."[79] Bertillon would himself come to a similar conclusion (see Figure 1.4), eventually supplementing his photographs with anthropometrical measurements of several parts of the body, and later with verbal descriptions of offenders.[80]

But Lombroso engaged and sought to deploy photographs differently, substituting a semiological or diagnostic reading for the "signaletic" practices of Bertillon. For positivist anthropologists, photographs served to make visible the atavistic or pathological aspects of dangerous individuals, who might or might not have transgressed the law. In this sense the criminological interest in the photograph differed from any possible criminalistic interest. Lombroso was certainly not indifferent to the problems of the police sciences; indeed several of his colleagues published important treatises in the field.[81] But the goal of the readings Lombroso performed—and invited others to perform— in the pages of *L'uomo delinquente* was not *identification*; it was instead the *recognition* of dangerousness. Signaletics and the semiology of dangerousness each engaged the individual body in a particular way.[82] Thus, for example, we can compare the photographs of ears included in Bertillon's book (Figure 1.5) with the woodcut of the "criminal ear" included in Lombroso's *Criminal Man* (Figure 1.6); although the first were intended to aid in the accurate identification of individual offenders, the second is meant to stand as an example of the atavistic and anomalous features typical of the bodies of dangerous individuals.[83]

In Lombroso's writings, although the photographs ostensibly were included simply as verifications of arguments made on the basis of anthropometry or pathological anatomy, they also struggled to make concrete and visible the abstract notion of dangerousness.[84] Lombroso's method was, in this respect, also rather different from the "pictorial statistics" elaborated by Francis Galton.[85] Galton, at the suggestion of the Director-General of Prisons Edmund Du Cane (1830–1903), superimposed the photographs of criminals to produce composite images.[86] In the discussion of Galton's paper, Du Cane expressed the hope that the process might enable scientists to establish whether criminals have "certain special types of features"; if so, "the tendency to crime is in those persons born or bred in them, and either they are incurable or the tendency can only be checked by taking them in hand at the earliest periods of life." [87]

Although Lombroso would include examples of Galtonian composites in his books (see Figure 1.7) his own goal was not to construct

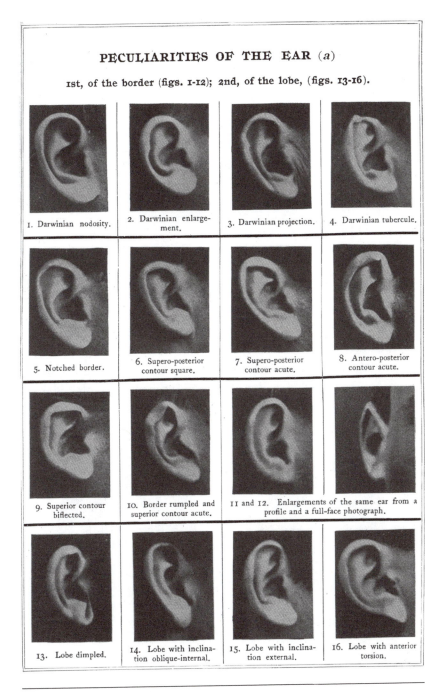

PECULIARITIES OF THE EAR (a)

1st, of the border (figs. 1-12); 2nd, of the lobe, (figs. 13-16).

1. Darwinian nodosity.

2. Darwinian enlargement.

3. Darwinian projection.

4. Darwinian tubercule.

5. Notched border.

6. Supero-posterior contour square.

7. Supero-posterior contour acute.

8. Antero-posterior contour acute.

9. Superior contour biflected.

10. Border rumpled and superior contour acute.

11 and 12. Enlargements of the same ear from a profile and a full-face photograph.

13. Lobe dimpled.

14. Lobe with inclination oblique-internal.

15. Lobe with inclination external.

16. Lobe with anterior torsion.

Fig. 1.5 Peculiarities of the Ear.

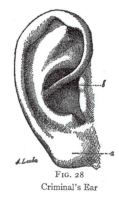

FIG. 28
Criminal's Ear

Fig. 1.6 Criminal's Ear.

---

a composite image of "the criminal," and then to extract typical (in this case average) features, but to identify a range of anomalies and deviations from commonsensical norms that might be used as aids in reading *individual* bodies. In Lombroso's text, unlike in Galton's work, photographs needed to resist what Sekula has called "taming," the transformation of the idiosyncratic into the typical.[88] Although Lombroso ignored or erased the "messy contingency of the photograph,"[89] he was obliged to acknowledge again the rarity of the criminal "type," offering

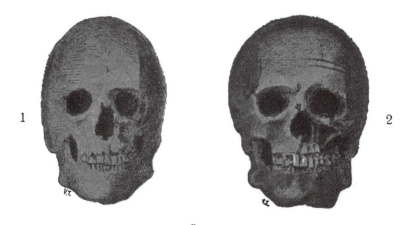

Fotografie composite Galtoniane di crani di delinquenti.

Fig. 1.7 Galtonian Composite Photographs.

up the metaphor of a "physiognomic kinship" to describe the patterned distributions of visible anomalies.[90] Precisely because the "type" was *not common*, it was necessary to multiply rather than collapse or superimpose the pictures of the heads and faces of the dangerous, and to look and read with an attention both to family resemblance and to idiosyncratic difference. In the end, Lombroso's deployment of photographs had more in common with the uses of photography in psychiatry, where it was hoped it could have a diagnostic or semiological function.[91]

A similar story can be told of the fingerprint.[92] In Italy, as elsewhere in Europe, police and forensic scientists used the fingerprint chiefly to fix the legal identity of suspects and to identify recidivists. The fingerprint was imagined to be a corrective to the problems associated with photography, anthropometry, and verbal portraits. But in a pair of studies, psychiatrist Giuseppe d'Abundo (b. 1860) sought evidence of the *anomalous character* of the fingerprints of the mentally ill and criminals.[93] D'Abundo complained in 1891 that the designs of the fingerprints had never before been studied as an object of medical pathology.[94] He found, however, that the designs of the fingertips in each of seven idiots showed a "remarkable" resemblance, such that there is really "only one design for all ten fingers."[95] The author claimed never to have observed this in normal men, and found other anomalies to be common among some criminals. D'Abundo also argued that fingerprint designs could be inherited, and planned to study the relations between fingerprints and sensitivity. Sante De Sanctis (1865–1935) and P. Toscano later found anomalies such as "simplicity of design" and "excessive uniformity" among phrenasthenics and deaf-mutes.[96]

Physician and medicolegal expert Attilio Ascarelli undertook a study of the fingerprints of prostitutes, hoping to confirm that these women exhibited degenerate and pathological characteristics more frequently than their normal counterparts.[97] Ascarelli compared the fingerprints of 100 "professional prostitutes" at the hospital in San Gallicano with those of 200 women of varied professions at the Polyclinic in Rome. Dividing the patterns into "evolved" (Figure 1.8) and "inferior" (as De Sanctis and Toscano had done) Ascarelli found not only that abnormal forms were more frequent among prostitutes (the disparity was greatest for the most primitive designs), but also that

IMPRÕNTE EUÕLVTE

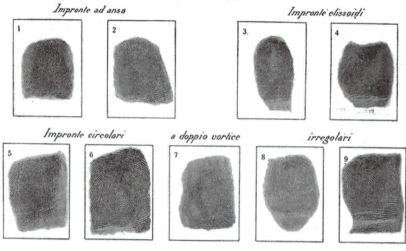

Fig. 1.8   Evolved Fingerprints.

these forms tended to exhibit more uniformity from one finger to the next. All of the evidence appeared to confirm that the professional prostitute was "anthropologically inferior" to the normal woman.

Finally, Lombroso reported that the French anatomist Alix had found that the great apes exhibited a distinctive pattern of papillary ridges that he called a "primitive system." The criminologist René Forgeot (b. 1865) had then examined 1,800 fingers of criminals, finding 416 cases of this primitive design; Charles Féré (1852–1907) had meanwhile found this pattern in 16.8 percent of the epileptics he examined.[98]

Similar projects had been proposed and later abandoned by Henry Faulds (1843–1930), who was interested in the ethnological uses of prints and the heritability of patterns from parents to offspring, and by Galton, who hoped that fingerprints would reveal differences among social classes and races. Galton found instead that "no indications of temperament, character or ability are to be found in finger marks, so far as I have been able to discover."[99] Lombroso was forced to a similar conclusion, but he held out the hope that palm prints might yet reveal links between savages, primates, and criminals (Figure 1.9).

Indeed, as we will see, criminal anthropologists were animated by the hope and expectation that virtually any body part (or physiological response, or gesture, or utterance) could serve to differentiate individuals

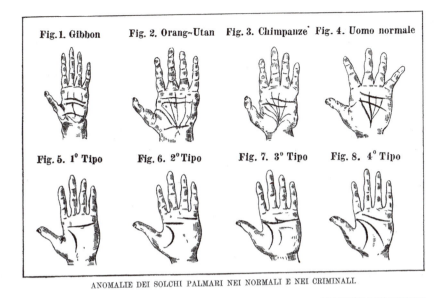

Fig. 1. Gibbon   Fig. 2. Orang-Utan   Fig. 3. Chimpanze   Fig. 4. Uomo normale

Fig. 5. 1° Tipo   Fig. 6. 2° Tipo   Fig. 7. 3° Tipo   Fig. 8. 4° Tipo

ANOMALIE DEI SOLCHI PALMARI NEI NORMALI E NEI CRIMINALI.

Fig. 1.9   Anomalies of the Palm.

and to help estimate social risks. Thus, one of Lombroso's assistants proposed an anthropological classification of fingernails, which could be sorted on the model of skulls (dolico-onychy, brachy-onychy, plagio-onychy, and the like.) Among born criminals and the mentally ill, there was a much higher frequency of morphological anomalies, representing "a deviation from the ethnic ungual type or else a morbid conformation."[100] Not every dangerous body would turn out to be typical, but many were imagined to bear traces that were both legible and quantifiable.

VI. The Argument Ahead

The remainder of this book is devoted to the playing out of the idea that the bodies of criminals—or potential criminals—give themselves away, testifying to their own dangers. The next chapter, "The Savage and the Modern," explores the construction of the criminal body as atavistic. For Lombroso and his contemporaries, fixing the criminal in space and time required ambivalent engagements with Italy's present (imagined as an incomplete modernity) and past. Claims about the atavistic nature of criminality were dependent, finally, not only on evolutionary and national narratives, but also on generative analogies that linked the bodies and behaviors of criminals, animals, children, savages, and women.

Chapter 3, "Making Criminologists," focuses on the production of the criminologist—on the fashioning of a new kind of medicolegal expert qualified to read the deviant body and to diagnose social dangers. Criminology's claims to the status of science were dependent on a political economy of bodies that made them available to practices of discriminating quantification: in the laboratory, the prison, the university lecture hall, and the courtroom the expert would be required to point with some measure of confidence to bodies that were marked off from the normal, that announced their difference and their dangerousness. At the same time, criminal anthropology felt the need to mark its distance from alternative knowledges of embodied dangerousness, including physiognomy, phrenology, folklore, and proverbial wisdom. In the end, the authority of criminological sciences had much to do with the *practical* abilities of physicians and others to regularize tools and measurements, to stabilize mobile readings and interpretations, and to compel—with the aid of graphical instruments—the criminal body to write the evidence of its own difference.

Chapter 4, "The Shock of Recognition," dwells in more detail on techniques and technologies of measurement, paying particular attention to the calculation of thresholds of pain sensitivity in criminals and normal persons. Sensitivity to pain (and pleasure) was imagined by many scientists to be an index of evolutionary progress, of "civilization," and of the relative dangerousness of individuals and groups. In this chapter, we examine how it came to appear commonsensical that the body's suffering and vulnerability could testify to the qualities of populations. We trace the development of the tools and devices (algometers, algesimeters) used to administer graduated electrical shocks to those parts of the body identified as reliable indicators of sensitivity (the hands, the neck and face, and the genitals), and we follow the gendered narratives that reworked relations of physical and moral sensitivity in women and men.

Chapter 5, "Blood Will Tell," explores the ways in which a wide range of new meanings came to be linked to the dilation of blood vessels in the face and other parts of the body. The criminal anthropologist's interest in the reddened face was part of a broad popular and scientific engagement with blushing at the end of the nineteenth century. Movements of blood, like the ability to feel pain, figured in conversations in and outside the biological disciplines about what it meant to be savage or civilized, male or female, black or white. And with the invention by Italian, French, and German physiologists of new instruments to chart changes in blood flow and pressure, it became possible to imagine that one could measure and record traces of the emotions on both the surface and the interior of the body—that one could quantify an emotional potentiality or proficiency. Indeed, the body's vascular system would be reconfigured as an instrument that could, with the aid of inscription devices, *write itself*, registering its perturbations on smoked paper.

The conclusion, "After Lombroso," sketches the fate in the twentieth century of the body Lombroso worked to construct. This is, in part, a story about the unmaking of expertise—about criminal anthropology's failure to shore up its authority in the courtroom, to have its readings of the body pass for scientific common sense. But this is, at the same time, a story about the persistence of scientific practices and social technologies, and about the increasingly porous boundaries between the normal and the pathological. The book ends by suggesting a genealogical connection between nineteenth-century criminology and more recent efforts to make the body testify to its potential to do harm.

The Savage and the Modern

I. Introduction: Origin Stories

Shortly before his death in 1909, Lombroso helped his daughter Gina to prepare a summary of *L'uomo delinquente* for an English-speaking readership. In a brief introduction to the volume, Lombroso offered a narrative of the birth of criminal anthropology that culminated in a visual discovery. The two orienting principles of the new discipline— to study not the crime but the criminal, and to classify the congenital criminal as "an anomaly, partly pathological and partly atavistic, a revival of the primitive savage"—did not, Lombroso advised, "suggest themselves to [him] instantaneously," but were rather "the offspring of a series of impressions."[1] Lombroso pointed first to 1864, when he had been a doctor in the Italian army. Filling his "ample leisure" with examinations of the men with whom he served, Lombroso had been struck by the extent to which the skin of some soldiers was covered by tattoos, as well as by the indecency of the tattoos' designs. He had been excited, too, by the prospect that these surface markings could be used to distinguish "the honest soldier from his vicious comrade," but this idea had "[borne] no fruit."[2]

Two years later, Lombroso had attempted to extend the experimental method to the study of psychiatry, specifically by "applying to the clinical examination of mental alienation the study of the skull, with measurements and weights, by means of the esthesiometer and craniometer." Lombroso reported that he had been encouraged by the results of these experiments to apply the same method to the study of the criminal. Although his measurements proved "useless for determining the differences between criminals and lunatics," they instead indicated a new method for the study of penal jurisprudence. A priori studies of crime in the abstract, Lombroso concluded, should be

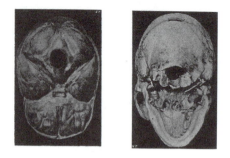

Fig. 2.1   Skull of Villella.

"superseded by the direct analytical study of the criminal, compared with normal people and the insane."[3]

Finally, Lombroso told of an encounter with Giuseppe Villella, an elderly Calabrian peasant who had been imprisoned for theft and arson.[4] Lombroso (we learn elsewhere) had been conducting research for several months in the prisons and asylums of Pavia, on both cadavers and living beings, in an attempt to "fix the substantial differences between madmen and criminals."[5] He had been having little success when he made the acquaintance of "the famous brigand" some days before his death; Lombroso was then charged with performing a post-mortem examination.[6] Laying open Villella's skull, Lombroso noticed a depression in the middle of the occipital part of the skull, which he named the "median occipital fossa."[7] (Figure 2.1) The depression, not typically found in primates but in lower orders such as lemurs and rodents, was accompanied by a "hypertrophy of the *vermis*, known in birds as the middle cerebellum." In an often-quoted passage, Lombroso reported:

> This was not merely an idea, but a revelation. At the sight of that skull, I seemed to see all of a sudden, lighted up as a vast plain under a flaming sky, the problem of the nature of the criminal—an atavistic being who reproduces in his person the ferocious instincts of primitive humanity and the inferior animals. Thus were explained anatomically the enormous jaws, high cheek-bones, prominent superciliary arches, solitary lines in the palms, extreme size of the orbits, handle-shaped or sessile ears found in criminals, savages, and apes, insensibility to pain, extremely acute sight,

tattooing, excessive idleness, love of orgies, and the irresistible craving for evil for its own sake, the desire not only to extinguish life in the victim, but to mutilate the corpse, tear its flesh, and drink its blood.[8]

Historians have tended to discount the significance of this origin story, in part because it contains several exaggerations and inconsistencies.[9] If we compare the 1871 article in which Lombroso first reported the examination of Villella with later texts in which the exam figures as a turning point in the formation of the discipline, we find that the month, the year, the conditions of the examination—even the spelling of the brigand's name—vary considerably. Most remarkable, perhaps, is the transformation Villella himself undergoes: a "miserable" 69-year-old, whose body was contorted by the pains of rheumatism and who was dying from a combination of tuberculosis, scurvy, and typhus,[10] is made into a "famous brigand" possessed of "extraordinary agility," and whose "cynical effrontery was such that he openly boasted of his crimes."[11] The reinvention of Villella was continued even by his Lombroso's daughter, who in 1911 referred to the man as "an Italian Jack the Ripper."[12]

But if the stories told by Lombroso near the end of his life have a mythic quality, there are already indications in the 1871 paper of the importance Villella's skull would have for Lombroso.[13] Indeed, the article began by announcing that the anomaly which Lombroso had witnessed was "unique in the natural and pathological history of man," and concluded by emphasizing its significance for theories of human evolution.[14] In particular, Lombroso found the fossa to be a confirmation of the work of the Italian zoologist Giovanni Canestrini (1835–1900). According to Lombroso, Canestrini had shown that man "is not a transformation of some anthropomorphic animal (as Vogt argues), still less of some animal intermediate between the anthropomorphs and man, but instead a successive transformation of a progenitor of both the bimanes and the quadrumanes."[15]

Lombroso offered the fossa—and the enlarged median lobe of the cerebellum that must, the author reasoned, have occupied it—both as an example of arrested development (the cerebellum resembled that of five-month-old human fetuses) and as a visual confirmation of the possibility of monstrous reversions in modern humans (such a structure was not, after all, to be found among the higher apes or even some quadrumanous monkeys).[16] Lombroso also took the opportunity to undercut the claims made by phrenologists (see Chapter 3) about the location of the "genital faculty" in the middle cerebellum: although in Villella this "organ" was enlarged, Villella had not exhibited any exaggerated sexual appetites—at least these had never emerged in any of his three trials, nor in the reports on Villella that Lombroso collected from his cellmates.[17]

Most important for Lombroso was the fact that this unusual structure, which he would later name as "atavistic," was found in "that unhappy variety of humans which is, in my opinion, more pathological than the lunatic: criminal man."[18] In 1874, Lombroso would expand on this point, drawing the conclusion that the "extraordinary anomaly of the organ most important for intellectual functions" must lead medicolegal experts to modify their views of criminal responsibility: "Since with a cerebral anomaly that made him descend below the primates, he certainly could not offer the same resistance to brutal and morbid instincts that a well-shaped brain would have allowed."[19] In 1895, Lombroso would again affirm that a brain that is *different* must indicate a different level of responsibility.[20]

We may still wish to ask what, if anything, Lombroso *discovered* about the atavistic nature of the born criminal when he held Villella's bisected skull in his hands. As Giuliano Pancaldi has argued, Lombroso's writings on psychiatry published in the 1850s already showed an interest in recapitulation theory, applying "teratological and embryological concepts to psychological phenomena."[21] And Lombroso's daughter reports that the idea of comparing "criminals, the mentally ill, savages and prehistoric men" had suggested itself at least a year before the article on Villella, when Lombroso had completed work on *L'uomo bianco e l'uomo di colore* [The White Man and the Man of Color].[22]

But I suggest that we begin with a set of questions that complicate in a different way Lombroso's story of simply *looking* and *seeing*. We have already asked what led scientists to examine the bodies of criminals for clues to their dangerousness—what enabled, in other words, an attention to criminals rather than crimes? In the next chapter, we ask about the material conditions of this looking—about the relations of power and knowledge that allowed Lombroso to circulate in prisons, to cut apart the dead body of a inmate, and to leave with Villella's skull; and about the tools, techniques, and practices of collection that made possible the skull's measurement and comparison with other "normal" skulls (human and animal). Here, we focus on what structured Lombroso's scrutiny of the criminal body, making it possible to see in certain ways and not in others. On one hand, I want to call attention to the political and historical context, and explore the ways in which the anthropology of the criminal body was tied up with a coming-to-terms with the Italian nation. On the other hand, I want to ask about the ways in which metaphors and analogies made Villella's skull intelligible as a recurrence of a biological past: How did readings of the bodies of savages, women, children, criminals enable one another, transferring meanings, and making the bodies of each legible in particular and productive ways?

II. Atavism and Modernity

For Lombroso and his contemporaries, fixing the criminal in space and time required ambivalent engagements with Europe's past and present; indeed, we might say that a tension between the modern and the atavistic was played out at the level of both the body and the nation. Thus, Lombroso's anthropology sought, among other things, to trace historical shifts in the nature of crime and criminality, to locate Italy in relation to other—more uniformly modern—nations in Europe, and to draw boundaries around an imagined Italian citizenry.[23]

In the decades following unification, the gaze of Italian anthropologists tended to be turned inward rather than toward exotic locales abroad: ethnological surveys of urban poverty or of sanitary conditions in rural areas promised to assess the health of the young nation at the level of individual bodies. In 1871, for example, one of the first acts of the newly formed *Società italiana di antropologia e di etnologia* [Italian Society of Anthropology and Ethnology] was to charge a group of four scientists (Lombroso, Paolo Mantegazza, Moritz Schiff, and Arturo Zannetti) with mapping the "anatomo-physical character" of the Italian population. The four developed an anthropological questionnaire for distribution to the towns throughout the kingdom, and especially to the district physicians, that included sixteen questions touching on matters as diverse as the pulse, diet, menstruation, and the prevalence of red hair.[24]

The anthropology of the criminal was also concerned with the progress and state of health of the Italian nation, developing both an evolutionary history and a geography of crime. Lombroso argued that "violent and bloody offenses predominated exclusively in ancient times and among the least evolved peoples, while those of forgery and fraud prevail among the most modern."[25] Just as, in matters of property, possession by force of arms had given way to contracts, criminal violence had over time, and through the work of civilization, been displaced by "trickery." The increase in crimes against morality was part of a more general shift, Lombroso argued, away from ferocious crimes that damaged persons to crimes that damaged things.[26]

At the same time, Lombroso argued that acts such as murder among savages and prehistoric peoples were not really crimes at all, but rather customary and natural behaviors. Transgressions of law or morality were in a sense not possible among "savages" because they lacked the capacity of moral judgment.[27] Even among uncivilized Italians, *vendetta* killings were duties rather than crimes, and adultery, rape and sodomy (as the stories of Boccaccio and Sacchetti revealed) were almost "comical transgressions."[28] In keeping with this relativistic stance, a person could not be a "criminal" by reproducing the traditions of the population in which he or she lived; the true delinquent in the historical and evolutionary pasts was not the murderer but the violator of "custom" [*delinquente contro l'uso*].

Thus, "civilization" could be characterized both by an increase in crimes and a shift in its objects, or rather by the addition of new "civilized" crimes to those of "barbaric times."[29] The increase in crimes was facilitated by the introduction of new technologies: not only was train robbery unthinkable without trains, but "modern" crimes often depended on practices of life insurance, telephones, and electricity.[30] Other new crimes, Lombroso suggested, were facilitated by the invention of tunnels, chloroform, lock picks, and hypnotism.[31] Fortunately, Lombroso added, new sciences and technologies, including the social technologies of criminology, also made possible a more effective policing of crime.

In some cases, however, an increase in crime could signal something else, a new *social danger*. This was true, Lombroso proposed, in both the United States and Italy.[32] In the United States, the increase was to be explained in large part by the "colored population" and its inferior stage of *civiltà*.[33] Though Lombroso acknowledged that blacks had been "unfairly treated," he went on to decry their lack of foresight, and noted that black criminals failed to cover their tracks and confessed easily. Above all, blacks failed to be modern: "No matter that he is covered in the dress and habits of modern civilization, the American black too often retains that disregard for the lives of others, that lack of pity that is common to all savage peoples."[34]

The problem facing Italy after unification was rather different, although also shaped by the tension between the savage and the modern. Again, it was not a numerical increase alone that worried Lombroso: the causes for this could be found in Italy's increased population and in the progressive work of civilization.[35] But in 1878, for example, the increase had been "all out of proportion,"[36] and Italy had not yet experienced the shift away from violent crime (that symbol of barbarity) that had been achieved by other modern nations, including Italy's neighbors. Much of the violence in Italy was directed, Lombroso further noted, against the nation itself, taking as its objects civil and social institutions (Giuseppe Villella, after all, was a brigand).

Even worse, in fact, was the existence of regional *differences* in rates of criminality revealed by the collection of statistics (Figure 2.2). How could the social expert account for the fact that in Cantanzaro homicides were fourteen times more frequent than in Turin, and twenty times higher in Naples than in Venice? What sense could be made of the fact that there were twenty-three times more thefts in Rome than in Florence?[37] The fact that the regions of the south—those that had in the past been "poorly tamed"—always "topped the lists" indicated the presence of a "profound evil" that required "serious and energetic measures."[38] These were regions, Lombroso suggested, where internationalism, organized crime, and criminal "associations" found a natural home; where "social hybridity" and poverty created instability; and where weapons and alcohol were too easily available.[39]

But Lombroso also pointed to the poverty of the new nation's social technologies, especially as these were deployed in the south: the uncertainty and mildness of penalties, delays in punishment, excessive

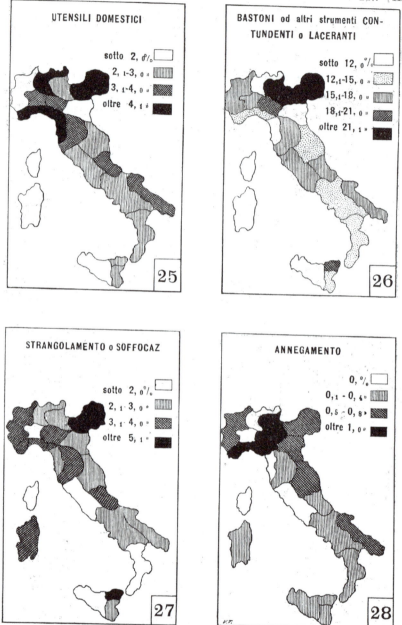

Fig. 2.2   Means of Murder.

appeals, and an undue reliance on the "subjective evaluations" of juries. Lombroso was particularly critical of the dispensation of *grazia* by the king, which "reproduced one of effects of religion with which modern criminal law purports to have broken."[40] Lombroso was not, as we have seen, arguing that all violators of the law should be treated uniformly—far from it. Indeed, he suggested that the creation and application of a uniform penal code, which might have been appropriate "for a people that has reached the acme of civilization," could be *disastrous* for Italy, "in which in many regions an almost medieval barbarism still reigns supreme."[41] Lombroso suggested that in regions where "*vendetta* homicide is almost a duty, it seems to me a grave error to punish it in the same manner as in regions where it provokes a profound disgust."[42] As he put it a decade later, "In order to unify the law, truly and not only on paper, it would be necessary to level customs, birth rates, ages of sexual development, and even climates, soils, and farming."[43]

Underlying all of these critiques was, as we saw in the last chapter, a challenge to prevailing penal theories and their focus on criminal *responsibility*. In Lombroso's view, the new nation needed to substitute strategies of social defense for "metaphysics," and evaluations of social dangers for worries about free will and intention. In sum, the unity (and modernity) of Italy were not to be guaranteed by the application of uniform codes linking transgressions and penalties, but by measures of social defense flexible enough to evaluate the potential social dangerousness of individual offenders. In the south, a vendetta homicide might not indicate any social danger, while in the north the same *act* might be an index of something altogether different. Building a nation and suppressing crime were both seen to require detailed knowledge about and management of difference.

Lombroso's project, finally, was to make dangerous difference visible at the level of the body, so that the larger body of Italy might be defended against risks, and made modern. However, as we will see, Lombroso imagined that, in a certain sense, it was modernity itself that was responsible not only for increases in crime, but also for the appearance of the born criminal. For Lombroso, the very possibility of variation, and thus the possibility of deviation from norms, was linked to both historical and evolutionary progress: neither the born criminal nor his counterpart—the genius—was imaginable outside modernity.[44]

III. Natural Histories of Crime: Plants, Animals, and Children

A number of scholars have observed that Lombroso's theory of atavism owes more to pre-Darwinian comparative anatomy, medicine, and linguistics than to the work of Darwin.[45] Renzo Villa has emphasized, for example, the importance for Lombroso of Giambattista Vico's (1668–1744) philosophy of history and Paolo Marzolo's (1811–1868) "natural history of languages."[46] Pancaldi has argued that the roots of Lombroso's evolutionism are to be found in the genealogy of the human species offered by Canestrini, which "weakened the links between humans and other primates, locating them much earlier."[47]

However, the construction of the congenital criminal as an atavistic being was dependent also on new practices of measuring and documenting that sought to mark off deviant bodies from normal bodies, and on a whole series of analogies that made the bodies of criminals, animals, women, children, poor people, and savages intelligible in terms of each other. These analogies enabled not only transfers of meanings among bodies and organisms (from the criminal to the child, from the child to the savage, from the savage to the animal), but also layerings of various kinds of time: embryological, developmental, historical, and evolutionary. As Nancy Stepan has argued, such comparisons were the condition of possibility of both perceiving and explaining similarity and difference in a variety of biosocial sciences at the end of the nineteenth century.[48] Here, they made it possible to discover and to measure the "precocity" of the criminal, the "ferocity" of the child, or the "infantilism" of European women. Finally, these analogies legitimated the circulation of knowledge claims across disciplinary boundaries (from zoology to sexology, from physiology to psychology, from botany to anthropology), promising an intensification or multiplication of the authority of each discipline.

Lombroso sought (unsuccessfully if we judge by the critical reception) to make precisely this rhetorical move in the opening pages of *L'uomo delinquente*, which were dedicated to a discussion of the "embryology of crime."[49] Here, Lombroso offered a narrative of the natural history of crime that began in the plant and animal kingdoms. In an introductory chapter devoted to crime and inferior organisms,

Lombroso argued that it was only fitting for criminal anthropology to follow the example of the disciplines of sociology, economics, and psychology in building on a foundation of zoological and botanical knowledge.[50] Unlike (artificial) systems of *justice*, he suggested, *criminality* was both transhistorical and transspecific:

> The old jurists speak of a divine, eternal justice—almost inherent in nature. If instead we take a look at natural phenomena, we see that the acts held by us to be most criminal are the most natural.[51]

On one hand, Lombroso configured the whole of the organic world as a space of indifferent violence, citing Darwin's work to argue that insectivorous plants could be considered the "first dawning" of criminality.[52] On the other hand, Lombroso used nonhuman and nonanimal killing to mock the metaphysical worries of classical jurists: anyone unfamiliar with histology might suspect, Lombroso suggested, that such plants were guilty of premeditation, laying in wait, even exercising free will by refusing insects that were too small.[53]

The evidence against the animal kingdom was both more voluminous and more damning. Enrico Ferri, Lombroso reported, had identified twenty-two species of animals that "commit murder." Animals killed each other, Lombroso told his readers, to have access to females, to defend themselves, as acts of war, and to practice cannibalism. There were even cases of animals committing "regicide," as when excess queen bees were eliminated by workers.[54] However, in the later editions of *L'uomo delinquente* Lombroso was quick to acknowledge that calling these killings "crimes"—or adding others to the list such as the theft among apes, the abduction of minors among red ants, or the substitution of infants by the cuckoo—could have little meaning, as "these actions which to us appear misdeeds are instead a necessary effect of heredity or of the organic structure, or are imposed by the struggle for existence."[55] These examples were rather meant to show the "vanity of the concept of abstract justice." That is, the rhetorical goal was not to demonstrate that animals really transgressed codes, but to show that criminality was not best understood—among animals or humans—as a *transgression of codes*, or even as a series of *acts*. Lombroso's classical opponents could surely not have been expected to accede to this point, and today these examples strike historians as some of the most laughable examples of pseudoscience.[56]

The connection between criminality and animality was, Lombroso hoped, more convincingly established by analyzing domesticated animals, as well as those wild animals that lived in social groups; the pathologies of these animals, he suggested, truly showed human deviance "in embryonic form." Domestication and socialization were, he reasoned, comparable to civilization, as they taught individuals over generations to control their passions. But occasionally, among animals as among humans, individuals reverted to or showed signs of a former state of savagery—the "rogue elephant was but one example."[57] Individual animals could commit crimes because of hatred, old age, cranial anomalies, "irresistible impulses," pain, or love. In addition to murder, they were capable of theft, fraud, and infanticide, and could join together to form criminal associations. These behaviors, Lombroso suggested, came much closer to what civilized humans called crimes, precisely because of their individuality (in contrast to the innate habits acquired by particular species) and because they threatened rather than furthered the survival of species or a social group.[58] The perversity of the rogue elephant and the murderous horse were tendencies *personal* to the delinquent individual, unknown to others of the species.[59]

In the end, the most interesting analogy for Lombroso had to do with causes, which he supposed were identical for the animal and the human criminal. There was, Lombroso found, a continuity or an "insensible passage" from the acts of animals we would call criminal to the crimes of humans.[60] In both animals and humans, Lombroso concluded, crime is not only *linked* to the underlying conditions of organisms, but is a direct *result*.[61] The goal, again, was less to anthropomorphize animals than to see human crimes as the equivalent of a deviation from the nature of a species, and more particularly a reversion to an earlier stage of development.

Because Lombroso linked the biological development of the species, history, and the growth of the individual, criminal dangerousness could also be read as a form of immaturity. In a challenge to the Enlightenment understanding of childhood as a period of innocence, Lombroso turned his attention to the dangerousness of children (Figure 2.3). Just as the fetus displayed physical characteristics that in

Fig. 2.3   Criminal Child.

a full-grown adult would constitute monstrosity, he argued, the child exhibited moral qualities that in an adult would constitute a social danger. The child was an adult human "stripped of moral sense."[62]

Lombroso relied in part on Bernard Perez's (1836–1903) work on the moral development of young children. Perez's account of the anger of the one-year-old—expressed by hitting people, breaking dishes, and throwing himself against those who displeased him—recalled, for Lombroso, the behavior of the "savage Dakota, who become frenzied when they kill bison."[63] Children were vindictive, jealous—breaking toys rather than share them with another—vain, lazy, and habitual liars.[64] Cruelty was, according to Lombroso, one of the most common characteristics of the child:

> In general, [the child] prefers evil to good; he is more cruel than good because he feels greater emotion and can prove his unlimited power—this is why we see him take pleasure in breaking inanimate objects. He delights in stabbing animals, in drowning flies; he beats his dog, suffocates sparrows. Some can be seen coating cockroaches and stag-beetles with hot wax, dressing them up as soldiers and prolonging their agony for months at a time.

It was the child who invented the reed or wicker cage, traps, butterfly nets, and thousands of other little devices of destruction.[65]

Lombroso added that children were incapable of true affection; like prostitutes, they only pretended affection in expectation of a return or reward.[66]

The American criminologist Arthur MacDonald (1856–1936), summarizing and extending Lombroso's conclusions, found that "the germs of crime are met with, in a normal manner, during the first years of infancy."[67] Children even murdered, MacDonald reminded his readers, and if their murders were less cruel than those of adult criminals it was only because they lacked force, not ferocity.[68] British sexologist and criminologist Havelock Ellis (1859–1939) found that there was indeed a certain form of criminality *peculiar* to children: that is, moral insanity. One Italian study of 240 children between the ages of three and seven found that 45 percent were "morally anomalous," while 66 percent exhibited "morbid physical characteristics."[69] For Ellis, Richard Krafft-Ebing (1840–1902) and others, morally insane children were characterized by a "certain eccentricity of character, a dislike of family habits, an incapacity for education, a tendency to lying, together with astuteness and extraordinary cynicism, bad sexual habits, and cruelty toward animals and companions."[70] These characters, Ellis noted, were "but an exaggeration of the characters which in a less degree mark nearly all children." The child was by its nature, Ellis argued, closely related to the animal, the savage, and the criminal:

> The child lives in the present; the emotion or the desire of the moment is large enough to blot out for him the whole world; he has no foresight, and is the easier given up to his instincts and passions; our passions, as Hobbes said, bring us near to children. Children are naturally egoists; they will commit all enormities, sometimes, to enlarge their egoistic satisfaction. They are cruel and inflict suffering on animals out of curiosity, enjoying the manifestations of pain. They are thieves for the gratification of their appetites, especially the chief, gluttony, and they are unscrupulous and often cunning liars, not hesitating to put the blame on the innocent when their misdeeds are discovered.[71]

The criminal could be regarded, Ellis suggested, as an individual who, to some extent, remained a child for his entire life—"a child of larger growth and with greater capacity for evil."[72]

Most children, Lombroso advised teachers in an 1895 address, could be expected to outgrow their criminal tendencies, "just as in the fully developed foetus the traces of the lower animals gradually disappear which are so conspicuous in the first months of the foetal life." In cases of normal maturation, there was a "genuine ethical evolution" that corresponded to physical development.[73] However, he urged teachers to be on guard for children who exhibited "extraordinary anomalies of the face and head." In these cases, efforts at ethical instruction would pass over their "diseased brains, as oil does over marble, without penetrating it." Such children needed to be kept away from cities and even towns, perhaps sent to work on isolated farms or as cabin boys at sea. In the most extreme cases, Lombroso advised, it was necessary to "procure their isolation as if they were lunatics."[74]

IV. The Savage and the Criminal: Bodies and Language

No analogy was more important, or more productive, for criminal anthropology than that linking the European criminal and the non-European "savage."[75] For Lombroso, a wide range of disparate phenomena linked prehistoric peoples, contemporary "colored races," and criminals. These included:

> thinning hair, lack of strength and weight, low cranial capacity, receding foreheads, highly developed frontal sinuses, a high frequency of medio-frontal sutures, precocious synoteosis, especially frontal, protrusion of the curved line of the temporal, simplicity of the sutures. . . darker skin, thicker, curly hair, large or handleshaped ears, a greater analogy between the two sexes. . . indolence. . . facile superstition. . . and finally the relative concept of the divinity and morals.[76]

While savages might lack the ferocity of semibarbarous peoples, they had the "incapacity for continual work" that was "a constant among criminals."[77] Lombroso also found that savages shared the moral insensibility of criminals (see Chapter 4), and that both groups were marked by impetuosity and unstable passions.[78]

As we have seen, in savage societies as among animals, violent acts were imagined to be not the exception but the rule, and thus were not identified as "crimes" by anyone. If among animals the true equivalent of crime was behavior that worked in opposition to the interests of the species, among savages it was the violation of custom.[79] At the same time, because savages had failed to evolve, and thus to achieve the differentiation of bodies characteristic of European men, there was little that was anatomically distinctive about the savage violator of custom; deviance was, in a sense, a privilege of modern humans. The bodies of savages were imagined to be homogenous and biologically monotonous, exhibiting little variation. By contrast, the body of the modern born criminal *was* distinctive, precisely in its resemblance to the body of the unvarying savage. Paradoxically, Lombroso offered the *absence* of the criminal type among savages as a confirmation of the atavistic nature of the type:

> An eloquent demonstration of the fact that [the criminal] type is, in large measure, a return to the savage epoch or an anterior animality. . . is the observation, made by many, that among people who are barbaric or barely civilized this type is *completely absent*. This is no doubt because the regression of the race has already reached its limits, and because in the barbarian, in whom pity and a sense of justice are essentially lacking, the distance or deviation from crime—honesty—is also lacking.

Lombroso offered as examples studies of the physiognomies of Chinese criminals and Japanese prostitutes, and of the crania of Egyptian and Indian criminals, few of which exhibited any anomalies.[80] A study of Mongol criminals in Siberia concluded that the men exhibited no special physiognomic features; by contrast, the same researcher found European criminals *were* distinctive, appearing to be "*more Mongol* than the Mongols."[81] In other respects, too, the modern criminal was imagined to be more savage than the savage.

The raced, savage body was, in turn, compared to those of other primates. Lombroso repeated the nineteenth-century commonplaces that blacks had smaller brains than whites, and that the eyes of blacks resembled those of apes. He also reported that the sutures in the skull on infants fused more readily in blacks, idiots, and apes; that blacks and apes had a precocious, but then arrested, intellectual development; and that they exhibited less sexual dimorphism than adult whites. There was, he imagined, a chain of regressions: if the criminal sometimes reverted to the savage, the savage also reverted to the animal: "The principal index of the kinship between man and other animals is offered

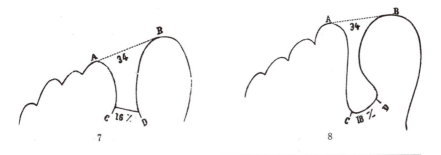

Fig. 2.4 Prehensile Toes.

by that constant regression of pithecoid characteristics that we find in the melanic races."[82]

Anatomical features such as prehensile toes worked, for Lombroso, to complete this chain of association among animals, savages, and criminals. In *L'uomo delinquente* Lombroso reported the results of a comparative study of the space between the first and second toes.[83] Salvatore Ottolenghi (1861–1934) and Mario Carrara (b. 1866) had examined normal women and men, criminals, prostitutes, epileptics, and idiots, tracing for each individual two outlines of the feet—the first with the toes relaxed and the second with the toes abducted, or spread apart (Figure 2.4). Criminals were three times more likely than normal men to have an interdigital space of 3 mm or greater when the toes were relaxed, and four times more likely to have a space greater than 22 mm when the toes were spread.[84] To these results, Lombroso added his own anecdotal observations: "M," a baker convicted of assault, was able to lift a heavy bottle of water with his toes without spilling a drop, while "V," an "epileptic criminaloid," had used his foot as a hand since childhood, an ability he shared with other members of his family.[85] Neither occupational habits nor walking barefoot, Lombroso reported, could account for such anomalies; instead, prehensility was intelligible only as an atavistic characteristic that recalled the function of the foot in the progenitors of modern humans—not only the "anthropomorphs," but also members of such human societies as the Kachin and the Annamese. Indeed, Lombroso saw represented in the collected tracings of feet an entire map of degrees of degeneration, from normal men, to normal and criminal women, to prostitutes, to criminals and epileptics.[86]

Lombroso also worked to link the *cultural* practices of criminals and savages; language is a case in point. Lombroso characterized the spoken languages of primitive humans and contemporary savages as incomplete—they lacked consonants, articles, gender, number, grammar[87]—and as excessively reliant on onomatopoeia and personification, characteristics shared with the slang of criminals. Because criminal slang enabled the Lombard thief to understand the Calabrian,[88] its existence could be understood simultaneously as a social danger (aiding secret communication among criminals), a national political problem (pointing once again to the disunity of the nation), and a sign of atavism (like the speech of savages and children). Lombroso concluded that criminals "speak differently because they feel differently. They speak like savages because they are savages living in the midst of a flowering European civilization; they often adopt, therefore, like savages, the use of onomatopoeia, automatism, the personification of abstract objects."[89]

Lombroso also worked to link the mark making of savages, criminals, and madmen. In a study of a monomaniac, for example, Lombroso and Toselli found the writings of their subject to be atavistic: this "mixture of letters, hieroglyphs, and figurative signs constitutes an interesting writing, as it recalls the phono-ideographic period through which early peoples (certainly the Mexicans and the Chinese) will pass. . . before inventing alphabetic writing."[90] In *L'uomo bianco e uomo di colore*, Lombroso developed a more general argument. "Everyone," Lombroso observed, "is aware of the inequalities of the various races concerning writing."[91] He traced an evolution from sketched figures—among savages these served not as writing proper but as mnemonic devices—to cuneiform and hieroglyphs, to the "pure alphabet." Only alphabetic writing, he suggested, was well suited to the "unfolding of ideas."[92] The "crude writing" of ancient Chinese, by contrast, revealed that the rhetorical tropes favored by pedants were "an expression of the poverty and not the richness of the intellect; in fact, they are found with frequency in the speech of idiots and educated deaf-mutes."[93] The deficiencies of savage and prehistoric speech and writing were accompanied, moreover, by an underdevelopment of arts and industries.[94] The sculptures of the Peruvians and the paintings of the "redskins," we are told, scarcely differed from the "scrawling of our children."[95]

President of Tribunal

Judge

Police Inspector

Public Prosecutor

Carbineer

Theft

Commissary of Police

Camorrist

FIG. 10
Drawings in Script.
Discovered by De Blasio

Fig. 2.5   Drawings in Script.

Lombroso's treatment of the mark making of criminals followed a similar (evolutionary) scheme. Lombroso first noted the "singular" tendency of criminals to express their thoughts with images; even when they were capable of writing words they resorted to "pictography" to narrate their lives of crime or to argue for their innocence, just as they sometimes used slang not to hide their thoughts but indeed to "versify."[96] For Lombroso, the graphical equivalents of slang were criminal "hieroglyphs"—symbols whose meanings were understood only by delinquents and by the scientists who collected the graphical traces left on prison walls, bedpans, and drinking jugs.[97] Prostitutes might, for example, be represented by mice, judges by scorpions, "liberty" by an image of a rooster, and a variety of criminal acts by more abstract symbols that appeared to vary little across Italy (Figure 2.5).[98] In some cases, hieroglyphs were used phonetically or to form epigrams (Figure 2.6). Criminals and prison inmates were dependent on such symbols, Lombroso reasoned, because of their need for secrecy and their frequent illiteracy. But the scientist could not help but see in them "traces of ancient medieval customs and of

FIG. 11
Alphabet
Discovered
by
De Blasio

Fig. 2.6   Alphabet.

atavism." Like prehistoric man, the criminal was "driven" to express himself in pictures, though even when he did write his marks on paper might also give him away.[99] And despite "the thousands of years" separating the criminal and the prehistoric savage, the art of the first faithfully reproduced that of the second. Gina Lombroso-Ferrero noted that her father's museum contained numerous specimens of criminal art: "stones shaped to resemble human figures, like those found in Australia, rude pottery covered with designs that recall Egyptian decorations, or scenes fashioned in terra-cotta that resemble the grotesque creations of children or savages (Figure 2.7)."[100]

Nowhere was the traffic linking savages and criminals heavier than at the intersection of mark making and the body constituted by the tattoo. As we have seen, Lombroso's interest in decorated skin went back to his days as an army doctor in the 1860s, when he was struck by the prevalence of tattoos among soldiers with discipline problems; he would later undertake studies of the frequency, form, and content

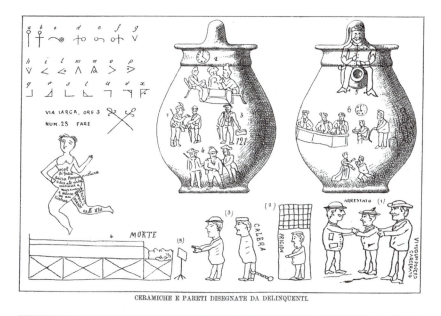

CERAMICHE E PARETI DISEGNATE DA DELINQUENTI.

Fig. 2.7   Ceramics and Walls Decorated by Criminals.

of tattoos among prison inmates and prostitutes. For Lombroso, tattoos also offered further evidence of the link between criminals and primitive people.[101] In an article that appeared in the American magazine *Popular Science Monthly*, Lombroso explained the "savage origin of tattooing."[102] Noting that the fashion of tattooing the arm was gaining popularity among "women of prominence" in London, Lombroso took the occasion to denounce the practice as "contrary to progress, for all exaggerations of dress are atavistic."[103] But above all he was anxious to point out the prevalence of tattooing among criminals:

> While out of 2,739 soldiers I have found tattoo marks only among 1.2 per cent, always limited to the arms and the breast; among 5,348 criminals, 667 were tattooed, or ten per cent of the adults and 3.9 per cent of the minors.[104]

Although Lombroso did not ignore the content of criminals' tattoos (their frequent obscenity or references to vengeance, for example),[105] he was particularly struck by their formal qualities—their reliance on cryptic forms of inscription, in which, once again, "ideographic hieroglyphs" took the place of alphabetic writing. Lombroso also noted criminals' tendency to cover the whole of the body (Figure 2.8), a sign

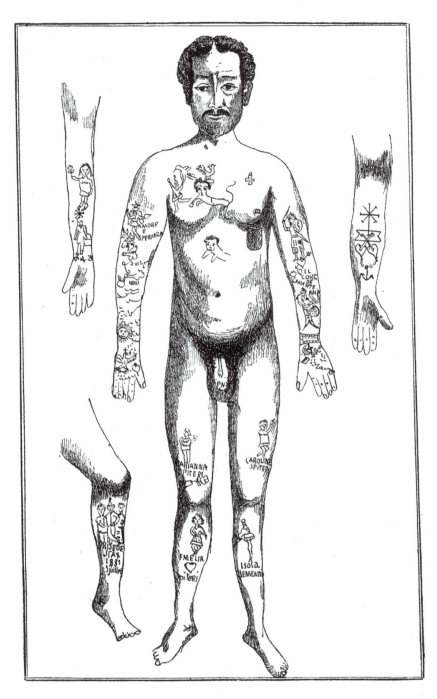

TATUAGGI SIMBOLICI.

Fig. 2.8 Symbolic Tattoos.

of their remarkable insensibility (see Chapter 4).[106] In both respects, the criminal could be linked to the "savage": "Tattooing is, in fact, one of the essential characteristics of primitive man, and of men who still live in the savage state."[107] Evidence of tattooing, argued Lombroso, could be found in the prehistoric grottoes of southern France, in the tombs of ancient Egypt, and throughout the ethnological literature: "I do not believe there is a single savage people that does not tattoo more or less." Indeed, Lombroso found that tattooing was "the true writing of savages, their first registry of civil condition."[108] The laws of atavism explained the reappearance of the practice among delinquents:

> Nothing is more natural than to see a usage so widespread among savages and prehistoric peoples reappear in classes which, as the deep-sea bottoms retain the same temperature, have preserved the customs and superstitions, even to the hymns, of the primitive peoples, and who have, like them, violent passions, a blunted sensibility, a puerile vanity, long-standing habits of inaction, and very often nudity.[109]

In at least one respect, criminals surpassed savages, tattooing even the penis. This practice proved not only the indecency of criminals, but also their strange insensibility. Even savages who covered almost their whole bodies in designs, Lombroso argued, usually spared the genitals.[110]

Tattoos were of limited use in identifying (in Bertillon's sense) individual criminals because they were not always permanent: experiments, including some performed by Lombroso, had shown they could be removed without a trace.[111] However, they did serve to mark criminals as a group, performing "the service among them of uniforms among our soldiers." More important, tattoos enabled the criminologist "to discern the obscurer sides of the criminal's soul, his remarkable vanity, his thirst for vengeance, and his atavistic character, even in his writing."[112] Indeed, tattoos helped to distinguish true criminals from others (especially the mad) with whom they had too often been confused. Although the madman resorted to the "strangest pastimes"—shredding his clothes and flesh, scribbling on walls and reams of paper—he almost never made designs on the skin. Since madness was, Lombroso had found, rarely congenital and even less often atavistic, this in turn appeared to confirm the link between tattooing and atavism.[113]

V. The Female Offender

Studies of female criminals came rather late in Lombroso's project to know the deviant body; *La donna delinquente, la prostituta e la donna normale* was first published in 1893, amid expanding debates on the scientific status of Lombroso's work.[114] Indeed, the volume, jointly authored by Lombroso's collaborator and son-in-law, Guglielmo Ferrero (1871–1942), assembled research on female criminals from around Europe largely to counter charges that the analogy between women and criminals *failed to hold*.[115] Critics had, in fact, pointed to two apparent contradictions: that female criminals seemed to be too few in number and that, though doubly other, they displayed few anatomical signs of their social dangerousness.[116] These results were unexpected only because Lombroso's anthropology had explicitly linked "woman" with others (criminals, savages, primates, and children) who had failed to achieve the evolutionary progress of European males.

The portrait of the normal woman provided in *La donna delinquente* depended upon, and worked to reinforce, precisely these analogies.[117] The normal woman, a figure that had no real counterpart in Lombroso's studies of male criminality,[118] was ostensibly constructed as a background against which the female offender might become distinct, visible, and legible. Much of the discussion was given over to detailing the continuities between European women and the females of other, less-advanced species. In Lombroso's formulations, which at times resembled the teleologies of Aristotle, woman was described as a "big child" and as a "man arrested in his intellectual and physical development."[119] The signs of woman's failure to evolve or mature were varied: ranging from an underdeveloped moral sense, to a predisposition to cruelty, to a "physiological incapacity" for truth telling. That women habitually lied was, the authors reported, confirmed by proverbs, and rooted both in atavistic biology ("savages always lie"), and more specifically in the social need to hide menstruation from men and sex from children.[120]

Women's bodies were, moreover, marked by traces of youth and the past: prehensile feet, left-handedness, dullness of the senses, an inability to experience pleasure, and a resistance to pain that could be measured in the laboratory (see Chapter 4). These characteristics were seen to link women not only to the indigenous peoples of Africa, but also to children and criminals. The irascibility, vengeance, jealousy and vanity common to all four meant none was able to achieve "equilibrium between rights and duties, egoism and altruism"—that crucial component of *political* participation in a modern, civilized state.[121]

Even Lombroso's critics could agree on the organic inferiority of women. Gabriel Tarde (1843–1904), for example, conceded a number of anatomical similarities between women and criminals:

[Women] have less voluminous crania and brains that are less heavy [than men's], even when the same size, and their cerebral forms have something infantile or embryonic about them; they are less frequently *right-handed*, more often left-handed or ambidextrous; they have, if I may say it, flatter and less shapely feet; finally, their muscles are weaker, and also completely smooth-faced despite being abundantly long-haired. So many traits common to our malefactors.[122]

But what was the criminologist to make of statistics showing women committed fewer crimes than did men, and that the heads and bodies of female criminals presented fewer signs of degeneration than did those of males?[123] The cranial anomalies of male criminals were, by Lombroso and Ferrero's count, three to four times more frequent, and the "complete criminal type," characterized by four or more atavistic characteristics, could be found in only 18 percent of female criminals (as compared with 31 percent of males).[124] The frequency of anomalies among normal women was also low. Lombroso recounted a day spent observing 560 women on a boulevard—only nine, he reported, presented the "complete degenerate type."[125]

Ironically, it was the preponderance of the norm among women that was marshaled to provide a solution: it emerged as a sign of the "diminished diversity" of the female relative to male, another sign of her failure fully to evolve and of her resemblance to females of lower species. Citing Charles Darwin (1809–1882) and Henri Milne-Edwards (1800–1885) on the "organic monotony" of females, a condition imagined to be necessary to the stable reproduction of species, Lombroso and Ferrero constructed both women and the female body as essentially conservative. Women's views of social order were weighed down by the "immobility of the ovum," their habits of dress remained relatively constant throughout history, and their anatomies showed few variations[126]: only the hymen and labia, the authors noted, were subject to great variability.[127] Even the tattoos of female criminals, Lombroso complained, were "monotonous and uniform," evidence of woman's "smaller ability and fancy" and the lower degree of differentiation in the female intellect.[128]

In the preface to later editions of *La donna delinquente* Lombroso and Ferrero were thus able to turn an apparent contradiction into a "vindication of the observational method." Although at first the evidence from anthropometry and pathological anatomy had seemed to call their assumptions and predictions into question, the two authors "remained faithful to the method," and followed the facts with "blind confidence."[129] The relative rarity of signs of degeneration on the female body, which had seemed potentially a sign of woman's superiority, could now be linked to a lesser degree of variability, itself a sign of inferiority and weakness.[130] Thus, ironically, at the precise moment that woman was identified as "normal" and "normalizing," as embodying and conserving the norms of the species, she was marked as other, if not pathological, and as opposed to history and civilization. Moreover, as we will see in a moment, this construction of the female body as closely bound to the norm presented additional reading difficulties for the anthropologist and the social worker: how might the deviant (and dangerous) female body be distinguished from the normal body?

The remaining problem—apparently low rates of "female criminality"—was solved by reconstructing this category in order to include prostitution. Among women, argued Lombroso and Ferrero, criminality had almost always taken the form of prostitution, from prehistory to the nineteenth century: "The primitive woman," they wrote, "was rarely a murderess; but she was always a prostitute."[131] This move, of course, required the authors to define prostitution rather broadly—to include, for example, all forms of marriage in "savage" societies[132] and the conduct of wealthy as well as poor women in modern Italy. Lombroso and Ferrero observed that even the Mediterranean rituals of hospitality (which have continued to attract the attention of ethnographers of the region) had their roots in savage and medieval practices of prostitution.[133]

If, in Lombroso and Ferrero's view, other female criminals rarely showed signs of degeneracy, this was far from the case among prostitutes, who were the very images of the evolutionary and historical pasts. Their developmental "precocity," minor degree of differentiation from males, and resemblance to Hottentot women[134] were all identified as signs of atavism, and 51 percent of prostitutes were found to have more than five anomalies.[135] There was, as Lombroso and Ferrero put it, a "crescendo of the peculiarities as we rise from the moral women, who are most free from anomalies, to prostitutes, who are free from none."[136]

A series of photographs were included to illustrate this argument (Figure 2.9). At times, the gaze of the anthropologist resembled that of the connoisseur or voyeur, delighting in surfaces and making frank aesthetic appraisals that the (presumed male) reader was invited to check and ratify.[137] Lombroso and Ferrero observed, for example, that French criminal women were "infinitely more typical and uglier" than Russian women, evidence of the fact that "the more refined a nation is, the further do its criminals differ from the average."[138] However, it was often the case that surface readings would not do, especially when anomalies might be hidden by women's makeup and clothing. Indeed, in Lombroso and Ferrero's view, the difficulties of reading the body, and of "positively affirming" anthropological conclusions, were multiplied in the case of prostitutes. After all, Lombroso wrote, prostitutes were unlike other female offenders because they were generally free from the anomalies that produced "ugliness," a result of the laws of sexual selection and of the marketplace.[139] "Let a female delinquent be young and we can overlook her degenerate type," Lombroso and Ferrero wrote, "and even regard her as beautiful; the sexual instinct misleading us here as it does in making us attribute to women more of sensitiveness and passion than they really possess."[140] Still, the outwardly beautiful prostitute concealed underlying signs of her degeneracy: internal anomalies (overlapping teeth and a divided palate), atavistic genitals, and facial signs that were covered by the mask of makeup or by the "freshness"

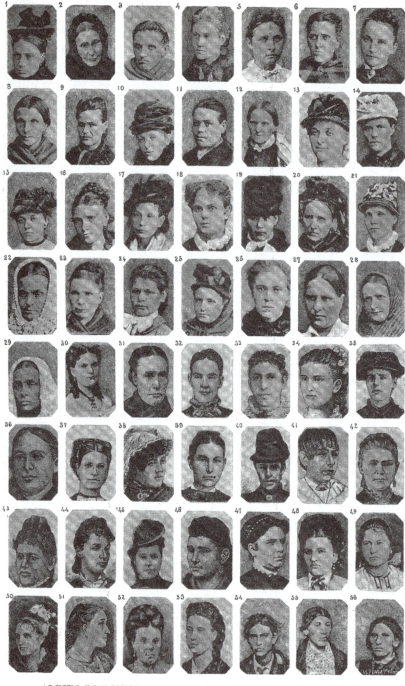

ALBUM DI DONNE DELINQUENTI TEDESCHE ED ITALIANE.

Fig. 2.9 Album of German and Italian Criminal Women.

and "plumpness" of youth.[141] The ugly truth was revealed only by the penetrating gaze of the scientist, able to see beyond seductive surfaces to detect anomalies, or (more surely) by the passage of time:

> [W]hen youth vanishes, the jaws, the cheek-bones, hidden by adipose tissue, emerge, salient angles stand out, and the face grows virile, uglier than a man's; wrinkles deepen into the likeness of scars, and the countenance, once attractive, exhibits the full degenerate type which early grace had concealed.[142]

Here, as elsewhere, the affirmation of the expert reading practices of the social scientist was accompanied by a recognition of the difficulty, if not impossibility, of any reliable readings of the deceptive female body. There was, in fact, a layering of uncertainties: the erosion of boundaries and taxonomic categories effected by a probabilistic understanding of criminal dangerousness, and the absence of adequate markers caused by the tendency of woman to adhere to the norm, were here joined by bodily acts of epistemological resistance. Together, these worked to blur the very boundaries between normal and deviant that criminal anthropology sought to draw, and to multiply the possible objects of social scientific concern and technical intervention.

And, as we will see in Chapter 6, it may be precisely through its *failure* to isolate the dangerous female body that Lombroso's anthropology establishes its links to the present, a present in which social life (including reproduction) is frequently imagined in actuarial terms, and in which the body continues to be pored over for signs of risks to be managed.

3

Making Criminologists

"Anthropology needs numbers."
—Cesare Lombroso, *L'uomo delinquente* (1896)

I. Introduction: Italians and Criminals

In his contribution to a jointly authored 1886 "Polemic in Defense of the Positive School of Criminal Anthropology," Lombroso struggled to salvage his notion of the "criminal type" from an international chorus of detractors.[1] Ten years earlier, as we have seen, Lombroso had proposed that the bodies of born criminals made visible, and in typical ways, their latent social dangerousness. Yet, by Lombroso's own calculations, some 60 percent of criminals bore no resemblance at all to the anatomical portraits he had constructed, appearing more or less "normal" even under the anatomizing gaze of the scientist—a fact that had not escaped the attention of French sociologists of crime.[2] In his polemic, Lombroso responded by pointing hopefully to the 40 percent of criminals who *did* possess some elements of the type, by emphasizing the "invisible passage" from one character to another that is the hallmark of biological variation among plants and animals, and by highlighting the increased variation among individuals that resulted from the perfection and civilization of the human species. "Besides," concluded Lombroso, "it is unlikely that you could find among one hundred Italians as many as five with the noted [Italian] type. . . . And yet it would never occur to anyone to deny the Italian type."[3]

Lombroso's move to shore up the embattled construct of the typical criminal by pointing his readers to the typical Italian is, perhaps, surprising. After all, just sixteen years after the unification of Italy, there could scarcely have been said to be common agreement about what it meant to be an Italian. Indeed, the very fabrication of the nation remained in doubt, fractured as it was by differences in language, economy, religion and, as Lombroso would point out, crime. "Even in evil," he wrote, "Italy is not unified."[4]

But I want instead to call attention to Lombroso's turn to the commonsensical—his invocation of a shared understanding that we all know the type (criminal or Italian) when we see it. This was, in fact, a move he made often in his studies of criminal anatomy and physiology. Indeed, as we will see, Lombroso wished at various times to foreground continuities between his readings of the criminal body, proverbial wisdom, and the earlier discourses of physiognomy, which had purported to find signs of interior intellectual and moral states on the body's surfaces, particularly at the level of the head and the face. And though he insisted on the modernity of criminal anthropology, Lombroso was also not above calling on "the ancients," and in particular Homer and Avicenna, to say there was little new about his scientific claims.[5] But if Lombroso frankly delighted in deploying traditional and popular culture to support his findings, and to undercut and isolate the "metaphysical" claims made by classical jurists, he and his colleagues were also aware of the risks these maneuvers posed to the credibility of an emergent scientific discipline. To count as *science*, criminal anthropology had to mark its distance, particularly through practices of quantification, from alternative knowledges of embodied dangerousness.[6]

The previous chapters have been focused on the production of "the criminal" in the late nineteenth century—on the practices and discourses that constituted the criminal and his body as objects of medical knowledge and sites of social prophylaxis. This chapter focuses, in a complementary fashion, on the production of the criminologist—on the fashioning of a new kind of medico-legal expert, qualified to read the deviant body and to diagnose social dangers. If we ask what it could have meant to be a criminal scientist toward the end of the nineteenth century, we are obliged first to recognize the relative absence of institutional markers of such a status. The identity of the new criminology was, at any moment, tied to the relative fluidity or fixity of disciplinary boundaries, to changes in the structure of the university, and to the evolving role of the physician in Italian culture.[7] The "Italian school" was, for a time, little more than an informal network of physicians, biological scientists, and jurists dispersed throughout Italy, committed to carving out a new epistemological space. Although many of its members taught in universities (in departments of pathology, physiology, law, and the like) there was no chair in criminal anthropology until 1905 (and this only an *ad personam* appointment to honor Lombroso at Turin).[8] Much of the making of the new science of criminals went on elsewhere: in laboratories, museums, journals, prisons, asylums, and, later, at international conferences.[9] Indeed, rather than speak of the *production* of criminologists in the nineteenth century, we might instead speak of a self-fashioning or, as Patrizia Guarnieri has suggested, of the cultivation of an "image."[10]

More concretely, criminology's claims to the status of science were dependent on access to bodies that lent themselves to a discriminating quantification. In the laboratory, the prison, the university lecture hall, and the courtroom the expert would be required to point with, some measure of confidence, to bodies that were marked off from the normal—that announced their difference and their dangerousness. At the same time, the facticity of "the criminal body" was dependent on the authority of figures such as Lombroso, who in publications and in testimony before juries had to struggle to contain the variability of real bodies' surfaces, to overcome criminals' multiple forms of resistance to scrutiny, and to disqualify competing knowledge claims. And this scientific authority had much to do with the *practical* abilities of physicians and others to regularize tools and measurements, to stabilize interpretations, and to deploy the rhetoric of the "expert."

II. Genealogies: Physiognomy and Phrenology

In his polemic, Lombroso found himself in the awkward position of having to refute both the charge that criminal anthropology was excessively "revolutionary" and the charge—leveled by those who "await the latest fashion from the Sorbonne"—that he had merely resuscitated an "antiquated theory."[11] He reached optimistically for an analogy with nineteenth-century molecular theory; like criminology, it was "fresh and lively even though [it] dated from the time of Pythagoras."[12] It was left to Lombroso's allies, for example, physician Giuseppe Antonini

(1874–1938), to flesh out this noble genealogy of the discipline.[13] The apologetic nature of Antonini's volume on the "precursors" of Lombroso is confirmed by the author's comparison of the treatment Lombroso received to the burning of Giordano Bruno, the condemnation of Galileo, the incarceration of Columbus, and the dismissal of Darwin.[14] Antonini, director of an asylum in Voghera, aimed to demonstrate that "criminal anthropology was not born like an armored Minerva by the will of a man"; instead, Lombroso's "genius" consisted in collecting, systematizing, ordering—"accelerating, in a word, the evolution of a doctrine, which because it was based on truth could not in fact remain completely unknown."[15] Knowledge about the precursors of Lombroso could serve, the author hoped, to increase the accessibility of the doctrine and the practical applications of the positive school. For Antonini, the school had had "representatives throughout the ages and among all kinds of observers, who intuited and presented at least a part of the Truth."[16]

For all its combativeness, the history that Antonini offered of efforts to "read" the body's exterior was a familiar one, and one that is more or less consistent with recent work on the history of physiognomy.[17] In a chapter on precursors in the ancient and medieval worlds, Antonini identified Aristotle as the founder of physiognomic observation,[18] then moved on to discuss Galenic medicine, medieval judicial astrology, palmistry, and metoposcopy (reading the wrinkles of the forehead), and Renaissance schools of physiognomy. Sometimes Antonini was anxious to assign credit to precursors, as when he suggested Gerolamo Cardano (1501–1576) had given Lombroso the idea of degenerative nature of genius.[19] There was even room to rehabilitate discredited knowledges such as astrology (Figure 3.1), by arguing that Lombroso had confirmed in his volume on *Pensiero e meteore* that celestial movements influence the comportment of criminals and others.[20] But Antonini was chiefly concerned to tell a story of progress from magic to science, in which physiognomy slowly took its distance, through the imposition of the positive method, from its "impure origins."[21]

This work of dissociating physiognomy from astrology was credited to the Neapolitan Giambattista della Porta (1535–1615), author of a treatise on human physiognomy.[22] Antonini praised in particular

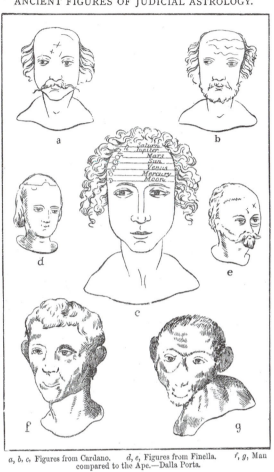

PLATE I. 311
ANCIENT FIGURES OF JUDICIAL ASTROLOGY.

a, b, c, Figures from Cardano.　d, e, Figures from Finella.　f, g, Man compared to the Ape.—Dalla Porta.

Fig. 3.1 Figures of Judicial Astrology.

della Porta's attention to cranial anomalies and deformations, to the degenerative character of dental diastemata, and to variations in the shape of the fingers. Della Porta's observations that short and fat fingers indicated ignorance and stolidity, whereas long fingers pointed to a healthy and good temperament (claims that would be "amply confirmed" by the research of Lombroso and others) stood as proof that he had "shed himself completely of any influence of chiromancy or astrology."[23] Although his text remained full of prejudices and errors, direct observation had enabled della Porta to separate himself from all who had come before him.

The ranks of precursors were not limited to philosophers and scientists, but also included painters, novelists, and playwrights; the artistic works of the great masters were, for Antonini, further proof that "there exists a type of criminal physiognomy easily revealed by those with keen powers of observation."[24] As Gina Lombroso-Ferrero put it:

> Painters and poets, unhampered by false doctrines, divined this type long before it became the subject of a special branch of study. The assassins, executioners, and devils painted by Mantegna, Titian, and Ribera the Spagnoletto embody with marvelous exactitude the characteristics of the born criminal; and the descriptions of great writers, Dante, Shakespeare, Dostoyevsky, and Ibsen, are equally faithful representations, physically and psychically, of this morbid type.[25]

Lombroso himself, in an effort to isolate his critics, observed that although every great artist had given violent criminals the same appearance he assigned to the born criminal, "the world refuses to accept the existence of the criminal type, the madness inherent in genius, the relations between epilepsy and crime, which it instead accepts in the novel or the play." Lombroso theorized that when people were in the presence of the "true representations" made by great artists, "the consciousness of the truth that lies dormant in all of us, compressed and disfigured by the forces of schools, wakes up and rebels against the conventional prejudices that have been imposed upon it." By comparison, the "cold statistics" generated by scientific observers of criminal bodies did not inspire rebellion against prejudice.[26]

Antonini's pre-Lombrosian history reached its climax with the "triumphant entrance" of physiognomy into the university in the late eighteenth century; for this achievement, the names of Johann Caspar Lavater (1741–1801) and Franz Joseph Gall (1758–1828) were to be "written in gold."[27] Although the language of Lavater had never been scientific, reported Antonini, his practices of observation and classification had resulted in a typology of humans who could be distinguished by their outward appearance. His studies of silhouettes had revealed, even before the research on facial angles undertaken by the Dutch anatomist Petrus Camper (1722–1789), the correlation of profiles with intellectual development.[28] More important, argued Antonini, Lavater

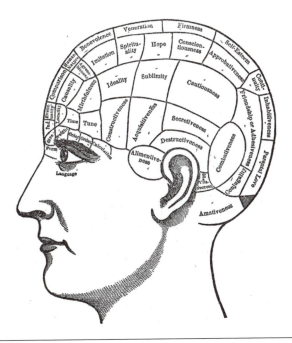

Fig. 3.2 Phrenological Map of the Faculties.

shared with Lombroso a determination to study bodies as harmonious wholes, and to regard certain features of the body as "pathognomic signs of dispositions."[29]

Antonini's discussion of Gall was scarcely less enthusiastic. He acknowledged that there were problems with Gall's central thesis—that "the brain is not a single organ, but a complex of special organs that are as numerous as the faculties of given individual." Indeed, later work in physiology and clinical medicine had, among other things, called into question Gall's cerebral geography of the faculties (Figure 3.2).[30] But Antonini nevertheless argued for the modernity of Gall's approach to the study of the brain and criminality: his arguments for an organic basis for violence, his reliance on direct observation of criminals in prisons, his distinction between crimes of passion and those due to instinct. Above all, Antonini wished to highlight Gall's demonstration that "sentiments, acts, intelligence—all of moral man—is localized in the brain."[31]

Although the principal aim of Antonini's book was to show, throughout the history of the West, that the relation of interior states to features of the body's surface was taken for granted, the links he established with physiognomy and phrenology entailed different rhetorical risks. In the first case, there was a general consensus among late-nineteenth-century human scientists—even among scholars who could not agree on much else—about the value of physiognomic studies. Augusto Tebaldi (b. 1833), a psychiatrist who headed an asylum in Pavia, may only have exaggerated slightly when he observed that "every discipline that has as its object a knowledge of man avails itself of, and profits from, the observation of physiognomy. Anthropology, Psychology, Medicine all read this book that reveals the interior life."[32] One of Lombroso's fiercest critics, anthropologist Paolo Mantegazza (1831–1910), would indeed devote an entire volume to the subject.[33] Later, in a review of Darwin's book on the expression of emotion, Mantegazza renewed his call that science "shed a bit of light" on the study of human facial features; by "ripping this research from the hands of divination and an almost cabalistic art," there was hope for the first lines of precise and incontrovertible knowledge. While he waited for science, however, "men and children, learned and uneducated, regard the human face with intense scrutiny, in order to read for hate or love, intelligence or idiocy, suspicion or trust, compassion or cruelty."[34] Even skeptics, observed Mantegazza, could agree that a man with a certain kind of face could not be a gentleman, and a man with another one must necessarily be stupid. Thus, while many might have laughed at the notion of drawing conclusions about the psychic or moral qualities of individuals from their features, these same people chose spouses or developed hatreds largely on the basis of physiognomy.[35]

Antonini's avowal of a kinship between criminal anthropology and phrenology was more problematic, and indeed Gall, Johann Cristoph Spurzheim (1776–1832), and George Combe (1788–1858) are, for the most part, absent from origin stories told by Lombroso and his allies, although they figure prominently in more recent histories of the deviant body.[36] Barbara Stafford has suggested Gall's "cranial criticism" was, in many ways, a "logical extension of a quantified physiognomics or calculating 'science' of the unseen," and work by twentieth-century historians has shown the importance of Gall's contributions to the development of brain physiology, neurology, criminology, and

psychiatry.[37] Renzo Villa has argued that phrenology played an important role in the formation of prison doctors in the nineteenth century,
and especially in the isolation of the single criminal as an object of
scientific knowledge.[38] A case in point is the 1841 study by Hubert
Lauvergne (1796–1859), *Les forçats*, a phrenological examination of the
convicts in the prison of Toulon.[39] For Villa, phrenology was a kind of
bridge between a "psychology of character" and a "materialistic natural-
ism," helping to fashion the corporeal reading practices of Lombrosian
anthropology.[40] Georges Lantéri-Laura argues for an even closer connection, suggesting that Lombroso borrowed from Gall's phrenology
both the idea that the true criminal has an instinctual penchant for
crime linked to a hypertrophied cerebral organ, and the techniques of
cranioscopic examination, designed to produce palpable evidence of
somatic anomalies.[41]

But phrenological sciences were already under attack by the middle
of the nineteenth century.[42] Indeed, as Marc Renville has observed,
it was part of the disciplinary formation of French anthropology to
efface or repudiate this part of its history[43]; by reducing Gall's work to
bump reading, critics hoped also to severe his ties to the histories of
neurology, physiology, and anatomy.[44] It is thus perhaps not surprising that French critics of the Italian school of criminology were, in
turn, anxious to link the fate of Lombroso's claims to those of Gall and
Spurzheim.[45] As we saw in Chapter 2, discussions of the significance of
the skull of Villella centered on the extent to which Lombroso seemed
to his opponents to be making a phrenological argument for localization. More broadly, Léonce Manouvrier (1850–1927) frequently compared Lombroso to Gall and criminal anthropology to neophrenology,
and it was widely understood that this was a move to deny the work
the status of science.[46] In a report to the second congress of criminal
anthropology, Manouvrier observed that Gall's phrenology had en-
joyed a popularity far greater than Lombroso's anthropology, which
had, he suggested, merely rejuvenated and refitted earlier claims about
the relations of the physical and the moral: "Rash conclusions and a
lack of scientific competence or scientific rigor discredited the former
phrenology and harmed its development; these must not be allowed
to do the same to its young offspring."[47] In Italy, Mantegazza predicted in a review of Manouvrier's work that Lombroso's anthropology

would share the fate of chiromancy and Gall's phrenology.[48] Indeed, allies of Lombroso were not above making this same rhetorical maneuver, as when Giovanni Mingazzini (1859–1929) compared the Russian anthropologist Pauline Tarnowsky to a phrenologist because she did not, in his view, know the relevant biological literature on prostitution.[49]

Defenders of Italian positivist anthropology sought to foreground discontinuities between Gall and Lombroso, in part by distinguishing the qualitative nature of phrenological readings from the quantitative measure anthropologists deployed. As early as 1866, when defending his work on mental illness and legal medicine, Lombroso had objected to a critic's having confounded craniometry—a "branch of applied anatomy, like pelvimetry"—with phrenology, "which is a fable concocted by Gall and Spurzheim." If there was a relation, Lombroso insisted, it was that the former had "unmasked and destroyed" the latter.[50] Twenty years later, in his polemic, Lombroso bristled anew at jurist Aristide Gabelli's (1830–1891) accusation that he had attempted to "restore" Gall's system, "going so far as to say...that I wish to condemn men only because of the shape of their cranium or their protruding ears or their thin lips; whereas I have never even considered this worth discussing, let alone approving."[51] Lombroso insisted his studies of the cranium had as little in common with phrenology as did surgical anatomy with palm reading.[52] As proof of a longstanding disavowal, Lombroso referred readers to an article he had published in 1878, a study of the exhumed cranium of the Italian physicist Alessandro Volta (1745–1827). After finding that Volta's skull (like that of other geniuses) bore indices of inferiority and signs of an anomalous structure of the brain, Lombroso had not been able to resist a mocking reference to the popularity of phrenology:

It would be ridiculous today to dwell on phrenological superstitions, but for those who still care it would be useful to know that no point of Volta's cranium protrudes notably, except that portion of the temporal region in which those alchemists of cerebral physiology would locate acquisitiveness, and others the instinct to steal or brawl; yet Volta was a model of modesty and generosity.[53]

III. Popular Culture and Proverbial Wisdom

If the knowledge physiognomists and artists had of criminals might plausibly have been gained through experiment and experience, Lombroso was convinced also that modern humans had an instinctive understanding of the criminal type. What some might have called an "intuitive sense" was for Lombroso more likely the result of a vaguely Lamarckian evolutionary process, a "phenomenon inherited from the epoch in which the weak, although fearing the violence of the wicked, were becoming a majority." Impressions of evildoers, he reasoned, had been transmitted from fathers to sons, eventually becoming a kind of "unconscious knowledge." The process was similar, he suggested, to what happened to domesticated birds: "born and raised in our houses, they are nevertheless frightened in their cages by the eagle and the predatory hawk who fly past in the distance, and whose image tormented their grandfathers and great-grandfathers."[54]

This "involuntary but universal consciousness" of a special physiognomy of criminals had led, in Lombroso's view, to phrases such as "face of a thief" and "mug of a murderer."[55] Indeed, an entire proverbial wisdom had developed, in Italy and elsewhere, which Lombroso proposed to use as a further support for the conclusions of criminologists. But in an 1882 article on "crime in popular consciousness," Lombroso was obliged to position himself carefully. On one hand, he wished to disqualify the "strange accusation" made by opponents of the positivist school that "its conclusions are at odds with popular convictions."[56] But at the same time he acknowledged a difficulty faced by any knowledge that wished to count as "science": "to overcome prejudices and preconceptions that are nothing other than a way of judging things according to one's own habits and those of one's ancestors." Equally damning, in other words, would be the charge that criminal anthropology had simply taken its conclusions from the wisdom of the folk.[57]

Here, Lombroso wished principally to suggest that the evidence in support of anthropological claims was so extensive and overwhelming that it had even found its way into the "the barley illuminated consciousness of the public; thus it leaves its traces in proverbs, in folksongs and in those verses composed by authors who have, as in a polished mirror, reflected the ideas of the folk."[58] For example, the "altogether distinctive physiognomy of the born criminal" was intuited in the Roman saying "There is nothing worse under the sky than a scanty beard and a colorless face" [*Poca barba e niun colore, sotto il ciel non vi ha peggiore*]. Venetian proverbs taught that one should "Greet from afar the red-haired man and the bearded woman" [*Omo rosso o femina barbuta da lontan xe mejo la saluta*] and warned "Beware the woman with a man's voice" [*Vardete de la donna che gha ose de omo*].[59]

At times, acknowledged Lombroso, proverbs went further than even the most daring anthropologists had been willing to venture, as when they spoke "with a singular accord" of "the wicked tendencies of the man with a turned up nose."[60] On the other hand, the "irresistibility of the impulse of the passions when excited and violent" was well expressed by the saying "The hand pulls the trigger, but the devil fires" [*La mano tira—il diavolo porta*]. And proverbs recognized, better than Lombroso's jurist critics, the recidivist nature of the true delinquent, independent of his or her economic circumstances, and the atavism of the born criminal.[61]

On this last point, Lombroso could rely on the support of Giuseppe Pitrè (1841–1916), the most prominent folklorist in Italy and the editor of the *Archivio per lo studio delle tradizioni popolari*.[62] Writing about atavism and folklore, Pitrè found that the concept of the inheritability of vices and virtues was "diffuse, indeed rooted in the folk. Rarely is the daughter of a bad woman honest, the son of a madman sane."[63] The experience of the people had resulted in the formulation of a "series of maxims" that, Pitrè suggested, could be a resource for the criminologist who wished to take account of folk ways of thought. Sicilians, for example, had observed that "the children of wolves are born with the canine tooth" [*Li figghi di lu lupu nàscinu cu lu scagghiuni*].[64] Lombroso, however, choosing his words carefully, avoided the idea of folklore as a "resource" for the production of scientific knowledge. It was enough (rhetorically) to silence his "metaphysical" critics—and to show that it was *they* who were at odds with common sense—by finding that the ideas of the anthropological school were "not merely echoed by, but . . . in complete accord with the popular imagination."[65]

An example of this kind of negotiation with common wisdom is provided by the anthropological discussions of left-handedness.

Left-handedness in Italy, as elsewhere, was linked linguistically and culturally with danger, dishonesty, and fraud. This was not only due to the plural connotations of the word "left" [*sinistra*], but also the multiple valences of "left-sidedness" [*mancinismo*]; the root *manco* signaling at once the left side of the body and a lack or absence. As Lombroso explained, there were a small number of people who worked more agilely "*a manca*," the so-called "*mancini*."[66] Left-sidedness was, he and fellow criminologists argued, more commonly to be found among children, women, savages, and in ancient times—a sure sign of the atavistic nature of mancinism. Even animals—crustaceans, parrots, lions, and monkeys—were more likely to be left-handed.[67]

For prison physician Carmelo Andronico, the pathological nature of left-handedness was well established. In contrast to the "nobility of right-handedness"—which had been confirmed by the Bible, Aristotle, and Avicenna, among others—left-handedness presented itself as an "anomaly." It was most prevalent, Andronico remarked, among savage peoples: "among Papuans in New Guinea, among the inhabitants of the islands of Pelew, where the men pierce their left ears; among the blacks of Sennaar and Dongola, who wear the leather purse in which they keep coins and tobacco on their left arms."[68] Lombroso cited as further evidence of the link between left-handedness and atavism the behavior of women and children:

> Some time ago Delaunay observed that the man holds out the right arm, which the woman takes with the left; that the woman buttons her clothes from right to left, while the man does so from left to right, and that women and children, when they trace a line or turn a key, for instance, of a watch, initiate the movement from right to left, while the adult man does always from left to right. This explains why, in early times, and still among people little civilized, such as Arabs, the writing was preferably from right to left, which is the habit of children until corrected.[69]

Lombroso proposed to build upon this "common wisdom" by exploring the relations of left-sidedness and criminality. The raw numbers appeared to be telling enough: mancinism had a frequency of 4 percent in normal men, 5.8 percent in normal women, 13 percent in male criminals, and 22 percent in female criminals. The mentally ill, by contrast, had roughly the same frequency of mancinism as normal women and men.[70] The presence of a single atavistic feature in an individual, Lombroso reminded his readers, did not mean his or her entire organism was in a state of arrested development or inferiority. Mancinism was by itself "only one musical note, which, taken alone, signifies nothing and gives no harmony." Anthropologists "[did] not dream of saying that all left-handed people are wicked, but that left-handedness, united to many other traits, may contribute to form one of the worst characters among the human species."[71]

Lombroso and his contemporaries associated left-sidedness with brain lateralization—"Everyone recognizes that mancinism . . . depends on the prevalence of the right hemisphere over the left"[72] —and relied also on research proposing to explain such asymmetries as due to inherited differences in blood supply (asymmetry of branches of the aorta) to the right and left brains.[73] As Lombroso summed it up, "while the honest person would think with the left brain, the criminal thinks with the right."[74] Lombroso would also undertake what he called a "bit of physiological police work," testing the sensitivity to touch and pain (see Chapter 4) of the right and left sides of subjects' bodies. By investigating friends, colleagues, and members of the working classes, as well as criminals, Lombroso was able to uncover a pervasive "sensory mancinism"—that is, a greater sensitivity on the left—that was much more frequent (26 percent) than mancinism in healthy people, and most frequent among lunatics.[75]

Finally, Lombroso reported that criminals almost always exhibited mancinism while walking. A study by a certain Peracchia had found that among normal men strides with the right leg averaged 65 centimeters, whereas those with the left averaged 63; by contrast, among criminals the averages were 70.6 on the right and 72 on the left. In addition, the "angle of deviation" of the left foot was, among criminals, greater than that of the right foot, while the lateral displacement [scartamento] was greater on the right. The longer strides of criminals were, Lombroso reasoned, a sign of their greater "robustness" (see Chapters 4 and 5), but the marked and inverted "lateralism" of their walk testified to their incomplete evolution. Indeed, a deviant stride offered itself as a "differential characteristic," making it possible to distinguish among thieves, murderers, and rapists—among the last, for example, the strides were small with only modest mancinism.

Again, argued Lombroso, this was something his countrymen already and instinctively knew, even at the level of their bodies. So when, in another experiment, a normal individual was told under hypnosis that he was a brigand, he unconsciously modified his walk to resemble that of a criminal. The lateral displacement of the stride extended on the right and declined on the left, the angle of deviation of the foot increased on the left and decreased on the right, and the stride grew in length by 11.6 centimeters on the right and 22.5 on the left.[76] Taken together, the results of laboratory experiments and anatomical measurements both extended and reconfirmed proverbial wisdom: "when the people, whether on the basis of their own observations or on the basis of figures of speech, are suspicious of the left-handed man, they have exaggerated and generalized a fact that is fundamentally true." Remarkably, the folk—and particularly the inhabitants of Emilia and Lombardy—had most closely associated left-handedness with the swindler, that variety of criminal in which experiments revealed "the highest quota (33 percent) of *mancini*."[77]

IV. Reading Bodies: The Child, the Savage, and the Scientist

If, to some extent, knowledge of criminal anatomy was instinctive, it was only logical to expect that it would also guide the reading practices of individuals. Lombroso pointed to the frequent cases on record of honest persons, "extraneous to the world of crime," who had escaped certain death by recognizing, in a "sinister glance," the intentions of an assailant.[78] Lombroso recounted that even his mother, who had lived "cut off from the world" and thus could not have gained any knowledge of men, twice guessed the criminal character of young men whom no one had suspected previously, but who revealed themselves to be wicked many years later.[79] Similarly, a sixteen-year-old noble girl who, according to Lombroso, had never left her ancestral manor and had no experience of life, refused to speak with a villager named Francesconi, treating him like a villain even though others in town acclaimed him. "If he is not an assassin," she correctly predicted, "he will become one." Although Lombroso himself found nothing in the man's photograph to signal his future ferocity, the girl had seen it "in his eyes."[80]

The reading practices of the lay public could, indeed, be put to the test. In his *Polemica*, Lombroso reported an experiment in which he had presented 200 photographs of young men to three physicians, asking them which in their opinion presented the "criminal type." All had agreed on a single individual. Next, Lombroso had shown the photographs to a twelve-year old girl; her judgment had been "perfectly in agreement with the others."[81] Lombroso was pleased to point out that the man identified by all four as a typical criminal had at the time of the identification committed no illegal acts. Later, however, having risen to a high position, he had "cruelly betrayed" those who had helped him to succeed. Thus, while he might not have been a criminal "*juridically*" when he was photographed, he was one "*anthropologically*."[82]

Lombroso often chose to rely on children, women, and even non-Western "primitives" as test subjects. On one occasion he solicited the help of a teacher who presented "20 portraits of thieves and 20 of great men"—we are told nothing further about the nature of these images—to 32 schools girls; 80 percent of the children were able to recognize "the first as wicked, evil and deceitful people."[83] In another experiment, Lombroso presented images of criminals to "young girls" who were, in his judgment, "inexpert in the world of good and evil." Nevertheless, the girls "almost always identified the criminal type."[84]

The "courtesy" of physician Cesare Nerazzini (b. 1849), the author of several books on Ethiopia, allowed Lombroso to perform an even more "curious" experiment.[85] The doctor had brought with him from Abyssinia a Somali servant named Mohamed Ismail, a "young man of lively intelligence," who in a conversation with Lombroso boasted of his ability to identify by sight the "rogues" of his native land. Ismail made his identifications by attending to the movements of the major blood vessels of the neck (see the discussion of the vascular system in Chapter 5). He went on to say he could also identify Italy's criminals, no matter how they were dressed, simply by looking at their faces: "They have necktie, but I look inside eye, nose, ears, and know bad man right away." Lombroso showed Ismail a series of images, including photographs, of "great men," ordinary men, and criminals, while Nerazzini recorded the Somali's judgments. Lombroso reports that the visitor correctly identified 148 of 162 images, declaring Michelangelo, for example, to be "good, serious, and big-brained." Lombroso delighted in contrasting the "savage's" ability to see with the stubborn blindness of his opponents (both the classical school and the French sociologists): "Oh, poor academic," he mused, "that a poor, savage Somali manages to correct your weakly supported assertions, and to serve as your teacher." When not led astray, the mind of a savage was "worth more than that of the most cultivated man who is trapped in old and new beliefs."[86]

But if folk typologies and lay reading practices served to reinforce the findings of the criminologists, and to defend them against charges of an "exaggerated somaticism,"[87] they might also have risked calling into question the privileged position of the anthropological observers, or (as some critics charged) the scientific status of their theories.[88] Gabelli, for example, accused Lombroso and his colleagues of an unscientific reliance on common wisdom. Like Lavater before them, argued Gabelli, criminal anthropologists were content to try to clarify and give order to those "popular instincts" that allow people, in their everyday lives, to pronounce a man a "gentleman" or a "rogue" on the basis of his appearance.[89] On one hand, Gabelli protested, such judgments were often wrong or impossible to make, and he invited his readers to repeat on the street an "anthropological" experiment he had often performed in the courtroom: "While we might be able quickly to recognize bricklayers, coal-sellers, and chimneysweeps, we would however confuse the lawyer with the doctor, and the shopkeeper with the clerk, not to mention the honest ones with those who are not."[90] On the other hand, Gabelli complained that science should combat rather than affirm the "human vanity" that forms a foundation of popular knowledges. Otherwise, he concluded, we would have "as many sciences as there are curiosities, desires, dreams, [and] prejudices among the masses."[91]

Lombroso, in turn, attacked Gabelli for concluding, on the basis of a single article (a piece in *Domenica del Fracassa*) that criminal anthropology took its conclusions from the wisdom of the folk, "which—it is true—often errs."[92] But, he continued, "we have never dreamed of turning to the folk for our conclusions." As proof, Lombroso cited the many elements of folk wisdom science had been unable to confirm. In the end, he said proverbial wisdom was cited only to show conclusions were not as far from "popular consciousness" as some people had claimed.[93] For Lombroso and his colleagues, the anthropologist was to be distinguished from the observant and instinctive folk by his specialized techniques for measuring and reading the body: by a corporeal literacy that made possible both an exegesis and a diagnosis. The anthropologist did not offer fortunetelling or prophecy, as the masses and critics believed, but a "reading." The criminal's body was a "palimpsest in reverse," made more easily legible because the anthropologist did not limit himself to the face, but also included "calligraphy, gestures, sensibility." [94]

On one hand, the gaze of the criminologist could be shown to be more practiced. Antonio Marro (d.1913), for example, invoked his experience as a physician attached to the judiciary prison of Turin to disqualify the amateur diagnoses of prison visitors: "People generally think they recognize the murderer or the assassin in the most striking physiognomies—protruding brows, a full and shaggy beard, and a surly gaze." For the expert, however, who had learned not to be deceived by appearances, an accused's steady, "glacial" gaze was far more significant than one that "spit flames and fury."[95] Still, Marro found he could not do without the rhetorical support of popular wisdom: "As the proverb says, still waters run deep, and the most bloodthirsty beasts are often hidden behind a hairless and pale face."

Lombroso cited examples of novelists who had given fictional criminals a too–frightening appearance, and complained physiognomists such as Casper had committed the opposite error, imagining no difference between delinquents and normal men. The point, claimed Lombroso, was not that the appearance of criminals was always *threatening*, but that it was "entirely *particular*"; indeed, it was "almost unique for each form of delinquency."[96] Thus, thieves were characterized by "a notable mobility of the face and hands," small eyes, and a thin beard, while arsonists displayed "feminine characteristics." However, as a *science*, forensic medicine could not content itself with these "generic and isolated descriptions": "Anthropology," argued Lombroso, "needs *numbers*."[97]

Stephen Jay Gould has identified the "allure of numbers" as an element of a faith that swept through the human sciences in the second half of the nineteenth century.[98] Despite this, there was always a danger that the data published by anthropologists could be seen as gratuitous quantification. For example, in a scathing review of Lombroso's *Pensiero e meteore*, a volume that argued for a causal connection between climate and criminal dangerousness, Mantegazza argued that the book was not scientific, but merely had the appearance of science: "the numbers and figures serve as an apparatus, not as a basis for arguments and conclusions."[99] What is more, some criminological readings remained avowedly qualitative—we might even say aesthetic.

But there is another sense in which it is misleading to suggest that "numbers" alone distinguished criminal anthropology from alternative and popular knowledges. In practice, what differentiated the scientist from the popular reader of faces was the ability to enter prisons, asylums, schools, and orphanages to perform tests; the authority to enlist "volunteers" from the populations of "normal" women and men; the access to instruments that were expensive and often difficult to manipulate; and the means to disseminate results (journals, conferences, university lecture halls, and, of course, the witness stand). On one hand, we need to keep in view the power relations that enabled physicians and biological scientists to move freely in nonpublic spaces, to compel subjects to remove their clothes, to probe and manipulate the body, and even to inflict pain. On the other hand, in this chapter and those that follow, we need to explore further the roles played by tools, techniques, manuals and other elements of *practice* in the elaboration and consolidation of a criminological science.[100] In so doing, we may call attention to the performative qualities of the new anthropology—to the acts of manipulating instruments, tabulating measurements, and testifying about numbers that aimed at elevating the work of criminologists above the level of popular wisdom, and at the same time sought to create a new kind of scientific "common sense." What I have in mind is to attend to the varied and messy kinds of work (manual, theoretical, interpretive, rhetorical) that were required to go from the manufacture, say, of a Zwaardesmaker double olfactometer in Geneva, to its manipulation in a cramped prison cell in Turin, to the transcription of olfactory thresholds in a pre-printed form, to testimony on the witness stand about the sensory atavism of a criminal defendant—testimony meant both to speak to the particular circumstances of the defendant,

and to affirm the competence of the scientific criminologist, and him
alone, to recognize social dangers.

V. Making Numbers: Bodies and Tools

Historian Renzo Villa, piecing together accounts from the local press,
tells the story of a tour of the city of Turin led by Lombroso during
the Sixth International Congress of Criminal Anthropology in 1906.
Lombroso guided a delegation of male and female visitors to a variety of sites of production of criminological knowledge, ending in the
local prison. While touring the cells, reports Villa, Lombroso and his
party came upon a boy who displayed "certain physical particularities
that could be catalogued as degenerative stigmata." Lombroso did not
hesitate, after the women were excused, to have the boy undressed,
with the goal of searching on his naked body for other signs of his
criminal type.[101] For the next hour, delegates to the congress watched
Lombroso examine other "sad specimens" collected by the head guard:
a shoemaker convicted of sexual molestation, a recidivist thief, and
particularly a second thief whose body was covered with tattoos. As
Villa reports, the "clinical" examination of these subjects included a
cataloging of surface anomalies and pathologies, measurement and
palpation of the body, interrogations, even a diagnosis of the subject's
handwriting.[102]

The ability of the criminal anthropologist to command the presence
of the criminal body, to compel it to be undressed, to be felt, even
to yield to painful manipulations, was in many ways an example of
the relations of power that characterized the practice of medicine—
particularly in prisons—at the beginning of the twentieth century.[103]
But if in 1906 the prison could be said to constitute the laboratory of the
criminologist,[104] only a few years earlier Lombroso had been greeted
with hostility in similar spaces, and had had considerable difficulty
gaining access to the bodies of criminals.

Biographer Luigi Ferrio reports that Lombroso received an "icy
reception" in Turin in 1876; when he went there to assume a chair
in Legal Medicine, Lombroso was obliged to set up a laboratory at
his own expense, and found prisons and asylums locked their doors
to him.[105] Lombroso's daughter, Gina, explains that her father first

obtained clients for his psychiatric practice by putting a handwritten sign on his door offering free consultations—the reputation of the doctor, "contested" at the university, was well established among the populace, his daughter reports.[106] The patients who came in turn allowed him to teach a course on psychiatry at the university that he had been denied on the excuse that he had no patients to present. It was, however, decidedly more difficult to study the "living criminal." Criminals did not present themselves at the door of Lombroso's laboratory, even when they were offered cash. Lombroso therefore enlisted his assistant Giovanni Cabria, by trade a bookbinder and lithographer, to go out and find criminals and bring them back to the lab. In a few months, Lombroso-Ferrero reports, Cabria became a "veritable bloodhound for criminals." He searched the arcades and taverns, and when he had found a potential client, convinced him of the need to visit the lab, negotiated a price, and walked him to the lab.[107] Cabria also was responsible for collecting hundreds of skulls unearthed by the urban renovation of Turin, which destroyed the cemeteries of criminals, soldiers, Jews, and monks, furnishing valuable material for a comparative anthropology.[108]

Many of Lombroso's later collaborators would be directors of asylums, hospitals, and orphanages, and could therefore rely on captive populations for observation, measurement, and experimentation. But even many of these also needed to recruit others, and in particular those normal or healthy women and men who served as points of comparison. Although it is clear that there was a somewhat regular supply of ordinary citizens willing to give their bodies over, even to embarrassing and uncomfortable experiments, we learn little about their recruitment, class positions, or levels of education. At times, as we will see in the next chapter, criminologists—like others working in experimental medicine or physiology—were obliged to rely on their own bodies to construct norms for the healthy body.

There were other limits to the power of the physician to read the body. For example, Lombroso complained in his study of criminal women and prostitutes about his inability to use pictures of Italian women because of a prohibition in his own country against measuring, studying, or photographing criminals once they had been convicted; instead, he was obliged to reproduce images of Russian and French prostitutes collected by Pauline Tarnowsky. The same prohibition had required Lombroso in *L'uomo delinquente* to rely on photographs from the German prison *Album*, the *National Police Gazette* (New York) and the *Illustrated Police News* (Boston) (see Figures 1.3 and 2.9).[109] "As long as there is a presumption of innocence," remarked a sarcastic Lombroso, "as long as [criminals] are only indicted or accused, you can defame them in any way you like and give them maximum publicity. . . But when they are recognized once and for all as rogues, when they are locked up forever in prison—oh, then they become sacred. Woe to those who touch them. Woe to those who study them." What is more, these limits on the power of social experts contrasted with the rules governing the training of physicians: "Consumptive patients [and] pregnant women may be manipulated, even to their hurt, by students for the good of science, but rogues—God help us!"[110]

The access of criminologists to the dead bodies of criminals was, for a time, also restricted. As we saw, scientists could be forced to scavenge for the crania of criminals or to rely on the generosity of family members for the skeletal remains of normal people or "geniuses." Anthropologists also participated in an informal international exchange of body parts to build their collections—a gift economy in which a personal friendship might bring the skulls of decapitated Indian criminals into a laboratory in Turin.[111] It was not until 1883 that an accord between the Ministries of the Interior and Public Education allowed university professors to perform autopsies on Italian criminals who died while in the prison infirmary.[112] Ezio Sciamanna, who prepared a guide for anatomical and anthropological research on the cadavers of convicts, noted that such research could result in the compilation of statistics that would help scientists to address two important social problems: the links between criminal acts and states of health and disease, and the physical consequences of incarceration. The autopsies Sciamanna proposed involved a variety of anthropometrical measurements, and a section on "special investigations" recommended that doctors keep parts of the brain and head, and that tattooed skin be cut and preserved.[113]

Augusto Tamburini (1848–1914), the director of an asylum in Reggio d'Emilia, and Giulio Benelli, employed by a house of corrections in Reggio, later campaigned to have the same kind of research undertaken on all *living* prisoners. In an open letter to the inspector of prisons Martino Beltrani-Scalia, Tamburini argued that material that was "too precious" and in great supply was being lost to science. "The careful and conscientious study of the entire criminal population enclosed therein, conducted without prejudice and with precision and uniformity of method, would certainly furnish, in a few years, an immense amount of material that would serve to solve a great many problems pertaining to penal and criminal disciplines."[114] Tamburini proposed creating a manual for the anthropological study of living inmates, similar to that developed by Sciamanna for autopsies. Each establishment would be furnished with a low-cost craniometer and a dynamometer. As Benelli noted, the first edition of Lombroso's *L'uomo delinquente* had summarized results from 830 criminals; the third edition 3,839. "But this number must grow further," wrote Benelli, calling for uniform studies on 100,00 criminals that would include eight tests of sensitivity.[115] Yet Lombroso would lament ten years later that there were no provisions in Italy for even routine judicial anthropometry. One of his "dearest disciples," Luigi Anfosso, had invented an instrument he called the "tachianthropometer" (Figure 3.3). Although this anthropometer allowed a series of measurements of the body to be made very rapidly (Lombroso dubbed the device an "anthropometric guillotine") after "much negotiation" the Italian government had rejected it.[116]

Anthropometry and physiological experiments were, in obvious ways, dependent on the availability not only of docile subjects (and dead bodies), but also on an appropriate selection of reliable instruments. The coherence and authority of criminology would come to depend on scientists' ability to contain a potentially limitless proliferation of measurements and to deploy those instruments that promised to demonstrate systematic and significant difference between pathological and normal bodies. Lombroso, in his handbook for forensic experts, suggested that a well-appointed laboratory would include the Anfosso tachianthropometer, Broca's auricular goniometer, Sieweking's esthesiometer, a Eulenberg baristesiometer, a Nothnagel thermesthesiometer, a Zwaardesmaker olfactometer, a Regnier-Mathieu dynamometer, a Mosso ergograph, and a modified campimeter, as well as a more mundane selection of compasses, measuring tapes, eye charts, magnets, and

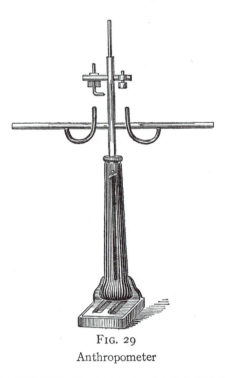

FIG. 29
Anthropometer

Fig. 3.3   Anthropometer.

odoriferous substances.[117] We might well ask how this bewildering array of instruments came to be found in medical laboratories, a question that might lead us to the conditions of the instruments' design, manufacture, and international circulation (Figure 3.4). But the selection of instruments (why each of these, and not others?) also tells us something about which measurements could and could not count as significant at particular moments in the history of criminology, and about how the body was imagined and mapped *through* tools. In a sense, each instrument produced the body anew, giving rise to an index, a threshold, or a capacity that could not have mattered previously.[118] Of course, the rhetoric of anatomical and physiological measurement tended to deny the constructed nature of what was measured, relying on (and reproducing) the illusion that indices were *features of bodies*, simply to be found on its surfaces and structures.

Although there clearly was a vigorous circulation of devices across the boundaries of discipline and nation, it is difficult to reconstruct this

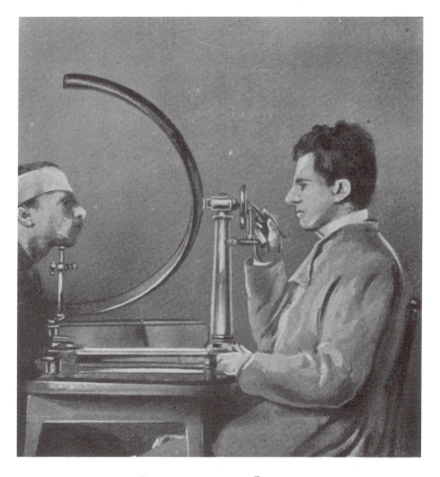

CAMPIMETER OF LANDOLT

Fig. 3.4 Landolt Campimeter.

traffic from anthropological journals and conference proceedings. It is striking, for example, that there was no space provided for a display of tools at the first international congress of criminal anthropology in 1886; Severi and Lombroso complained of the absence of anthropometrical instruments (with the exception of a single example of a Regnier's graphical craniometer), arguing such an exhibit could have been of "greatest importance" and given rise to "productive comparisons."[119]

The occasional laments of criminologists are often as revealing as the announcements made of new or improved instruments. Many devices were, to judge by the published reports, very difficult to use properly. Giuseppe Sergi admitted that he struggled to manipulate a Benedikt craniophore—a device for holding and orienting skulls in order to make craniometric measurements—even though he had had it demonstrated by its inventor during a visit to Vienna. Use of the device remained "a long and difficult operation for those who do not have experience with instruments of precision."[120] Other researchers worried about the consistency of measurements made by a rapidly growing range of competing instruments. Carlo Gaudenzi, in an article devoted to the clinometer—a device to measure angles of the head—complained of the proliferation of "goniometric" instruments. The development of the field of craniometry required so many different single devices that there was, in addition to a concern about time and money, a danger of multiplying possible errors. These errors were not avoided, Gaudenzi warned, by graphical instruments such as craniographs and cephalographs because these provided no direct measurements. The central problem was to choose a consistent point of orientation for subsequent measurements, and he offered as a solution a device that allowed more than three dozen measurements to be taken on a skull or the head of a living person.[121] Paolo Mantegazza also worried in print about the errors and inconsistencies introduced by scientists, especially in comparative work: while all anthropologists measured the cranium, they used different methods and instruments to collect their observations. In order for these measurements to "have the same value" and serve as bases for comparison, it was necessary that each procedure be "diligently described."[122]

A number of devices sought to overcome both the sloppiness of scientists and the requirement of an accompanying narrative by calculating indices themselves; for example, Lombroso described an index-craniograph (Figure 3.5) as "automatically giving" an index as a relation of two cranial diameters.[123] Such devices, in fact, appeared to read or record indices directly from the body and in an unmediated way; in a sense, it was the criminal body itself that produced the index, telling the story of its own dangerousness. Ironically, the scientist, who was elsewhere so insistent on his special ability to read the body, was in the act of collecting an index made to withdraw from view.

Fɪɢ. 30
Craniograph Anfossi

Fig. 3.5 Anfossi Craniograph.

VI. The Writing Body

This tension, as we will see in coming chapters, was particularly marked for graphical instruments, that array of devices (cardiographs, ergographs, pneumographs, mylographs) that produced inscriptions from the criminal and the normal body, and that promised to overcome the limits and fallibility of the human senses.[124] As Robert Frank observes, although some instruments such as the microscope sharpened or extended a perception or sense, others such as the sphygmograph (Figure 3.6) "took a human sense that was imprecise, variable, fleeting and translated it into the movement of an instrument." They "made possible the rearrangement of sense experience into some new format."[125] As Etienne Jules Marey (1830–1904) argued in 1885:

> Not only are these instruments sometimes destined to replace the observer, and in such circumstances to carry out their role with an incontestable superiority, but they also have their own domain where nothing can replace them. When the eye ceases to see, the ear to hear, touch to feel, or indeed when our senses give deceptive appearances, these instruments are like new senses of astonishing precision.[126]

If the graphical method sought, on one hand, to overcome the deficiencies and vagaries of the observer's senses, it also promised, in

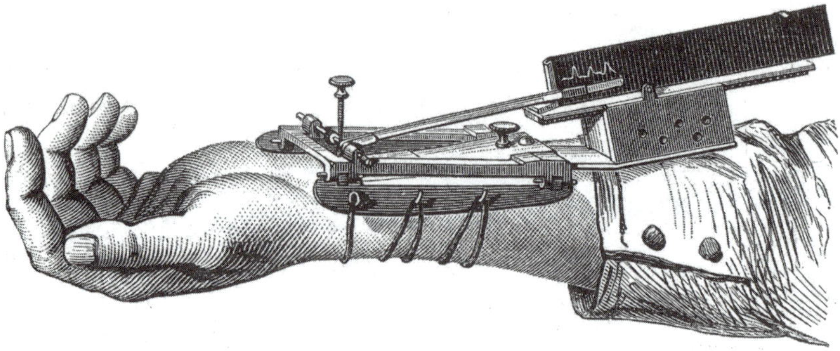

Fig. 370. — Sphygmographe direct (Marey).

Fig. 3.6 Marey Direct Sphygmograph.

Marey's view, to overcome the inadequacies of spoken language. It yielded a record ostensibly unaffected by the prejudices of the observer and that could speak across language barriers, circulating freely—in texts and in lecture halls—and with a particular rhetorical force.[127] The recorded traces were at times characterized as the language of science, at others as the language of the phenomena themselves, or of *life* itself. The fantasy, as Robert Brain puts it, was one in which "automatic recording instruments would generate a vast heterotopic space of inscription that would push out speech altogether and replace it with mechanized forms of thinking and communication."[128]

If the body of the scientist (marked by its sensory weaknesses and the imprecision of its utterances) receded into the background, the body of the experimental subject was at the same time foregrounded and given a new agency. Whether the brain "wrote" or the pulse was "armed with a pen,"[129] the body was imagined to tell its own truth, and to give itself away. In a lecture "On the Physiology of the Heart and its Relations with the Brain," experimental physiologist Claude Bernard (1813–1878) noted that with Marey's cardiograph the heart, a "veritable living machine," can "itself trace on paper each of its contraction with their slightest variations, and we can say, without metaphor, that we read in the human heart."[130]

4

The Shock of Recognition

"The instinctive criminal resembles the idiot to whom, as Galton remarks, pain is a 'welcome surprise.'"
—Havelock Ellis, *The Criminal* (1914)

I. Introduction: Autoexperiment

In 1867, Lombroso invited four male colleagues, whom he judged to be "free of cutaneous and nervous disease,"[1] to his laboratory in Pavia to conduct an unusual experiment. Lombroso proposed that the men apply the electrodes of a Ruhmkorff induction coil (Figure 4.1) to various parts of each other's bodies, gradually increasing the current until each man indicated that he felt pain. Lombroso had previously used the induction coil for therapeutic purposes[2]; on this day, the men held the electrodes, which had been fitted with sponges dipped in a saline solution, to their gums, nipples, tongues, lips, eyelids, the soles of the feet, and the glans of the penis—thirty-nine separate locations in all. Lombroso reports that the pains he and his associates sustained were of varied qualities. On the index finger, the pain was experienced as a "series of hot pricks"; on the palm of the hand, as a "cramping and tearing"; on the back as a "scalding pain"; on the penis as "though a red-hot wire were passed through it."[3] But though these qualitative differences evidently made an impression, it was *quantitative* differences that held the researchers' attention. For each application of the electrodes, Lombroso and his friends measured the distance between the inducing and induced coils when pain was first reported, and recorded this "threshold of sensibility" in a notebook.

The tabulated results first revealed that parts of the body varied consistently in their sensibility to pain. In all of the men, the gums, glans, tip of the tongue, lips, and nipples proved the most sensitive to pain; the soles of the feet and the big toe the least sensitive. In

ALGOMETER

Fig. 4.1 Algometer.

general, the top and front of the body proved more sensitive than the bottom and back. Lombroso explained these differences largely in terms of variations in the thickness of the skin (which accounted, in his view, for the sensibility of the penis and the tongue) and variations in the quantity and "nobility" of the nerves (which accounted for the sensibility of the face).[4] Second, and perhaps more important, the results suggested that individuals varied in their *overall* sensibility—it did not escape their attention that the "most intelligent" member of the group (who is never named) also proved the most sensitive to pain.[5]

But the real significance of the correlation between intellect and sensibility only became apparent when Lombroso examined the results of experiments on a different set of subjects: twenty-three male and female volunteers, whom Lombroso identified as mentally and physically "healthy," and sixty-three institutionalized persons, whom he identified as "mentally ill."[6] Here, it was not only individuals who demonstrated a patterned variability, but groups. Men, it appeared, were systematically less sensitive than women—a result, Lombroso speculated, of men's thicker skin. But after skin thickness, the most importance cause of differences appeared to Lombroso to be the "level of intelligence," or rather the state of mental health: the mentally ill were systematically and markedly less sensitive than healthy subjects. Lombroso found that the mad "seemed almost not to feel currents that were very painful for healthy men."[7] What is more, they could not properly identify the *site* of pain: one subject, for example, moaned that his tooth hurt, while in fact his hand was being shocked.

In the case of the mad, insensibility (or "obtuseness," as Lombroso called it) was taken to be a sign of an underlying organic defect. This suggested not only the possibility of mapping, through precise measurements of pain thresholds, madness in relation to sanity, but also of distinguishing experimentally among different kinds of mental illness: thus, while the demented, pellagroids, and apathetic melancholiacs presented diminished sensibility, erethismic melancholiacs presented increased sensibility.[8]

In order for us to make sense of these experiments (and we may at first be inclined to dismiss them), there is much we would need to know: about the history of categories of mental health and illness that made possible a confident sorting out of the "normal" and the "abnormal," the "apathetic" and the "erethismic"; about the late-nineteenth-century fascination with the therapeutic and diagnostic uses of electricity; and, of course, about the multiple understandings of pain that circulated in European philosophy, theology, psychology, and medicine.[9] In this chapter, we confine ourselves to exploring how it came to appear commonsensical that the body's suffering could be quantified, that it could testify to important qualities of individuals and groups, and that it could in particular signal a "criminal" nature.

What Lombroso's experiments seemed to promise, at least to his contemporaries, was not only a refined understanding of the nature and manifestations of organic anomalies of the mind, but also a means of a more general *diagnosis*: of making visible a wide variety of conditions that threatened to remain hidden but that might pose social dangers. Scientists in Europe and the United States would soon test the sensibility of epileptics, deaf mutes, under-achieving school children, and a whole range of suspected and convicted criminals.[10] In the case of criminals, *algometry*, as it came to be called, would be proposed as a routine part of the examinations performed by criminologists retained as expert witnesses in courts of law, as well as by prison physicians.[11] Pain was not enlisted to extract the truth about illegal *acts*, as had been the case with torture, but rather to produce evidence of the biological nature of individuals and groups, and about the *dangers* that accompanied a "failure to evolve."

II. Measuring Pain

Measurements of pain sensibility constituted simply one among many metrical practices at the disposal of anthropologists. To the extent that pain thresholds were stable, quantifiable, and served to differentiate, they could function interchangeably with the cephalic index, the angle of a jaw, or the bizygomatic diameter of the face. As we have seen, claims anthropologists made about the dangerousness of particular individuals typically involved *multiple* signs of the body's degeneration or atavism. But it is worth noting the boldness of the claim that *pain*, which many nineteenth-century scholars had identified as private, subjective, and highly variable—in sum, beyond the reach of quantification—could be made both objective and public.[12] Indeed, as we will see in a moment, it was the link that pain established *between* the body's surface and interior states (including the ability to feel "moral" anguish) that made algometers and algometry of particular interest to criminologists.

The relations of pain sensibility to pain perception and to endurance, which would come to preoccupy many late-nineteenth-century physiologists—and even some other criminal anthropologists—were never posed by Lombroso in a systematic way. Instead, he took for granted that painful sensations were unambiguously felt and would be faithfully reported. In this respect, pain experiments seemed to him to avoid precisely the problem of "subjectivity" that had plagued earlier tests of "general sensibility." Lombroso criticized Ernst von Leyden's (1832–1910) work in electrical esthesiometry and E. H. Weber's (1795–1878) work on tactile sensibility, which has used a compass (Figure 4.2) to test subjects' ability to distinguish two points on the skin,[13] on the grounds that the subjects might not always be "attentive" to their sensations; the problem of paying attention was

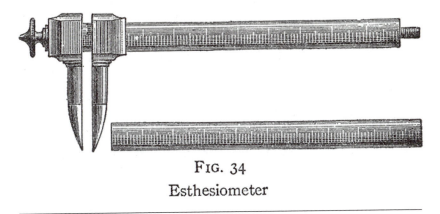

FIG. 34
Esthesiometer

Fig. 4.2   Esthesiometer.

greatest, Lombroso observed, in the lower classes.[14] By contrast, in experiments involving painful shocks, Lombroso assured his readers, there was no question of subjects' failing to pay attention. The only problem he acknowledged was with the mentally ill, who could not always be relied upon to describe the intensity or (as we saw) the *site* of their pain. But, in any event, argued Lombroso, the experimenter could rely on grimaces and involuntary contractions of the muscles.[15]

Other experimenters would offer more subtle accounts. Criminologist Salvatore Ottolenghi observed that the difficulties involved in measuring pain grew out of variations in the subject's attitude toward the experiment, his or her readiness to acknowledge pain when felt, the "sincerity of subjective phenomena," the difference between sensibility and excitability, variations in resistance, and the possibility of suggestion or autosuggestion.[16] Two other associates of Lombroso, surprised to find that "cultured" men seemed in one experiment to be less sensitive to pain than male hospital orderlies, reasoned the first group better understood the importance of the examination, and knew to wait until the pain reached levels that were truly unbearable.[17]

Some of Lombroso's contemporaries raised more troubling questions: about the stability of pain thresholds, about the physiological effects of pains of short duration, and about the suitability of electrical algometers for administering pain.[18] Lombroso argued that nothing was better suited to the measurement of sensibility than electricity because nothing was less harmful.[19] However, the anthropologist Paolo Mantegazza, author of a lengthy volume on the physiology of pain, found that electrical currents produced "disagreeable sensations" that were *different* from the majority of pains, and were differently tolerated by different individuals. Some, Mantegazza observed, even found these sensations to be *pleasurable*.[20] These questions were among those raised in what became a very public feud between Lombroso and Mantegazza, who at the time of Lombroso's first algometrical experiments in 1867 was professor of pathological physiology at Pavia and completing work on the first edition of *Fisiologia del dolore*. The debate, which by all accounts destroyed a professional and personal relationship, was ostensibly centered on the question of whether pain *increased* the pulse (as Lombroso had argued) or *decreased* it (as Mantegazza had earlier claimed on the basis of experiments with animals and humans). But also at issue were disciplinary boundaries (those dividing criminology, anthropology, and physiology), techniques for administering and measuring pain, and even the credit for coining the term "algometry."[21] In the end, the most serious charge Mantegazza leveled was that Lombroso had measured *nothing* and had merely observed the stimulant action of electricity on the muscles. (Mantegazza, for his part, preferred to administer traumatic pains by crushing the paws of animals, using sharp probes, or applying boiling water and ice cubes to the skin. None of these methods allowed for gradations, but Mantegazza's interests were in the physiological effects of traumatic experiences.)

Lombroso responded that, although there was admittedly was no evident correlation between sensibility to electrical shocks and sensibility to touch, there *were* more constant relations between sensibility to electrical pain and sensibility to pain generally, a correlation he sought to confirm by pricking and pinching his subjects, and by applying heated cylinders and pieces of ice to their bodies. Moreover, he noted, the loci identified as most sensitive to electrical shock were precisely those known to the ancients and to more recent practitioners of torture, and included the sites where pain is most strongly felt during illness (e.g., toothaches and migraines).[22]

III. Sensibility and Civilization

For all its purported utility in making distinctions, pain sensibility was, unlike say the "facial diameter," much more than indexical. In making sense of pain thresholds, Lombroso and his contemporaries drew on (and purported to confirm) the widespread notion that sensibility—not just to pain but also to sensory stimuli of varied kinds—was linked to levels of evolutionary progress, to race, and to "civilization."[23] The outlines of this hierarchy of suffering, what Martin Pernick has labeled a "great chain of feeling,"[24] were fairly consistent across disciplinary and national boundaries. The story told later by René Fülöp-Miller (1891–1963) in his volume *Triumph over Pain* is similar to late nineteenth-century accounts: plants and lower animals are less sensitive than higher animals, children less sensitive than adults, "savages" less sensitive than "the civilized," Eastern Europeans less sensitive than Western Europeans.[25] Also typical is the author's narrative style, weaving together anecdotes, published reports of experiments, and common wisdom:

> Women, upon whom nature imposes the painful and arduous task of childbearing can, in general, bear pain better than men. Electrical experiments have shown that women can endure exposure to an electrical current ranging up to 250 volts, whereas men can rarely endure more than 30 volts. Social circumstances, too, have a great deal to do with sensibility, the countryman being, as a rule, less sensitive than the townsman, and the mental workers more sensitive than manual workers. British and French investigators have proved that sensibility to pain diminishes with advancing years. Environment, temporal as well as physical, plays an important part in determining sensibility to pain. There have been periods, like that of the Thirty Years' War and that of the dominance of the Inquisition, when sensibility to pain was greatly blunted by the general prevalence of savagery. The sensitiveness of different races and peoples varies much. The European is at least twice as sensitive as the savage; and de Ségur, in his history of the Napoleonic campaign of 1812, reports that the Russian bore pain much better than did the French. But I need hardly say that these generalizations are often invalidated by experience of particular persons.[26]

The link between civilization and sensibility could be construed in a number of ways: that civilization made humans soft, vulnerable, and weak; or that is allowed them better to make aesthetic and other qualitative judgments.[27] For the eugenicist Francis Galton, for example, sensibility was intimately linked to the ability to *discriminate*: "the more perceptive the senses are of difference, the larger is the field upon

which our judgment and intelligence can act."[28] But underlying these
varied readings was the shared assumption that the uncivilized felt
no pain (and, for that matter, little pleasure). Travelers' accounts that
had affirmed the extraordinary sensory *abilities* of non-European peoples (and particularly the sense of smell) now found themselves under
attack.[29] This notion had become so much a part of common scientific
wisdom by the time Lombroso conducted his experiments in 1867 that
he could invoke it to counter the charges of his anthropologist critic:

> [Mantegazza] must be well aware that the Dakota [and] the Otomac
> exhibit a pain sensibility so obtuse as to sing war hymns while their limbs
> roast in a slow fire, that the Tahitian and the Negro feel pain so little as
> to invent for ornaments cuts made in the most sensitive regions of the
> body. The savage woman of Australia has gone so far as to contradict the
> most sacred laws of the Bible when it comes to the pains of childbirth,
> insomuch as in some tribes it is the husband who is confined while the
> wife who has given birth is obliged to work. And do we not see, we
> doctors, among our masses, the peasant who tolerates for several days in
> a row, without even noticing, pains due to pleurisy and wounds which for
> men of more refined intelligence would be intolerable?[30]

In fact, Mantegazza would make similar claims in his own work on the
physiology of pain, finding that sensibility is "certainly less among the
inferior races, both because their organization is simpler, and because
sensation is propagated in a more restricted field of sympathies."[31] For
Mantegazza, "ethnic differences in sensibility" were due not only to
biology, but also to "the habit of suffering," to the use of narcotics, and
to the presence or absence of stimulants (e.g., caffeine). He cited as
evidence his own experiences as a surgeon in the Americas, and ethnographic and anecdotal accounts of childhood games, rites of passage,
and expressions of grief.[32]

Not content to rely on folk wisdom or on a loosely organized ethnographic record, Lombroso and other human scientists would also proceed to measure variations in pain sensibility among males and females
of different age groups and social classes; the results appeared to give
new scientific support to received wisdom. Ottolenghi found children
to be less sensitive than mature men; although boys and girls between
the ages of six and nine refused to cooperate (Ottolenghi blamed their
"exaggerated excitability"), the results appeared to link the "deficient
moral sense" of children with a "deficient sensibility."[33] An examination

of 1,147 adults from different social classes revealed, meanwhile, that the poor were on the whole less sensitive to pain than the rich.[34]

Physician and anthropologist Robert William Felkin (1858–1922) reported on the "differences of sensibility between Europeans and Negroes," having examined tactile sensibility (using Weber's compass) "in twenty-six body parts of the body on 150 negroes and on 30 Soudanese (Arabs)." Felkin found Europeans could discriminate two points on the tip of the tongue at 1.1 mm, while Sudanese required 2.6 and "negroes" 3.0 mm. The rehabilitative power of civilization was not, however, to be underestimated: "after two negro boys had been educated for four years in England it was found that their tactile sensation had become more acute, and they could then distinguish the points of a pair of compasses at 2 mm."[35]

Lombroso was able to perform his own tests of primitive sensibility on a group of Dinka who were "visiting" Europe from central Africa (the German physiologist Rudolf Virchow (1821–1902) had also made them subjects of physiological experiments).[36] Algometrical experiments on the hands and the tongue, Lombroso reported, revealed the Dinka's "great obtuseness," more than three times the Italian norm. This finding appeared to be confirmed by the subjects' easy tolerance of syphilitic and scrofular sores, by a man who refused to allow doctors to remove a protruding nail from the heel of his shoe, and by the people's habits of scarification and breaking off teeth.[37] And lest we assume these experiments were undertaken only at the margins of the human sciences, it is worth noting that studies of sensibility (as well as other sensory capacities) would later be made parts of two important scientific expeditions: the Cambridge Anthropological Expedition to Torres Straits, headed by Alfred Cort Haddon (1855–1940),[38] and the expedition to Cape Horn undertaken by the French Academy of Sciences.[39]

By the end of the century, the insensibility of criminals had also become part of common wisdom. For example, American criminologist Arthur MacDonald wrote in 1893 that "It is generally admitted that sensibility is less among criminals."[40] In Britain, Havelock Ellis noted that "the physical insensibility of the criminal has indeed been observed by every one who is familiar with prisons. In this respect, the instinctive criminal resembles the idiot to whom, as Galton remarks, pain is a 'welcome surprise.'"[41] For Garofalo, the mere fact of widespread tattooing among prison populations offered itself as compelling evidence of a physiological incapacity[42]; Ellis noted that this tattooing did not spare "parts so sensitive as the sexual organs, which are rarely touched even in extensive tattooing among barbarous races."[43]

Lombroso, in the 1878 edition of *L'uomo delinquente*, repeated stories of criminals whose resistance to pain had been particularly impressive: one "old thief" did not even scream when red-hot metal was applied to his scrotum, and asked if they were finished "as if this were happening to someone else." Another had, with complete apathy, allowed his leg to be amputated, taking the leg in his hands and joking about it.[44] More mundane were the 483 cases of self-inflicted wounds in Chatham penitentiary in 1871.[45] But Lombroso found anecdotal evidence from prisons unsatisfactory, not least because many who were confined in prisons were, in his judgment, also mentally ill. Moreover, he wrote, "the subject of the pain sensibility of criminals was too important and delicate for [him] to be content with only approximate data, not verified through direct experiment."[46] Only such experiments, he argued, could offer the further precision that sensibility is highest in the case of con artists, and lowest for those who committed assaults and robberies, or that sensibility was greater on the left side of the body than on the right (as we saw in Chapter 3, the prevalence of left-sidedness was taken to be a further sign of the atavistic nature of criminality).[47]

Other experimenters found that criminals not only were less sensitive to pain but also had diminished "general" and tactile sensibility, and obtuse senses of smell, taste, and hearing.[48] Sensibility of smell could be judged by presenting subjects with solutions (most often essence of cloves) of varying strength. Salvatore Ottolenghi's subjects were asked to indicate the solution in which they could first detect an odor, and to arrange the solutions in order from weakest to strongest; 10 percent of criminals exhibited either "asnomia" (a complete lack of olfactory sensation) or "olfactory blindness" (the absence of any *specific* sensation).[49] Ottolenghi tested taste by placing drops of varying solutions of saccharine, strychnine, and salt on the subject's tongue. Although some evaluations relied on devices specifically developed for the task (Lombroso's algometer, Weber's esthesiometer, Nothnagel's thermesthesiometer, Landolt's campimeter, and Ottolenghi's graduated osmometer), others were decidedly low tech. To evaluate hearing, Lombroso recommended "speaking in a low voice at a certain distance from the patient, or . . . holding an ordinary watch a little way from his ear."[50]

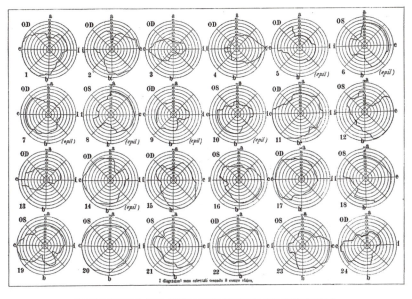

CAMPO VISIVO NEI DELINQUENTI-NATI ED EPILETTICI.

Fig. 4.3   Visual Fields of Born-Criminals and Epileptics.

If in most respects criminals were found to have deficient sensibilities, they proved more sensitive than normal people to the weather; a heightened "meteoric sensibility" meant that with variations in temperature and atmospheric pressure, "both criminals and lunatics become agitated and manifest changes of disposition and sensations of various kinds, which are rarely experienced by normal persons."[51] Criminals were also more likely to be sensitive to the effects of metals and magnets. In these experiments, researchers placed disks of copper, zinc, lead and gold, or the poles of a magnet, on the frontal and occipital parts of the subject's head. The reactions included "pricking or heat, giddiness, somnolence, or a sense of bodily well-being." Lombroso-Ferrero reported that in hysterical criminals sensibility to magnets reached such a degree of acuteness that other sensations became polarized: "what appeared white to them before becomes black; bitter, what was formerly sweet, or vice versa." This reaction, she suggested, provided a means of distinguishing real from simulated hysteria.[52] Finally, anthropologists tested the visual acuity, chromatic sensibility, and field of vision (Figure 4.3) of a wide range of normal and abnormal persons. Born criminals and epileptics typically suffered from peripheral "scotoma," and criminals had high rates of color blindness. Criminals were found to possess generally *acute* eyesight, but "in this," argued Lombroso-Ferrero, "the criminal resembles the savage."[53]

IV. Rewriting Women's Sensibility

If Lombroso's studies relied upon and worked to reinforce common wisdom about pain and civilization, they would also come to challenge popular beliefs, particularly in the case of women.[54] Recall that in Lombroso's 1867 study he had found women to be *more sensitive* to pain than men, a result that was subsequently confirmed by a number of other studies. But this conclusion proved to be at odds with an evolutionary model that, as we saw in Chapter 2, linked women with savages, criminals, and children as not fully developed, not yet civilized. By the early 1890s, Lombroso's algometrical experiments seemed, instead, to confirm that women possessed a *limited* ability to sense pain. In a summary of work on the "physical insensibility of women" translated for *The Fortnightly Review* in 1892, Lombroso reported on tests in his laboratory in Turin that revealed a "marked degree of sensory obtuseness."[55]

Lombroso would also argue that women were limited in their ability to experience pleasure. Lombroso assembled a series of literary, scientific and anecdotal sources—from Dante to Darwin—that agreed on the reduced sexual desire and "sexual sensibility" of women.[56] Lombroso focused in particular on a study by Harry Campbell, who interviewed fifty-two poor, working-class hospital patients about the sexual instincts of their wives. The men reported the presence of a sexual instinct before marriage in only twelve of the women; in twenty-seven the instinct had appeared only in special circumstances after marriage, and in thirteen the instinct had never manifested itself. Campbell concluded that the sexual instinct was not only less intense in women than in men, but also tended to atrophy over time.[57] Havelock Ellis had found a more pervasive sexual sensibility among bourgeois women he interviewed, but Lombroso suggested the different results had everything to do with the class standing of the women in the two groups. Indeed, Lombroso noted, the most intelligent women in Ellis's group experienced the strongest sexual emotions.[58] Lombroso felt safe in concluding that most women were "naturally and organically monogamous and frigid."[59]

Opinions to the contrary, he observed, resulted from a confusion of eroticism with the "satisfaction of maternal instincts," and from the fact that women had three "sexual centers" to men's one: "A woman studied by Moraglia," Lombroso remarked with evident wonder, "knew how to masturbate in 14 different ways."[60] Lawyer and anthropologist Giuseppe Sergi (1841–1936), author or a treatise on pain and pleasure, suggested that in other parts of the world practices such as subincision of the penis were performed in an effort to satisfy women, thus linking a savage male insensibility to pain to a female insensibility to pleasure.[61]

Aware that he was, at least in the case of pain, working against common sense as well as his own previous findings, Lombroso supplemented the algometrical results with "still further corroborative data." Some of the "principal surgeons in Europe" confirmed that women withstood pain during surgical operations better than men; some acted "as though the body beneath the surgeon's knife were that of another and not their own."[62] An obstetrician assured Lombroso that women suffered in childbirth "much less than might be supposed," and dentists spoke of women's courage and resistance. Even Italian proverbs observed that "A woman has seven skins" and that "A woman has a soul, but a little one."[63]

Lombroso and his collaborator Guglielmo Ferrero now felt they could dismiss the popular notion that women were *more* sensitive to pain: their earlier experiments, it seemed, had not taken into account that women react more *loudly* to pain, a sign of their "greater irritability."[64] Similarly, when the researchers Roncoroni and Albertotti found normal women to be generally less sensitive to touch than normal men, but more sensitive to pain, they pointed to a possible source of error in measurements of pain sensibility: "woman, having a more developed sense of fear, complains of pain when it is not yet unbearable; whereas men can better be persuaded to resist until the pain becomes truly vivid."[65] In a letter to Lombroso, Sergi sought to put such claims on surer footing, distinguishing between "irritability" and "sensibility." Irritability, he explained, which dominated in women, was "the incipient, brute form" of sensibility, and was quickly translated into movement. Because we are in the habit of judging sensibility by the "external signs of emotional expressions," we are misled by women's habit of manifesting signs of sensibility after any kind of irritation.[66]

A similar account was offered by Francis Galton in 1883: "At first, owing to my confusing the quality of which I am speaking [sensibility] with that of nervous irritability, I fancied that women of delicate nerves who are distressed by noise, sunshine, etc., would have acute powers of discrimination. But this I found not to be the case."[67] Women's inferior powers of sensory discrimination were, for Galton, confirmed by the "business experience of life" and by everyday social practices:

> The tuners of pianofortes are men, and so I understand are the tasters of tea and wine, the sorters of wool, and the like. . . . Ladies rarely distinguish the merits of wine at the dinner-table, and though custom allows them to preside at the breakfast-table, men think them on the whole to be far from successful makers of tea and coffee.[68]

Some eleven years later, in 1894, Galton arranged for his own set of own experiments on the tactile sensibility of women (377) and men (932), conducted by a Sergeant Randall over a period of months at Galton's anthropological laboratory. Randall used the points of a cran-iometer to test the powers of discrimination at the nape of the neck, a part of the body chosen because there were no variations in thickness of the cuticle caused by usage (as with the fingertips) and because the back of the neck was so "get-at-able" in clothed volunteers.[69] Galton found women had, on average, slightly greater delicacy of discrimi-nation, and also varied more in their discriminative powers than did men, but wondered whether the latter might be due in part to the fact that women varied much more than men in the "exercise of sustained attention." Some women, he noted, were "religiously painstaking," but "the frivolity of numerous girls, and their incapacity of, or unwilling-ness to give, serious attention, is certainly more marked than among men of similar ages."[70]

Salvatore Ottolenghi sought in 1896 to sort out these conflicting findings and opinions, studying 681 women in addition to the 400 men he had studied as part of his experiments on sensibility, age, and social class.[71] The experiments on women were conducted over a period of two years on students at the teaching colleges in Siena, various conser-vatories, and the Institute for Deaf-Mutes, as well as on other women of varied social classes, occupations, and ages. Ottolenghi used an

Edelmann Faradimeter applied to the moistened back of the hand; "general sensibility" was indicated by the subject's report of a slight tingling [*fourmillement*], while the onset of pain was judged by the subject's facial expression. Ottolenghi recounts that he observed a reaction in these experiments on women that he had only rarely encountered in his tests of men: when subjects began to feel a disagreeable sensation—but which (judging by the facial expression) was "not yet pain"—they tried abruptly to withdraw the hand. This movement was evidence, Ottolenghi concluded, of an "exaggerated excitability." Far from being associated with a *real sensibility*, it most often accompanied "obtuse sensibility."[72] Ottolenghi also warned against confusing sensibility to pain with the ability to *resist* pain; the latter was, he found, more variable but also much stronger among women. Prone to suggestion, including autosuggestion, women could with prompting from their peers resist electrical current that far exceeded their normal thresholds, an ability Ottolenghi said he had never encountered among men. But they could just as easily be led to protest extravagantly before suffering became real.[73]

In the end, Ottolenghi found he was able to resolve much of the controversy by declaring both Lombroso and Galton to be correct (and Mantegazza and others to be confused): women were more sensitive to touch, but less sensitive to pain.[74] Women's insensibility to pain was, however, a characteristic of inferiority that could not be "redeemed" by a superior general sensibility. The latter was, in fact, to be explained by the delicacy of women's skin, which enabled it better to transmit excitations, and which thus further highlighted the failure to feel pain. But this combination of abilities and defects left women, finally, "better armed" than men in the struggle for life:

These qualities, acquired at the expense of cerebral evolution, are necessary, indispensable to woman, in order to enable her to tolerate the difficulties of domestic life and the suffering to which her sex is exposed. They explain also her greater longevity.[75]

Lombroso, too, suspected insensibility to moral and physical suffering helped women to survive:

The greater physical frailty of women, and the extra element of danger to life involved in child-birth, being taken into consideration, the fact of the sex's greater average longevity will appear still more striking, and not to be satisfactorily explained otherwise than by the hypothesis of its inferior sensibility.[76]

As in the case of criminals, insensibility was tied to an increased vitality and longevity that won a grudging admiration from anthropologists.

In addition to telling a story about the evolutionary status of women and men generally, and in the context of debates over the political rights and duties of the sexes,[77] algometrical studies were also used to differentiate among women: to make claims for the atavistic nature of female criminals, and especially prostitutes, and to argue for the naturalness of maternity. Gurrieri and Fornasari's study is typical: the researchers found that prostitutes were generally more obtuse than normal women,[78] and that prostitutes who had never borne children showed a particular insensibility.[79] Lombroso's algometrical studies found the "greatest deadness" on the hands of peasant women and in the clitorises of prostitutes. Twenty-eight percent of prostitutes were found to be completely insensible to pain, although sensibility increased if the prostitutes had borne children.[80] These results could be taken to mean either that maternity restored a more proper level of sensibility, or that prostitutes with children represented a category of "occasional" criminals who were not, in fact, degenerate and atavistic.

The project of (re)writing women into the criminologists' story of pain, civilization, and social dangerousness has all the appearances of a salvage operation. And yet it was precisely the challenge algometrical experiments appeared to offer to common sense that was put forward by Lombroso and his colleagues as the mark of *science*—the very counterintuitiveness of the claim that women are less sensitive than men was imagined to stand as a vindication of the will to quantify.

V. Disvulnerability

Finally, criminologists worked to establish a link between *physical* sensibility and *moral* sensibility. As Ellis put it, criminals suffered from "psychical analgesia."[81] Psychologist G. B. Verga argued that moral sensibility was nothing other than a "perfection of peripheral sensibility, which conducts external impressions to the interior of the brain."[82] And if moral insensibility could be linked to an organic defect, it was only logical that it, too, could be investigated in the laboratory. Thus, as we will see in the next chapter, studies of the blushing reflex purported to show the criminal body's inability to react appropriately to "moral stimuli." The incapacity to feel pain was, for criminologists, not only a *sign* of an underlying social danger, but also a social danger in and of itself.[83] As Garofalo commented, "This physical insensibility . . . prevents any vivid representation in [criminals'] minds of the suffering which they cause to others, since they themselves either would not feel such suffering or would feel it but little."[84] More troubling still, the Hungarian-born criminologist Moriz Benedikt (1835–1920) cited examples of criminals who regarded their insensibility as a sign of *privilege*: they "hold the delicate and sensitive in contempt" and "take pleasure in tormenting others whom they regard as inferior creatures."[85]

Although human scientists may not have shared this admiration for the criminals' insensibility, preferring instead to read it as an *inability*, Lombroso and others did find that obtuseness was often accompanied by a remarkable *ability*: a recuperative power that Benedikt termed "disvulnerability." Criminals not only could withstand wounds that in others would have been fatal[86]; they could also recover more quickly from their injuries than could normal women and men. Havelock Ellis reported that the rapid recovery from wounds had been confirmed by a questionnaire he sent out to prison medical officers, and by an experiment by the Belgian philosopher and psychologist Joseph Delboeuf (1831–1896) that made disvulnerability into an effect of insensibility. Delboeuf had made two equal and symmetrical wounds on the right and left shoulders of a hypnotized subject, and had suggested to the subject that he was insensible on the right side. The wound on the right side had healed "much more rapidly."[87] This helped to explain, Lombroso suggested, the apparent "robustness" of many criminals—a robustness that, if left unaccounted for, might threaten (at least for judges and juries) the claim made by scientists that criminals were, in fact, sick (see below).

As might be expected, the criminal was imagined to have his counterpart in the disvulnerable savage, as well as the lower animals. Ellis cited, for example, the observations of Edward Tregear (1846–1931) on the New Zealand Maori, made in a series of responses to questions from J. G. Frazer. Tregear reports that among the Maori, wounds healed "in a manner an [sic] European could hardly believe."

I have seen a Maori speared with a big rafting spear (an iron-shod pole thicker than the wrist), the point driven through the breast (just under the collar-bone) and coming out at the back—in a week's time he walked fifteen miles crossing a mountain range—the wound being healed.[88]

Benedikt, for his part, relied on the research of Italian physician Cesare Nerazzini (b. 1849) who after treating wounds of African warriors had remarked, "Certainly one has the right to wonder whether one is operating on humans or animals."[89]

Much of the evidence for the recuperative power of the savage takes the form of decontextualized anecdote[90]; however, disvulnerability was a subject of considerable anthropological interest at the turn of the century. For George Harley (1829–1896), a physician and member of the Royal Anthropological Institute, the archaeological evidence of successful operations on the skull (trephination) during the Neolithic period—operations that if performed "upon highly civilised men would inevitably kill them"—had posed a challenge to common sense.[91] It was, in Harley's judgment, generally held that "the modern inhabitant of Europe vastly excels his predecessor of the neolithic period, both in bodily physique and mental power"; thus, it was to be expected that "men of the present period would be able to endure better and recover quicker from bodily injuries, whether accidental or intentional." Yet the evidence of trephination suggested men of the Stone Age might be "possessed, for some reason or another, of a much greater bodily recuperative capacity than their more highly developed civilised successors."[92]

For Harley, the most probable explanation was the "vital degeneracy of the present race of Europeans." The transition from a state of barbarism to one of *bien séance* and refinement had materially diminished the body's recuperative powers:

[E]very appliance adding to man's bodily comfort, every food pampering his palate and exciting his appetite, as well as all contrivances either stimulating or developing his mental faculties and powers of perception, while adding, no doubt, to his personal enjoyment, have a direct deteriorating influence on his animal vitality, rendering him less able to resist the lethal effects of bodily injuries, or to recover from them either as quickly or as well as individuals of the same race and temperament not having similar corporeal or mental advantages."[93]

For Harley proof of this thesis could be found in the recuperative abilities of contemporary "savages": a gored South African "Caffre" who rinsed his bowels and replaced them in his abdomen, returning to his "usual avocations in a few days," and a North American Indian man who had hacked off the lower part of his leg with a tomahawk to escape from a crane, and was hobbling about within a fortnight. But Harley, like several contemporaries, found examples of recovery from childbirth particularly compelling: "Childbirth being an identical physical process in all members of the human species, the comparative effects of it in a savage and in a civilised state admits of easy and definite comparison."[94] Whereas an "average healthy woman in the middle ranks of European life" required from four to fourteen days to recover from a natural birth, "rude savage" women needed as little as half an hour to labor, give birth, and return to their previous activities. Savage women appeared to have a "superrecuperative animal power."[95]

However, for Harley, unlike Lombroso, these differences did not point to race—that is, to "innate constitutional peculiarity"—but rather to modes of life that either sustained or undermined the essential qualities of the human: "the savage, owing to her mode of life, retains the natural *aboriginal* bodily recuperative capacity of the human species, which highly civilised woman has lost, by reason of her refined mode of living."[96] As evidence, Harley cited examples of women of the same race, living in the same locality, who manifested differing degrees of recuperative ability according to their habits and position in life. Thus, a "tramp" who accosted the author in Kent, planned to return to picking hops after a day or two of recovery, whereas a Scottish woman scarcely interrupted her clothes washing to deliver. "What gently reared Kentish or Lanarkshire lady would be found capable of accomplishing feats like these, and yet they are of the same flesh and blood as their less peculiarly favored sisters, whose recuperative powers, in my opinion, they have good reason to envy."[97]

The notion that painful labor was "an indication of a certain amount of elevation in the scale of civilization"—a rewriting, or transposing forward, of the biblical account—had widespread currency by the end of the nineteenth century. In a survey of studies on the meaning of *couvade*, H. Ling Roth (1854–1925) noted that the practice of confining the husband while the wife "gets up and returns to her normal duties" was less barbarous that it might at first seem, "for among savages we find almost everywhere that women are delivered with little pain or trouble."[98] But he also wished to correct the popular belief that the "wives of savages, like the majority of those of the civilised working classes," had become inured to suffering by a lifetime of hard work. Instead, Roth cited Galabin's manual of midwifery to link pain and risk in parturition to the increase in the size of the brain that accompanied civilization. Savage babies not only had smaller heads, but their mothers had larger, more accommodating pelvises.[99] But Roth could not resist reporting on correspondence from an "eminent London professor" who wrote to remind him that if savages "had such constitutions as many of us possess. . . they could not exist in the conditions of life to which they are exposed. With us the evil [morbid sensibility] and the alleviation go hand in hand to a great extent."[100]

Lombroso found that the resistance of the insane and of criminals to morbid causes—their relatively greater vitality—was confirmed by Venetian and Tuscan proverbs: "Weeds grow quickly" [*Erba cativa cresce presto*] and "Madmen grow without being watered" [*I pazzi crescono senza inaffiarli*].[101] And, as we will see in the next chapter, Lombroso would explore both the analgesia and disvulnerability of criminals by measuring their vascular reactions with a hydrosphygmograph. But the robustness of criminals also posed a problem, Lombroso acknowledged, for the expert witness wishing to convince a jury that the criminal was a sick person requiring treatment and isolation. There were, in fact, two apparent contradictions: first, that criminals exhibited "glowing health" [*floridezza*] despite being "gravely ill in their nervous centers"; second, that criminals were resistant to disease and trauma, despite the "rule of pathology that someone already suffering from a disease is more exposed to the attacks of every new infirmity." The "incredulity of judges and the public" concerning the gravely diseased nature of criminals was, Lombroso conceded, "understandable."[102]

5

Blood Will Tell

"'How can those be trusted, who know not how to blush,' says the European."
—Alexander von Humboldt and Aimé Bonpland,
Personal Narrative of Travels (1818)

"Every emotional excitement speaks in the blood supply of every limb."
—Hugo Münsterberg, *On the Witness Stand* (1908)

I. Introduction: The Absent Blush

Criminals, observed Lombroso, do not blush. Indeed, the Italian folk had "for centuries" considered the absence of blushing to be "the equivalent of a dishonest and savage life."[1] In Lombroso's view, it was not simply that criminals had inappropriate emotional responses to particular situations (an absence of shame at the transgression of law or custom, pleasure at the suffering of another, joking indifference in the face of imminent execution), but that they lacked, in a certain sense, a normal *affective capacity*.[2] The blush, for Lombroso and other human scientists, linked the exterior of the criminal body with its interior, an atavistic physiology with an aberrant psychology. Blushes and their absences were only infrequently imagined as guides to individuals' guilt or innocence. Instead, the ability or inability to blush confronted the scientist as evidence of an individual's embodied *dangerousness*.

In this chapter, we explore the ways in which a wide range of new meanings came to be linked to the dilation of blood vessels in the face and other parts of the body. As we will see, the criminal anthropologist's interest in the reddened face was part of a broad popular and scientific engagement with blushing at the end of the nineteenth century. Movements of blood, like the ability to feel pain, figured in conversations in and outside the biological disciplines about what it meant to be savage or civilized, male or female, black or white. And with the invention by Italian, French, and German physiologists of new instruments to chart changes in blood flow and pressure, it became possible to imagine that one could measure and record traces of the emotions on both the surface and the interior of the body—that one could quantify an emotional potentiality or proficiency. Indeed, the body's vascular system would be reconfigured as an instrument that could, with the aid of inscription devices, *write itself*, registering its perturbations on smoked paper.

Many of Lombroso's studies of blushing were, to be sure, strikingly unsophisticated. In the fifth edition of *L'uomo delinquente*, Lombroso summarized results of a number of experiments he and others performed to test the "blushing reflex," juxtaposing these with anecdotal evidence supplied by correspondents.[3] One series of tests focused on ninety-one male criminals between ages 19 and 26. In this case, Lombroso's procedure involved scolding his subjects or fixing them with a stare (we learn nothing more about an experimental protocol). In response to this treatment, Lombroso tells us, only forty-one subjects blushed; three instead grew pale.[4] Moreover, the blushes that were elicited were often, in Lombroso's judgment, incomplete—twenty-four of the forty-one blushed only on the cheeks (and not on the ears, the throat, or the chest)—or were otherwise anomalous and therefore significant. For example, Lombroso found that five thieves exhibited an "exaggerated" blush that could be "easily produced"; further examination found that three of these men were intelligent and displayed a "normal physiognomy," while two were of the upper class. Here—as in the case of pain—class standing, intelligence, and certain physiological capacities appeared to be directly related.

In another study of male juvenile offenders, Lombroso found that when blushing occurred in the presence of the researcher, it was often because the subjects became too agitated in discussions, made themselves laugh, or were instead startled by the scientist's sudden entry into the cell. These reactions, which other researchers would characterize as "flushes," were to be distinguished, Lombroso admonished, from the "physiological" reactions produced by the scientist's reproachful gaze or by the subjects' memories of the crimes they had committed.[5]

Among women criminals, the failure to blush was both more pro-
nounced and more telling, as women were imagined normally to blush
more easily than men.[6] Lombroso relayed to his readers the "precious
observations" reported in a letter from Carmelo Andronico, a physician charged with the care of prostitutes and young female criminals
at a prison in Messina:

> Of the registered prostitutes, none blushes when asked for information
> about her sordid occupation. I have seen one blush when she is reproached
> for having gone against nature in the act of coitus.
>
> Among the convicts at the prison house I have observed the following
> facts: prisoners who have committed a violent homicide recount the deed
> sincerely without blushing at all. Those who have killed their own spouses
> by poisoning, or have had them killed, do blush, and a great deal. Prisoners
> convicted of theft blush first on the ears and then on the face. Those
> convicted of incitement to commit prostitution do not blush at all; neither
> do those convicted of perjury.
>
> Two women convicted of attempted arson do not blush, but instead
> laugh when talking about their crime; it bears noting, however, that both
> are incorrigible mattoids; one of these is twice a recidivist, and speaks in
> a loud voice.[7]

Lombroso and an assistant named Pasini had also examined 122
women and found 81 percent unable to blush (79 percent of murderers,
80 percent of poisoners, 82 percent of infanticides, and 90 percent of
thieves). What is more, the women who did blush did not do so when
asked about their crimes, but rather when "interrogated about menstrual disorders,"[8] suggesting a distinction between true shame and
mere embarrassment.

However, if both here and in the studies of young boys the nature of
the stimulus appeared to matter—to help the scientist to distinguish
a blush from a flush, or a "physiological" event from a meaningless
reddening—there was also an insistence that the defect was not strictly
speaking *moral* but *vascular*. This was confirmed for Lombroso by experiments with amyl nitrite in which researchers attempted to produce
a reddening of the face in nineteen male criminals. Here the results
showed that the "vaso-motor reaction" was often delayed (by up to
50 seconds), less intense, and more circumscribed in criminals than in
normal men—each criminal required at least two drops, while ten of

thirteen normal men required only one to produce a rapid and extensive flush. The exception appeared to be young offenders and criminals
who had murdered out of passion, whose reactions resembled those of
normal subjects.[9]

It is, as we have seen, a notable feature of Lombroso's texts that case
studies and experiments are not accompanied by much commentary or
interpretation, that the results are imagined to speak for themselves.
In this case, Lombroso is counting on his readers to share a "folk"
understanding of blushing and the "dishonest" life that was pervasive
at the end of the nineteenth century. But he would also work to but-
tress his claims by analogy to the insane and to savages, two other
categories of persons who, in the judgement of scientists, "failed" to
blush. In an experiment performed on institutionalized "mad" women,
Bartolomeo Bergesio had attempted to produce a blushing reflex by "allowing the discussion to turn to the functions of the reproductive organs
and to menstruation, and by posing questions tinged with malice."[10]
In another experiment performed on men by Lombroso's students,
the stimulus used was a prolonged and serious fixing of the gaze of
the subject, and an unexpected and brusque reproach.[11] Both studies
had, in Lombroso's judgment, confirmed that the ability to blush was
impaired among the insane; however, Lombroso noted that the absence of blushing was twice as frequent among criminals as among the
mad.[12]

Lombroso concluded his discussion of the blush in *L'uomo delinquente* by evoking what he took to be the lessons of evolutionary biology. Paraphrasing Darwin's *The Expression of the Emotions in Man and
Animals*, which had appeared in 1872, Lombroso wrote:

> Darwin teaches us that an albino negress and mulattos, the Lepchas
> and the Chinese, the Aymara and the Polynesians all blush. But even he
> admits that the Chinese and Malays blush little [and] the Hindoos rarely,
> and that the South Americans blush so rarely that the Spanish used to
> say "How can those be trusted, who know not how to blush?" Martius
> noted that the Aborigines of Brazil blushed only after a long period of
> contact with whites.[13]

Lombroso's reading of Darwin, arguably an interested misreading of
what was a layered set of citations and anecdotes,[14] reauthorized an

analogy of the criminal and the savage (see Chapter 2) and enabled a scientific scrutiny of the absent blush. But Lombroso would also, through the work of physiologist Angelo Mosso, seek to go beyond Darwin.

II. The Natural History of the Blush

Attention to blushing gained a new seriousness with the publication in 1872 of Darwin's *The Expression of the Emotions in Man and Animals*, but the blush had already been a topic of both literary and scientific interest.[15] Like pain (Chapter 4), the blush was part of a conversation about what it meant to be human, and about the contradictory effects of being or becoming civilized. This was a conversation that had everything to do with race, imperialism, and the power of scientists and others to manipulate bodies.

For some time, blushing had served as a link between the surface of the body and interior states, the visible sign of a conscience. As Janet Browne remarks, in the mid-nineteenth century it was imagined that only blushing could prove that men and women *had* a conscience: "Only the hot flush of embarrassment could establish that people had the ability to reflect upon themselves and their behavior, were alive to their situation, could feel *self-conscious* in the literal sense of that term. Completely bypassing the will, and surfacing despite all our efforts to subdue it, blushing was seen to be a direct manifestation of our innermost thoughts and feelings. It was a window to the soul far more revealing than those other windows, the eyes."[16]

But the blush became an object of scientific scrutiny as well with the publication of Thomas Henry Burgess' *The Physiology or Mechanism of Blushing* in 1839.[17] For the physician Burgess (d. 1865), blushing was interesting as an example of "an involuntary act of the mind upon the vital organs and their several functions."[18] In what Browne identifies as a natural theological argument, Burgess claimed that blushing was both uniquely human and had been designed by the creator in "order that the soul might have sovereign power of displaying in the cheeks the various internal emotions of the moral feelings."[19]

Yet modernity had brought with it an acquired sensibility that Burgess likened to a diseased state; examples included young men who were "sensitive, timid and abashed in society."[20] Refinement and civilization had "perverted the original intent" of blushing, such that it was now "difficult to judge whether the blush be from an impulse of shame, or merely from a sensibility that is overwrought."[21] Civilization was marked by the "uncalled-for blush," due to an "irritability of the sensorium arising from an over refinement, and want of early education."[22] By contrast, the blush of the unrefined savage was *authentic*, as well as more easily legible:

> Who ever heard of an American savage blushing from morbid sensibility? and yet is he on this account the less liable to the impulse of shame or disgrace, according to his own views or interpretations of such feelings? No! the change of colour in him is a genuine example of *moral instinct*.[23]

By contrast, Burgess did assert the inability of the "congenital idiot" to blush, not because of a somatic (vasomotor) defect, but because of his lack of reasoning power.[24]

Burgess also confronted the claim made by Alexander von Humboldt (1769–1859) that "the dark races" were incapable of giving external evidence by blushing of their deep internal feelings.[25] Humboldt had concluded a "physical sketch" of the Chaymas with the following observations:

> If the variety and mobility of the features embellish the domain of animated nature, we must admit also, that both increase by civilization, without being produced by it alone. In the great family of nations, no other race unites these advantages to a higher degree than that of Caucasus, or the European. It is only in white men, that the instantaneous penetration of the dermoidal system by the blood can take place; that slight change of the colour of the skin, which adds so powerful an expression to the emotions of the soul. "How can those be trusted, who know not how to blush" says the European, in his inveterate hatred to the Negro and the Indian. We must also admit, that this insensibility of the features is not peculiar to every race of men of a very dark complexion; it is much less apparent in the African, than in the natives of America.[26]

In Burgess's view, the problem here was one of legibility: "Because the increased redness peculiar to blushing is not observed in the negro's face, which nature seems to have screened by a dark veil—therefore, it has been taken for granted that he is incapable of blushing."[27] For Burgess, blacks might be intellectually inferior without also being morally inferior. As proof of an obscured or screened moral sensibility, Burgess offered the example of a black woman whose white scars "invariably became *red* whenever she was abruptly spoken to, or charged with any trivial offense."[28] The story of the scar, imagined as a window to a shadowed interior, is offered as a counter to Humboldt's racism.[29] But this anecdote and others like it also point to the acts of violence that produced the conditions of visibility—the startling reproach, the unwarranted accusation, indeed the scar itself—that make it possible for physicians and colonists (like criminologists) to test the ability to blush.[30]

Meanwhile, in civilized Europe, even a striking reddening of the face could not be reliably read. For Burgess, the "false blush," the "deceptive blush," the "hectic flush," and the "flush of rage"[31] threatened the scientist's ability to link interior and exterior, moral and emotional states with movements of blood.

As Janet Browne has argued, Darwin's volume on the expression of emotions was intended as a defense of his theory of evolution, and is thus usefully read as a sequel to the *Descent of Man*; its goal, in short, was to demonstrate that human emotional expressions were continuous with those of animals.[32] Darwin hoped to show that all the "chief expressions exhibited by man were the same throughout the world," and that even the "highest," or "most human" of human characteristics were, at root, derived from animals. This was in marked contrast, for example, to Burgess's claim that human blushing was a "special creation," or Charles Bell's argument that human facial muscles were a "special provision" for the sole object of enabling human expression.[33] As Browne puts it, for Darwin "No mental or moral faculty was . . . special to man alone; the difference was only one of degree, not kind."[34]

Yet if the goal of Darwin's natural history of expression was to establish a continuity between animals and men, Darwin began his chapter on "Self Attention, Shame, Shyness, Modesty," by asserting a *difference*—that "Blushing is the most peculiar and the most human of all expressions. Monkeys redden from passion, but it would require an overwhelming amount of evidence to make us believe that any animal could blush."[35] As Browne notes, the finding that animals cannot blush appears to undercut Darwin's claims for continuity. Darwin would hope to solve the problem by a turn to "self-attention," the mechanism that accounts for the outward appearance of shame, guilt, and embarrassment.

Darwin followed Burgess in asserting that the true blush could not be produced by any physical means or action on the body: "It is the mind which must be affected."[36] What is more, the mind was powerless to prevent the translation of its "affected" state onto the surface of the body: "Blushing is not only involuntary; but the wish to restrain it, by leading to self-attention actually increases the tendency."[37] Darwin turned to the work of Henry Holland (1788–1873), Henry Maudsley (1835–1918), and Pierre Gratiolet (1815–1865) for other examples of mental attention having power to influence the circulation of blood, the movements of the intestines, and the activity of glands.[38]

Mental states that induced blushing consisted of shyness, shame, and modesty: "the essential element in all being self-attention."[39] Attention to moral conduct was, from an evolutionary point of view, secondary. For Darwin, attention originally directed to personal appearance, in relation to the opinion of others, was the exciting cause. The same effect was subsequently produced, through the force of association, by self-attention in relation to moral conduct: "It is not the simple act of reflecting on our own appearance, but the thinking what others think of us, which excites a blush."[40]

Because the face was the "most considered and regarded" part of the body, it had been "subjected during many generations to much closer and more earnest self-attention than any other part of the body,"[41] although in primeval man and races who now go naked, attention, and thus the blush, spreads to rest of body.[42] Darwin cited the example of a woman whose body blushed progressively as the gaze of the physician (and hence the attention of the patient) traveled from the face to the neck to the breasts.[43]

When Darwin turned his attention to the question of "guilt," or blushing from "strictly moral causes," he found that the opinion of others was still of primary importance. In a move that marked a break with much of nineteenth-century thought, Darwin sought in fact to sever the blush and the conscience: "It is not the conscience which raises a blush . . . . It is not the sense of guilt, but the thought that others think or know us to be guilty which crimsons the face."[44] Relying, it would appear, on anecdotal evidence, Darwin observed that "Many a person has blushed intensely when accused of some crime, though completely innocent of it."[45] At the same time, he asserted, "A man reflecting on a crime committed in solitude, and stung by his conscience, does not blush; yet he will blush under the vivid recollection of a detected fault, or of one committed in the presence of others, the degree of blushing being closely related to the feeling of regard for those who have detected, witnessed, or suspected his fault."[46]

Darwin's effort to establish when self-attention and thus blushing emerged in our evolutionary history led him also to explore the comportment of the insane. Darwin argued in his introduction that, just as infants "exhibit many emotions, as Sir C. Bell remarks, 'with extraordinary force,'" purity and simplicity, the insane "ought to be studied, as they are liable to the strongest passions, and give uncontrolled vent to them."[47] Darwin relied, in particular, on observations of "idiots" and "the deranged" made at his request by the psychiatrist James Crichton-Browne (1840–1938), who from 1866 served as medical director of the West Riding Asylum.[48] Crichton-Browne reported that he had never seen a "genuine blush" among those under his care, "though he has seen their faces flush, apparently from joy, when food was placed before them, and from anger."[49] This flush could also be produced, Crichton-Browne found, by administering amyl nitrite to his patients.

Yet, as Janet Browne observes, Crichton-Browne and others had argued that because blushing was an effect of a conscience, dependent on a moral sense, those suffering from a disease of the will could not blush, or else were liable to a morbid sensitivity. Darwin, by contrast, wished to break the association of blushing and the will. As Browne notes, Darwin preferred to see blushing as a product of *consciousness* rather than *conscience*: idiots, like infants, were not aware of their behavior, and thus were not capable of attending to themselves.[50] We are reminded here of the productive power of the metaphorical association of children, the insane, and racialized others (Chapter 2). This association allowed Darwin to link the emergence of blushing, in both developmental and evolutionary terms, with the emergence of consciousness. Although a recently developed mental attribute, Darwin could argue, it was expressed using ordinary mechanisms of the body that had been inherited from animals.

In order to "ascertain whether the same expressions and gestures prevail, as has often been asserted without much evidence, with all the races of mankind, especially with those who have associated but little with Europeans,"[51] Darwin circulated in 1867 a printed questionnaire to Europeans living abroad, including missionaries and "protectors of aborigines"; thirty-six responded. The second question read as follows:

> 2) Does shame excite a blush when the colour of the skin allows it to be visible? And especially how far down the body does the blush extend?[52]

The responses Darwin collected tell us as much about the work of missionaries and colonialism as about the differences among the races of man, for they speak again and directly to the conditions under which a blush is or is not produced: the reproach, the accusation, compulsory undressing. O'Farrell has noted "the ease of Darwin's simple registry of the blithe unconsciousness and active disregard with which traders, missionaries, and doctors have noted the instances of painful self-consciousness they have provoked and exploited."[53] For O'Farrell, Darwin's record of blushes among "all the races of mankind" is "a record also of vigilance and of accusation."[54]

But Darwin also struggled to take his distance from many of these reports, as well as from earlier published accounts. For example, Darwin referred readers to the assertion made by the German naturalists Johann Baptist von Spix (1781–1826) and Karl Friedrich Philipp von Martius (1794–1868) that the aborigines of Brazil could not properly be said to blush.[55] But Darwin called into question the authors' further claim that "it was only after long intercourse with the whites, and after receiving some education, that we perceived in the Indians a change of colour expressive of the emotions of their minds."[56] Darwin argued it was "incredible that the power of blushing could have thus originated," even if "the habit of self-attention, consequent on their education and new course of life, would have much increased any innate tendency to blush."[57]

Darwin found that "there can be no doubt that negroes blush, although no redness is visible on the skin."[58] In support of this claim he cited reports that the faces of blacks get not only darker but warmer. He concluded that, though many of his informants had suggested varied peoples did not blush: "The facts now given are sufficient to show that blushing, whether or not there is any change of colour, is common to most, probably to all, of the races of man."[59] Darwin used this as a final proof that blushing was not "specially designed by the Creator" to make interior states visible, as Burgess had argued. "Those who believe in design . . . will find it difficult to account for negroes and other dark-coloured races blushing, in whom a change or colour is scarcely or not at all visible."[60]

III. Graphical Instruments and the Vascular System

If we return now to Lombroso's citation of Darwin in support of an assertion of a similarity of the nonblushing criminal and the savage, it may be tempting to dismiss it as both a misreading and misappropriation of Darwin. But it may be more accurate to see it as another in a series of rhetorical moves made by Martius, von Spix, Prichard, and Darwin that positioned the othered body differently, but always in relation to a question of visibility and truthtelling, and always on the condition of a violent compulsion (undressing, accusing, cutting). It is also clear, however, that Lombroso meant to move beyond Darwin, to undercut the vestigial humanism of his evolutionary theory, and to quantify what remained qualified in Darwin's narrative. In the work of the physiologist Angelo Mosso, Lombroso found the means to do all three.

Mosso (1846–1910) has been identified by Otniel Dror as the first scientist to undertake the systematic laboratory-based research on the emotions.[61] A self-described materialist who studied under Moritz Schiff and Carl Ludwig (1816–1895), Mosso sought to reduce the blush to an example among many of vasomotor responses to emotional states.[62] In contrast to Bell, Burgess, and Darwin, Mosso saw nothing distinctively *human* about these responses: "blushing was deemed a privilege of man, which, however, is not the case."[63] In a popular treatise on fear, Mosso announced: "The time has come when we must throw off our professorial robes, tie on our aprons, roll up our sleeves, and begin the vivisection of the human heart according to scientific methods."[64] Such an approach promised to reveal that "Blushing—that ideal token of innocence and purity—is no accidental fact; it was not given to man as sign of nobility, nor as a mirror to reflect the agitation of his heart; it is a fact rendered necessary by bodily functions and which the will can neither produce nor suppress. It is simply caused by the structure of our vital machine, by the activity of the blood-vessels in all organs and in all animals."[65] Mirroring the disqualification of the will in criminological discourse, Mosso found that Darwin had attributed "too much importance to the will considered as the cause of expression. We younger physiologists are more mechanical: we examine the organism more minutely, and it is in the structure of the organs that we seek the reasons of their functions."[66]

Blushing was, for Mosso, linked to the needs of the animal brain during emotional disturbances, and it was by no means confined to the face. Studies of rabbits showed that "the circulation of blood in the ears reflects the psychic condition of the animal, and that nothing takes place either in itself or in its surroundings without immediately acting upon these blood-vessels." What is more, different rabbits had a different "facility for blushing."[67] Humans, too, varied in their ability to redden, for example according to age: "An old lady does not blush under those moral emotions which used to betray her feelings as a girl; and this, not because she has overcome the timidity of youth, or because the hard struggles of life have blunted her sensibility, but because the blood-vessels of the face have, in course of time, become less yielding."[68] Even young girls did not respond to the same stimuli in the same way: "One must not ascribe the difference solely to shyness or modesty, since the blood-vessels of different persons respond in various ways."[69]

When the boundary between the human and the animal was thus breached, and when blushing was extended from the face to the entire body, it became possible to imagine that a whole range of vasomotor phenomena might serve as indices of emotional disturbance, if only they could be rendered accessible to the scientist.[70] Indeed, this rereading of the blush shifted the attention of the scientist from the body's surface to its interior. While Darwin had imagined that the blush moved inward, at times causing mental confusion,[71] Mosso and later researchers would follow the blush from the interior *outward*. Psychologist G. E. Partridge, for example, found the reddening of the face to be an effect of an inner "organic turmoil." Students he surveyed at the State Normal School in Trenton, New Jersey, reported feelings of engorgement, fear, and confusion as the first symptoms of the blush, with the actual redness of the face coming "late in the nerve storm" and constituting but "a very small part of it."[72] This suggested the blush was no "mere local hyperaemia of the surface":

> The diffused bodily feeling, pressure on the chest, general discomfort, increased heart-beat, dizziness, pressure in the head, confusion, dread, all evidence a profound disturbance of the vaso-motor functions, and strong emotion.[73]

Scientists would seek to uncover, beneath the surface, the material manifestations of emotion, following what Mariano Luigi Patrizi would call "the *internal* blushes and pallor."[74] In no other way, advised Mosso, could "the slender link which connects psychological phenomena with the material functions of the organism be rendered evident."[75]

One such opportunity was provided Mosso by "Bertino," an eleven-year-old boy with an opening in his forehead that was covered with skin.[76] Bertino's condition allowed Mosso and his collaborator Giovanni Albertotti to investigate the "blushing" of the brain caused by a variety of emotional events. A graphical "apparatus" was applied to the boy's forehead while he lay on a sofa, and the movements of blood in and out of the head were recorded by a stylus on paper. As Mosso reports: "The reproofs and threats which I uttered to Bertino when he was hindering my experiments by moving his head or his hands, the disagreeable things which I sometimes purposely said to him, were always followed by very strong pulsations; the brain-pulse became six, seven times higher than before, the blood-vessels dilated, the brain swelled and palpitated with such violence that physiologists were astonished when they saw the reproductions of the curves."[77] Mosso called these curves cerebral "autographs," inscriptions produced by the brain itself. Autographs did more than render visible the dilation of blood vessels in the brain; they enabled scientists, in Mosso's words, to "see how the brain writes when it guides the pen itself."[78]

As we saw in Chapter 3, graphical instruments developed in the nineteenth century promised both a new quantification and a new kind of visibility. In this case, inscription devices transformed the study of vasomotor reactions and appeared to make newly accessible the phenomena of feeling and thinking. For Patrizi, who would succeed Lombroso to the chair in criminal anthropology in Turin in 1911, technological improvements allowed scientists "to measure and quantify the features of a soul [*anima*], which had been thought to elude the experimentalist, or else to be accessible only with the misleading instrument of introspection."[79]

The sphygmograph (Figure 3.6), a "pulse writer" that could be applied to unbroken skin, had been presented by Etienne-Jules Marey to the Academie des Sciences in 1860,[80] and was quickly employed in a variety of experiments that explored the effects of varied mental processes on blood pressure, the pulse rate, and the shape of the pulse curve. As Braun puts it, "The sphygmograph transformed the subjective character of pulse feeling into an objective, visual, graphic representation that was a permanent record of the transient event, a record that could be studied and criticized by a single physician or by groups of physicians."[81]

Physiologist Eugène Gley (1857–1930), psychologists Alfred Binet (1857–1911), J. Courtier, and N. Vaschide, and a wide variety of others used the sphygmograph to follow the physiological effects of emotions, thinking, and calculation.[82] Binet and Courtier explored the effects of painful and pleasurable stimuli—needle pricks, strong odors, varied kinds of music, and surprising news (such as the promise made to a child of an unexpected gift)—on the circulation. Gley's research, together with that of Binet and Vaschide, sought to distinguish the circulatory effects of intellectual work from those of other kinds of external stimuli. Each of these experiments, of course, required comparisons of states of stimulation with states of nonstimulation. Gley, who performed many of his experiments on his own body, describes in some detail how he constructed a state of "rest" that might allow him to record the "normal pulse" or *tracé-type*: he would sit alone in a chair with his head slightly inclined to the right, elbows on a table, and breathing through his nose. If the experiment to be performed involved the stimulus of a written text (Gley preferred philosophy and

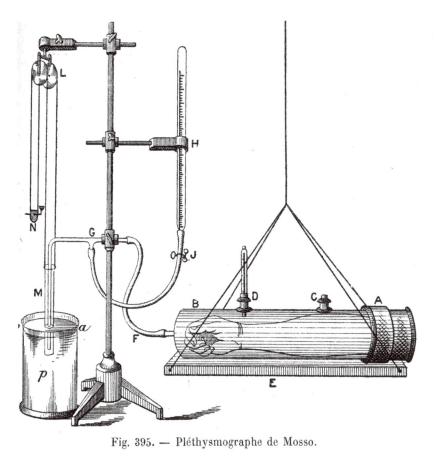

Fig. 395. — Pléthysmographe de Mosso.

Fig. 5.1 Mosso Plethysmograph.

geometry), he would hold the book in his hands, regularly turning the pages, though he made sure to hold it upside so he would not be tempted actually to read. In this way, and with a sphygmograph positioned over the artery in his neck, Gley felt he could achieve a state free of emotion and reasoning.[83] It is also worth noting that while all of these researchers acknowledged variations among individuals, and worked to distinguish the effects of varied stimuli, none exhibited an interest in establishing claims for groups.

Mosso's own contribution to the scientific study of emotion was the plethysmograph (Figure 5.1), a meter and recorder of changes of volume that enabled the study of variations in circulation in the extremities. To construct the first device, Mosso had taken a long, narrow bottle and broken out its bottom. After inserting his brother's hand and forearm, Mosso sealed the bottle hermetically with putty. In the neck of the bottle, Mosso fastened a stopper through which a long slender glass tube passed, and filled the bottle and glass tube with tepid water: "I thought if a greater quantity of blood flows into the hand, an amount of water corresponding to the increased quantity of blood will be forced out of the bottle."[84] In a series of experiments performed in Italy on his brother, Mosso was struck by "the great instability of the blood-vessels of the hand, in consequence of which it changed in volume under the slightest emotions in the most surprising manner, whether the subject were awake or asleep."[85] Any "movement of the soul" sufficed to disturb the equilibrium of the vascular system.[86]

Later, Mosso traveled to Leipzig to demonstrate the instrument to Carl Ludwig. Mosso recounts that he was assisted in his Leipzig experiments on circulation and respiration by the future hygienist Luigi Pagliani (b. 1847), who on one occasion had both arms in cylinders when Ludwig entered the room. The graph produced by the sudden decrease in blood volume in the forearm was so remarkable, Mosso recounts, that Ludwig wrote "Enter the Lion" on the paper.[87] In further experiments, the tracings produced by Mosso and Pagliani's arms would repeatedly register the comings and goings of Ludwig; even the sound of his familiar footsteps in the hall would produce a characteristic reduction of the blood volume in the forearm. After eliminating fear and anxiety as possible explanations, the researchers agreed that they had captured on paper the emotion of "veneration." Their instrument enabled the writing even of "those emotions that are not depicted on the face."[88]

Later researchers would modify and refine Mosso's arm plethysmograph: François-Frank developed a hand and wrist plethysmograph (Figure 5.2), while Patrizi would develop a volumetric glove (Figure 5.3). Plethysmographic studies were also extended to other parts of the body: for example, to the ear (Figure 5.4), in which case the device seemed to capture and quantify the blushing of the face, and to the bladder, which was imagined to function as a particularly sensitive esthesiometer. As Ellis notes, the influence of emotions on the bladder had been well known before Mosso and Paolo Pellacani used

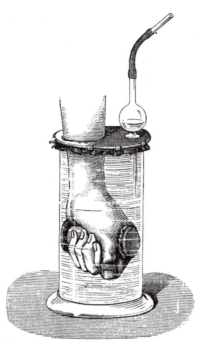

Fig. 394. — Appareil de François Franck.

Fig. 5.2   François-Franck Plethysmograph.

a catheter and plethysmograph to demonstrate the "delicate character of the reactions of the bladder to psychic stimuli."[89] In experiments performed on girls of about 20 years of age, they found trivial remarks, the touch of the scientist's finger, mental calculations, and the psychic representation of pain could produce a legible reaction. The researchers concluded that "every psychic event and every mental effort is accompanied by a contraction of the bladder."[90] The bladder, the researchers concluded, constituted "an esthesiometer more certain than the blood pressure, and not inferior to the iris."[91]

Scientists would eventually attach a plethysmograph to the penis (see below). Ellis quoted an unnamed source as saying "an erection is a blushing of the penis,"[92] and others took male sexual arousal as the model for the emotional states registered by the new graphical devices. For Charles Féré, "exciting irritations that lead in the end to agreeable emotions are translated by a state of erection of the organism, while

FIG. 25

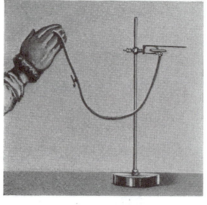

A VOLUMETRIC GLOVE

Fig. 5.3 Volumetric Glove.

excessive irritations or the absence of excitation that correspond to unpleasant emotions are translated by a state of flaccidity."[93] Indeed, the whole body could be imagined as an instrument for quantifying and recording emotional reactions. Mosso devised a "balance," a kind

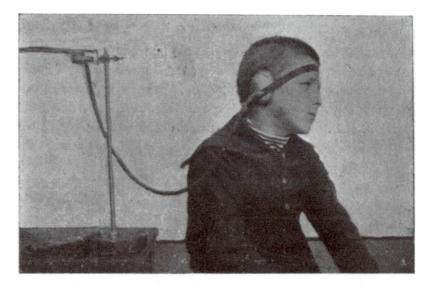

Fig. 22. — Pletismografo auricolare, di cui è derivazione il pletismografo faciale descritto nel testo.

Fig. 5.4 Ear Plethysmograph.

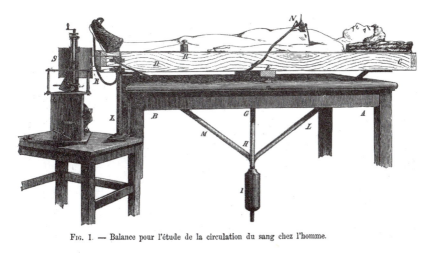

Fig. 1. — Balance pour l'étude de la circulation du sang chez l'homme.

Fig. 5.5 Balance.

of seesaw on which subjects could lie fully extended (Figure 5.5). Every shift in the circulation of blood tipped the balance either toward the feet (as in the case of normal respiration) or toward the head (as in the case of intellectual efforts). Mosso found that for the demonstration of psychic influences on circulation it was superior to the plethysmograph.[94]

As we saw in Chapter 3, while graphical instruments worked to make the body of the scientist (marked by its sensory weaknesses and the imprecision of its utterances) recede into the background, they pulled the body of the experimental subject into the foreground and gave it a new agency. Whether the brain, the ear, or the bladder "wrote," or the pulse was "armed with a pen,"[95] the blushing body was imagined to tell its own truth, and to give itself away. Here, as in other experiments on the physiology of emotion, the inscribing body was reconstituted as what Dror calls an "emotio-meter."[96] This notion of bodies testifying—of intimate truths made objective and public—would take on particular meanings in relation to criminality, where the hiding of the intimate posed particular social dangers.

IV. The Sphygmography and Plethysmography of Delinquents

Lombroso was attracted to the work of the physiologists of emotion, and especially to the research of Mosso, by the promise of making visible not just a transient emotional experience, but also an affective capacity that might be deficient or otherwise abnormal.[97] Lombroso's experiments with the vascular system, first reported in 1881 and 1884,[98] aimed both to confirm the more general claim that certain criminals were biologically distinctive—linked by their physiology and anatomy to savages and lower animals—and to aid in the diagnosis of individuals, whose relative ability to feel might serve as an index of their relative dangerousness.

As Lombroso's daughter reports in her posthumous popularization of his work, the "affections" could often be tested by a simple oral examination. The investigator might, for example, ask: "'Is your father a bad man?' or 'Are your neighbors worthless people? Do they treat you with due respect? Has any one a spite against you? Are you fond of your parents? Are you aware that your brother (or mother) is seriously ill?' "[99] The goal was not, strictly speaking, to elicit information; rather, the examiner sought to determine whether the questions themselves caused the subject "emotion of any kind, whether he has real affection for those beings to whom normal persons are attached, but towards whom born criminals and the insane in general do not manifest love." In the absence of instruments, affection might be judged by the contents of the responses and by any accompanying facial expressions. However, Gina Lombroso-Ferrero reminded her readers that "medico-legal experts naturally prefer a scientific test by means of accurate instruments, by which the exact degree of emotion is registered."[100]

Lombroso reports in the fifth edition of *L'uomo delinquente* on a series of 1881 experiments using a hydraulic variant of the sphygmograph; for these experiments he and his assistant, Filippo Cougnet, chose "robust" individuals who were multiple recidivists and shared "the usual psychical and physical characteristics of the criminal," as well as normal subjects and causal offenders.[101] The experimenters connected the left arm of the subject to a hydrosphygmograph, and on the right arm affixed the terminals of a Ruhmkorff induction coil, having previously determined the pain and sensitivity thresholds for each subject. Another device recorded the elapsed time of the experiment.

In addition to studying the changes in blood pressure produced by the administration of electrical shocks and other unpleasant stimuli (the sudden firing of a pistol, for example), the experiments sought to quantify reactions to *pleasurable* stimuli, including varied kinds of

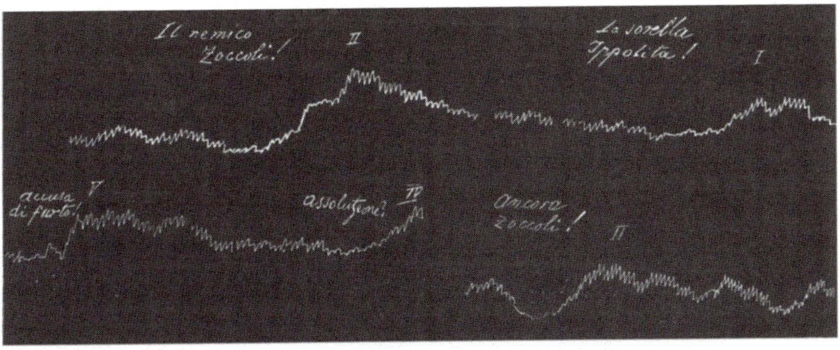

(Leggere da destra a sinistra).
Fig. 29. — Cinque forti diminuzioni della mano destra di Musolino e perciò altrettante inflessioni della curva, per le diverse emozioni accennate con parole sul fondo.

Fig. 5.6 Plethysmography of Musolino.

recorded music. Another series of tests involved an apparatus for visual stimulation: a shutter suspended by an electric magnet was opened to reveal a variety of images that were designed to produce excitement, and that had been "specially selected" for each experimental subject: a bottle of wine, a cigar, a nude woman, food, or money. Finally, a third set of experiments sought to measure responses to "purely psychic phenomena": mathematical calculations, good and bad news, or the sudden mention of the judge who had tried the subject's case. In contrast, say, to the work of Binet and Courtier (see above), which also explored differential effects of various stimuli, Lombroso was interested in making visible differences *between* subjects and categories of subjects that he took to be indices of social danger (Figure 5.6).

The fragmentary nature of the reported results (some two dozen abbreviated case studies) makes it impossible to determine which of these tests was administered to which subjects, and under what circumstances. What struck Lombroso as most significant was the "almost total lack of vaso-motor reactions" in some of the subjects. "Ausano," for example, was characterized as:

> prognathous, tattooed, receding forehead, with marked frontal sinuses, criminal uncle, drunkard father, neurotic mother; thief since childhood, who declares he would sell his soul for cash; does not like his friends, but together with them squanders his pitiful earnings—never demonstrated any reaction, neither to music, a pistol shot, unpleasant news, nor calculations; only [an image of] wine produced a slight rise [in blood pressure] for 18 pulses.[102]

"Comino," a seventeen-year-old "thief and recidivist, of criminal type," similarly showed "no reaction to seeing [an image of] a knife, to very strong electrical shock, to seeing [an image of] a nude woman; only seeing [an image of] a skull produces slight increase of the sphygmic line; same for an image of a pistol."[103] Finally, there was "Agagliate":

> Thief, recidivist, very young, presented reaction of descent and slowed pulse to melancholy music; and to a light aria, a rise for ten pulsations and an acceleration of the pulse. No reaction to calculation, puncture.
>
> Instead the revolver caused the sphygmic line to rise, but for only 4 beats; the same for vanity [flattering comments].
>
> Electricity did nothing one time; a second time lowered the line of the pulse.
>
> Thinking about the electrical machine flattened the pulse, to render it almost barely detectable at the apices, for six pulsations (fear?).
>
> Another day, neither the pistol, nor the dagger, nor the wine, nor a head of a dead man, produced a clear effect.[104]

In some cases, Lombroso tells us, the pulse was so weak that even after feeding the subjects "lavishly" (following Mosso's suggestion), the researchers were unable to obtain a clear figure of the pulse. With these subjects (three of whom are described), Lombroso and Cougnet instead resorted to the plethysmograph, which Lombroso elsewhere described as "a marvelous instrument," enabling researchers to "descend into the penetralia of the most thoroughly dissimulating man, and with an accuracy that could be called mathematical."[105] The plethysmograph expressed "in millimeters," wrote Lombroso, any emotional and psychic reaction."[106]

The device was applied to the likes of "Barelli," characterized as a

> thief, epileptic, 23 years old, very impudent and an informer in the prisons, so habituated to prison life that he speaks in slang even with us and tells us he couldn't go to sleep peacefully unless he had stolen something.
>
> On the plethysmograph gives rather uncertain reactions: rise of 2 mm after 15 seconds of light music; of 1 mm to wine. Whispering to him in his ear and in slang that he is an informer causes a progressive rise of 4 mm that lasts 2 minutes."[107]

Although these experiments were repeated over the course of an entire year, Lombroso found it difficult to reach a definite

conclusion, given "the many causes influencing this important vasomotor reaction."[108] Nevertheless, the researchers were struck by the
frequent absence of a vasomotor response to strong electrical current,
which seemed to correspond to analgesia. As they put it, "pain in fact
being absent, the stimulus does not seize the [subject's] attention, does
not arrive at the psychic centers; it is as if it had never happened."[109]
By contrast, in cases that involved a more specific, individuated stimulus (for example, the fear of a particular judge), a pleasurable stimulus
(wine, women, gold), or above all vanity, the reactions of criminal
subjects were *greater* than those of normal men. These results, argued Lombroso, allowed researchers to discover that pleasure, vanity
and the fear of pain were, for criminals—as for women, children, and
savages—more effective forces than pain itself.

V. Simulation, Deception, and Danger

More broadly, experiments on the vascular system seemed to promise
what forensic scientist Salvatore Ottolenghi called a "means of differential diagnosis of varied delinquents."[110] By comparing characteristic
tracings, researchers had established the probability that certain categories of delinquents—the habitual criminal, the morally mad, and the
demented—but not others would "present either minimal or no vascular reaction to stimuli." By contrast, Lombroso predicted, the reactions
of "criminals of passion" would be similar to, and perhaps more pro-
nounced than, the normal man's.[111] Augusto Tamburini, in a review of
Mosso's work, characterized the plethysmograph as a "true psychome-
ter" that could enable comparisons among the mentally ill—in whom
the normal means of making the psychic life visible were "altered and
absolutely defective"—by quantifying "the degree of alteration of the
principal nervous centers."[112] Later research, he reported, found that
the sphygmic curves of the mad [*pazzi*] had a characteristic shape.[113]

Finally, the sphygmograph and plethysmograph could aid in the
detection of feigned mental illness. Because intelligent subjects and
known "simulators" typically had more marked vascular reactions to
stimuli than the criminally insane, the plethysmograph would enable
police and jurists to uncover those who might pretend to be defective
in order to mitigate their punishment.

In an least a few instances, Gina Lombroso-Ferrero reports, her father used the plethysmograph to discover whether a subject might be guilty or innocent of a particular charge, "by mentioning it suddenly while his hands were in the plethysmograph or placing a photograph of the victim unexpectedly before his eyes."[114] In one widely reported case, a coachman named Tosetti was shown to be innocent of the murder of a six-year-old girl in Turin in 1902. An anthropometric exam showed him to be "devoid of any degenerate characteristics except excessive maxillary development." His sensibility was "almost normal," his field of vision "not much reduced," and "his natural affections were normal"; "he was a good son and brother; he was excessively timid and disconcerted by the slightest reproof from his brothers." The examination, on Lombroso-Ferrero's telling, "proved beyond a doubt that Tosetti was not a born criminal, and was incapable of committing the action of which he was suspected—the murder of a child for purely bestial pleasure."

"To obtain stronger proof," however, Lombroso used the plethysmograph. He found a slight diminution of the pulse when Tosetti was asked to compute a sum. When, however, skulls and portraits of children covered with wounds were placed before him, the line registered no sudden variation, not even at the sight of the little victim's photograph. The results of the examination, we are told, "proved conclusively that Tosetti was innocent of a crime which can only be committed by sadists, idiots, and the most degenerate types of madmen."[115]

This and similar cases have led some scholars to suggest that Lombroso's experiments on the vascular system be read as part of the genealogy of the lie detector, and certainly there is a technical kinship among the sphygmograph, the plethysmograph, and the later polygraph.[116] However, as the Tosetti case makes clear, the goal of Lombroso's experiments was not to distinguish truthful from untruthful utterances in order to assign legal responsibility for particular acts, but rather to identify the physiological and psychological states that might or might not have *enabled* an individual to commit a particular act. As Lombroso-Ferrero put it, the goal was to detect the presence or absence of "natural affections":

> If after talking to the patient on indifferent subjects, the examiner suddenly mentions persons, friends, or relatives, who interest him and cause

him a certain amount of emotion, the curve registered on the revolving
cylinder suddenly drops and rises rapidly, thus proving that he possesses
natural affections. If, on the other hand, when alluding to relatives and
their illnesses, or vice-versa, no corresponding movement is registered on
the cylinder, it may be assumed that the patient does not possess much
affection.[117]

In both Lombroso's work and later research on the detection
of deceit, it was expected that the body would betray or honestly
write itself, that interior states would insist on being known, that
the "non-transparency" of the body would be overcome.[118] As Hugo
Münsterberg would later put it, "the lips and hands and arms and legs,
which are under our control, are never the only witnesses to the drama
which goes on inside—if they keep silent, others will speak."[119] Even
subjects who might be able to control, through acts of will, certain of
the external signs of internal events, proved unable to suppress changes
in the pulse, in respiration, and later in the conductivity of the skin.[120]
This "useful inability," as Benussi put it, meant that techniques of visualization, of measurement, and of recording could serve as humane
alternatives to torture.[121]

But the polygraph and the plethysmograph were also technologies
for the production of different *kinds* of truth. Although the lie detector
could be understood as a "mental microscope," able to discern "whether
there are lies in the mind of the suspect,"[122] the plethysmograph in
Lombroso's hands functioned as a *danger detector.* The body did not, in
the second case, betray the mind as much as its own organic pathologies. Indeed, the truths revealed by the plethysmograph were truths
that might not even be available to the subject, let alone articulable
in his or her speech; only the criminologist was positioned to diagnose an affective defect that put the social at risk. Perhaps the heir to
Lombroso's work is not the lie detector but the penile plethysmograph,
a device created in the 1908 and used since the 1970s to help in the
identification of sex offenders.[123] It is there, as well in a variety of imaging technologies, that the fantasy of the confessing body—a body that
can alert scientists and others to the presence of a social danger—is
sustained.

6

After Lombroso

"Every crime is committed by a born criminal."
—Mariano Patrizi, *Dopo Lombroso* (1916)

I. Introduction: The Unmaking of Expertise

The claims made on and about the criminal body by Lombroso and his colleagues did not go unchallenged: they were resisted by criminologists in France and elsewhere who rejected the model of atavism; they were resisted by legislators who refused to replace a system of penalties with measures of social defense; they were resisted by juries unwilling to abandon a discourse of legal responsibility. And, finally, they were resisted by the bodies of criminals, which frustrated, again and again, the unmasking readings of the scientist.

We might, then, be tempted to conclude that criminologists failed in their efforts to draw stable and reliable boundaries dividing the bodies of criminals from those of "normal" women and men. Neither pain measurements, nor plethysmographic inscriptions, nor cranial capacities, it would seem, could resolve the messiness of legal responsibilities into questions of social hygiene. But we risk mistaking the project: criminal anthropology helped to produce the social world *as messy*, produced social dangerousness as ubiquitous, indeed produced the criminal body as never fully legible. The elusive body called forth measurement after measurement, just as society conceived as a locus of risk called for unbounded practices of prevention.

Of course, for many anthropological claims to have the *effects* desired by criminologists, it was necessary that they leave the confines of the laboratory or the scholarly journal. As we have seen, spaces for recording anthropometrical measurements, pathological anatomical features, even thresholds of pain sensitivity would be routinely provided in the forms used by Italian prison administrators and asylum doctors at the beginning of the twentieth century.[1] But quantifying measures and the diagnoses they enabled were supposed to matter, above all, in the decisions of judges and juries. Lombroso envisioned, for example, that tests of pain sensitivity and plethysmographic reactions could be of particular usefulness to courts in cases where the simulation of mental illness was suspected—even if the simulator attempted to mask his or her reaction, the contractions of the face or the blood flow to the limbs would give the accused away. And Lombroso could point to a handful of other cases in which these measurements had had decisive results: once, for example, algometrical tests on a deaf-mute girl who was a victim of sexual assault showed that she was "not unintelligent," a finding that spared her aggressor a charge of aggravated rape.[2]

But the criminal anthropologists had, of course, hoped for much more. In 1879, Lombroso had imagined that the introduction of the experimental method to legal medicine would effect a radical transformation. In the past, judges and juries might have smiled when alienists spoke of an accused's "degree of imputability," of variations in "free will," or of "transitory madness." But experimental phreniatry would "put an end to all of this." In place of the "inconclusive formulations and imprecise abstractions" of experts who failed even to use their senses, the new science would substitute "a few arid facts, but facts nevertheless: the weight of the body; the condition of the skin and hair; measurements of the cranium; evaluations of temperature, urine, muscular force, sensibility, writing and pronunciation."[3]

In practice, however, the authority of the new criminological experts, and of the medical and social facts they deployed, was frequently compromised. As Garofalo complained, judges and legislators persisted in "abstracting the crime from the criminal," and were therefore reluctant to reform codes of criminal procedure. This meant that the unfolding of expert testimony occurred under conditions ill suited to the pursuit of scientific truths: experts did not have adequate time to prepare, to construct family histories, or to conduct experiments on the body, all of which made it difficult to reach reliable conclusions.[4] But the *performance* of expertise in the courtroom was also problematic: "The experts, wishing to show off their science, vie with one another in a

Greek technical language that the jury cannot begin to comprehend."
The result of the hastily arranged "scientific jousting tournament" was
that jurors became bored and confused—overwhelmed by divergent
opinions they ended by having none of their own.[5]

Indeed, the very continued presence of the jury in the Italian courtroom testified to the failures of procedural reform, to an inability
practically to "set aside legality."[6] But the jury's presence was also an
embarrassing reminder of the proximity of folk and medical discourses,
and threatened to collapse the spaces of medical authority. Juries, as
Lombroso put it, did not simply represent the *volgo*, but "an armed
and powerful *volgo*."[7] For Antonio Raffaele, the persistence of the jury
meant not only that justice was "compromised," but that the dignity of
the medical profession was routinely "offended." The physician "feels
a justifiable resentment when he sees jurors, who are ignorant of science, choose not to trust in his judgment but arrogate unto themselves
the right to examine what they cannot comprehend."[8] And as Patrizia
Guarnieri has shown, criminological theories, for all their reliance on
folk wisdom, ran up against the common sense of juries when they
suggested criminals should not be held responsible for their crimes.[9]
Jurors, complained Lombroso, were "blind in acquitting and even more
so in convicting"; they "followed their hearts rather than the findings
of science, and pursued a social vendetta."[10] The situation was, in any
event, far removed from one in which, as Raffaele envisioned, "both
judges and juries [would] be obliged to accept, without reservation, the
judgments of men who occupy themselves exclusively with research and
scientific laws."[11]

One sign of the crisis in medical authority in the courtroom was the
publication in 1905 of Lombroso's *La perizia pschiatrico-legale*, a manual for psychiatric expert witnesses. Although Lombroso would soon
be honored by his colleagues for his life's accomplishments, 1905 could
hardly be called a triumphant year for the Italian School, which had
weathered attacks from abroad and had become internally fractured.
La perizia was, in some sense, aimed at consolidation rather than further elaboration. There is none of the brashness and excitement that
mark the tone of Lombroso's early scientific reports. Nor does the text
have the scope and pastiche qualities of the various editions of *L'uomo
delinquente*.[12] The manual reflects in its organization and contents a

renewed tension between the scientific and the commonsensical. Designed for the educated layman (and thus implying that almost anyone
can become a forensic expert) it sought at the same time to shore up
the wall dividing science from other cultural practices. It did this by
constructing forensic expertise as a form of *practice* or *discipline*—with
its own tools, procedures, conventions, and specialized vocabulary.

The first part of the volume consists of a series of summarized
case studies provided by various criminologists and alienists, many of
which conclude in a perfunctory but triumphant declaration: "a clear
case of irresponsibility" or "a true cretin." These examples of "classic
expert testimony" were marshaled both to "confirm with secure doc-
uments the theories advanced in *L'uomo delinquente*," and "to guide
the hand of the forensic neophyte."[13] The second part, devoted to expert witness methodology, was intended to "meet the needs of those
who complain they cannot follow these [earlier] studies because they
lack . . . a familiarity with specialized techniques." Lombroso proposed
to teach readers "the few maneuvers necessary for anthropometric
and psycho-physical measurements and research, and [to] show how
to apply these to expert testimony and to scientific investigations."[14]
Finally, the text included a glossary of the most important terms in scientific criminology—terms whose meanings might otherwise remain
elusive.

In his discussion of expert practices (part 2), Lombroso distinguished between "common" or "ordinary" kinds of forensic investigations, and cases of a particular or historic importance that demanded
more detailed study. In either kind of case, Lombroso advised, the
work of the forensic expert ought properly to resemble scientific research: "both aim at the accumulation of objective proofs," and should
therefore confine themselves to a somatic and psychological study of
the accused.[15] However, cautioned the author, the authority of science in the courtroom was far from assured: "since judges and, even
more so, members of the jury are not scientists, and are instead for
the most part averse to science, they would become fed up by an excess of subtle scientific analyses and would not be able to follow the
witness; they might indeed arrive at a contrary verdict out of spite or
boredom."[16] Thus, in the case of ordinary expert reports, Lombroso
recommended that witnesses restrict their research and testimony.

After a brief exposition of the case, he advised, experts should report the weight and height of the accused, then move quickly to the general anthropological characteristics, including thresholds of sensitivity. He further suggested that witnesses have before them one of the forms developed by Tamburini and Benelli, or by Carrara and Strassmann, "which in a few lines group together the most necessary investigations and determine the order in which one should proceed." The expert's final tasks were to link the anthropological characteristics to the acts in question, and to provide a synthesis that would "illuminate" the judge.[17] If the lists Lombroso recommended may strike us as fairly exhaustive (including, for example, craniometry, anthropometry, plethysmographic and sphygmographic studies, and assessments of reflexes, muscular force, respiration, digestion, and handwriting), and therefore likely to try the patience of any judge or jury, Lombroso insisted upon a much more detailed investigation in criminal cases of special import. Here, as in scientific research, there were "never enough data."[18]

In both kinds of cases, experts were advised to conduct measurements of pain sensitivity (along with eight other sensory thresholds). And here there was no longer any question whether the Lombroso algometer, for example, was an appropriate device, whether it measured anything real, or whether the pain threshold was significant. Instead, the question with which the expert had to contend was whether a diminished sensitivity to pain was one of the facts that might productively be presented to a wary and disrespectful jury. When the expert took up his pen to complete the Tamburini–Benelli form, and came to the line for pain threshold, the competition among instruments makers, the contests between anthropologists and physiologists, the debates about electricity and excitability, and the other ambiguities that attend the elaboration of a new science, disappeared.

This is not to say criminology had, by 1905, put an end to such contingencies. Indeed, it would not have taken much for things to unravel: the expert might skip over the line in question, or a jury might scoff at the evidence when it was presented. And what was implicit in *La perizia*—that anyone with the right stuff (tools, techniques, rhetorics) might become a forensic expert—might actually have worked to undermine the authority of the scientist.

As we explore the genealogy of the body-as-evidence, we may wish to attend not only to the struggle between science and law, but also to medicine's confrontation with another stubborn force: popular culture. This was at once the condition of possibility of a medicalizing, somaticizing discourse of crime, and also for a time set limits to the authority of physicians to decide the facts of the matter, to treat deviant individuals and to elaborate solutions to social problems. Yet it is also clear that by 1905 both criminological debates and trials were unfolding on a modified terrain where a certain kind of attending to bodies could be taken for granted, and where quantification proceeded silently and inexorably. An unobtrusive circulation of tools and techniques, across both national and disciplinary boundaries, played a crucial role in reworking this terrain. More detailed—and comparative—research may enable us to understand the ways in which shared practices crosscut discursive and theoretical debates (and not only between the "Italians" and the "French"), and helped to diffuse the scientific project of knowing the deviant body, producing tangible—if sometimes unintended—effects.

II. Practices of Risk

Lombroso himself was not sanguine about the impact his work had or might have in Italy. In 1895, he remarked that he was "fairly startled" when asked by the editors of *The Forum* to give an account of the applications made in Italy of his ideas. It was easy enough for him to see what these *might* have been: radical revisions of Italy's code of criminal procedure and criminal code, which had been "conceived through the study of crime as an abstraction."[19] The new codes should have been organized around nothing other than the defense of society. As he observed in his article for *The Forum*,

> The greatest criminal anomaly—even insanity—should not be considered an extenuating circumstance. Even lunatics should be arrested in order to protect society, especially the morally insane, who are a great peril, and the masked epileptics. In the punishment of crime the tendency of its authors should be considered. If the author is a born criminal, he must be confined for life, though the crime itself is not great. On the other hand, a crime committed by an honest man impelled by some strong motive should be

punished with much indulgence, especially political and religious crimes, which often anticipate by some centuries the thought of the people.[20]

But none of this, Lombroso lamented, had happened in Italy. "What can one expect," he asked his American readers, "from a race of advocates and rhetoricians?"[21] The United States alone could "boast of having conscientiously applied scientific knowledge of criminal anthropology to criminal therapeutics." Lombroso cited as examples the opening of a bureau for degenerates and abnormal people in Washington, and the founding of the Elmira Reformatory.[22]

Even within Italy, however, positive anthropology would have its effects; although Lombroso himself might be "discredited," the political rationality of social defense would have more lasting implications. These were most fully sketched out in a draft revision of the penal code authored by Enrico Ferri in 1921. But though this draft was not adopted, many practices of social defense were built into the fascist penal code in 1930.[23] And as Mary Gibson has argued, the work of criminal anthropologists (and especially Salvatore Ottolenghi) also shaped the development of "scientific policing" in Italy.[24]

More broadly, I want to suggest, the legacy of criminal anthropology, together with that of other humans sciences at the end of the nineteenth century, is linked to the development of what we might call a new culture of risk. Michel Foucault's genealogy of "dangerousness" makes it clear that a number of criminal anthropology's "most fundamental theses, often those most foreign to traditional law, have gradually taken root in penal thought and practice."[25] This did not happen, Foucault argues, because of the truth value or persuasive power of positive theories of criminality. Rather, he suggests, it was changes in *civil* law—around the notions of accidents, risk, and responsibility—that made possible "the articulation of the legal code and of science in penal law."[26] Other scholars have explored the ways in which a new logic of risk has sustained new social technologies—practices of preventive detention, parole, probation—substituting for punishment the assessment and management of risk.[27]

All of this is dependent upon a generalized suspicion, a construction of the social that has been linked, paradoxically, to the *inability* of criminal anthropology to isolate the criminal type. Indeed, this apparent failure can also be read in another way, as producing a more mobile and flexible attention to bodies and the signs of their dangerousness. By the end of his career, Lombroso had, in fact, multiplied the categories of possible criminals, to include not only the moral madman and the epileptic criminal, but also occasional offenders, criminals of passion, juridical criminals, and other "criminaloids." *Each* of these—not only the atavistic monster—was constituted as a proper anthropological object, requiring scrutiny and, possibly, intervention if society was to be defended. As two historians put it, "Everyone came under [the category of] the pathological, a dark crucible into which disappeared not only individuals, but the peculiarities between and internal to each listed category. These could be interchanged, transfigured in the condensation. The only thing that was clear was that [society] had to be defended against all of them." [28]

III. The Normal and the Pathological

As we saw in Chapter 2, the problem of recognizing social danger was perhaps greatest for women. In the end, what emerged from Lombroso's studies was less the (hoped for) transparent pathology of the female offender than the barely legible *potential* dangerousness of the normal woman. As a result, not only were the criminal woman and the prostitute made objects of new practices of surveillance, prevention, and punishment, but the normal woman was placed at the center of a whole range of modern discourses and technologies called "social," ranging from social medicine, to social hygiene, to social work. Against the background of struggles for women's suffrage, anthropologists constructed women as beings who were incapable of balancing rights and duties, who lacked an innate respect for property, and who embodied a latent criminality that could be held in check only by the experience of maternity and the action of new techniques of government.[29]

Ostensibly, Lombroso and Ferrero constructed a stable, triangular scheme announced by their book's title.[30] At one apex stood the prostitute, the true expression of female degeneration. At another apex was the born criminal, who in Lombroso's view was an entirely exceptional being. She was "doubly abnormal" because she did not follow the "natural" form of retrogression in women—that is, prostitution. Born female criminals were the true "monsters" of their sex, marked anatomically by virile characteristics that makeup could not disguise, and behaviorally by a rejection of maternity that typically took the form of infanticide.[31] Gender and sexual inversions were at once the signs and logical consequences of female criminality, since, as we have seen, neither the category "woman" nor the category "female" allowed for deviation from norms.

At the final apex stood the normal woman, the most unstable figure because she was physically indistinguishable from the "occasional criminal," and was indeed linked to her by a "fund of immorality" latent in all women, the principal sign of which was an innate lack of respect for property.[32] The normal woman, in a sense, embodied potential criminality. "In ordinary cases," wrote Lombroso and Ferrero, "the child-like defects of the semi-criminal are neutralized by piety, maternity, want of passion, sexual coldness, weakness, and undeveloped intelligence."[33] In sum, woman was constructed as both normal in her pathology, and pathological in her normality. This construction not only removed all women from the domain of rights, duties, and politics, but also inscribed them in the domain of the social. It made women suitable objects of an ongoing surveillance and of corrective interventions that, in an effort to restrict "opportunities" for criminality, blurred the lines between penal practices and social work.

The social technical interventions and punitive measures Lombroso and Ferrero proposed for female criminals were linked to this tripartite typology.[34] They argued, for example, for the social usefulness of prostitution, a "safety valve" that "serves to relieve the passions of men," and advised state regulation rather than penalization.[35] They recommended imprisonment (as in the case of men) only for the monstrous, born criminal who posed an ongoing social danger. By contrast, the "occasional criminal," who was presumed to be passive, determined by her environment, and open to the suggestions of others, was to be made the object of educational interventions and penalties appropriate to her sex: "in view . . . of the important part played by dress, ornaments, etc. in the feminine world, penalties inflicted on vanity—the cutting off of the hair, the obligation to wear a certain costume, etc., might with advantage be substituted for imprisonment."[36] In addition, Lombroso and Ferrero advocated special tribunals for women, adjusted to "the milder nature of feminine criminality, the usefulness of women in the home, and the serious injury inflicted on the family and the society in general by the segregation of the wife and mother (if only for a short period)."[37] Finally, Lombroso and Ferrero proposed a politics of prevention centered on the regulation of marriage and maternity. He recommended the liberalization of divorce and the prohibition of marriage before the age of 18 as a way of reducing violent crimes against husbands.[38] And, in a move that joined women's autonomy to her potential dangerousness, Lombroso argued that "the child bearing function" could act as "a moral antidote" to female criminality.[39]

However, to view Lombroso's anthropology simply as calling women back to their (maternal) natures is to overlook the construction of the female body as a *social* body—no longer enclosed in the private spaces of the home, but accessible in the social domain to the investigations and interventions of social scientists and social technicians (social workers, hygienists, home efficiency experts, nutritionists, and architects). In Italy, as elsewhere in Europe, the ongoing exclusion of woman from the political domain was accompanied by her location in the domain of the social, both as a special object of social science and social technics, and as a subject responsible for reproduction, for the welfare of the family, and by extension for the health of the larger social body.[40]

Of course, the male criminal—in all of his anthropological manifestations—remained at the center of the criminological project, but here, too, the lines of demarcation became increasingly hard to discern. Mariano Luigi Patrizi offered perhaps the boldest statement about the continuity of the normal and the pathological. Trained as a physiologist, Patrizi served (beginning in 1890) as an assistant to Angelo Mosso before assuming in 1911 the chair in criminal anthropology at the University of Turin created by Lombroso's death.[41] Later in his career, Patrizi's orientation was decidedly psychological. In a discussion of the "psychological phase of criminal anthropology," Patrizi proposed that Lombrosian criminal anthropology had moved gradually from the exterior of the body to its interior: "rising from physiology, to psycho-physiology, to psychology."[42] At the end of this evolution, and with the aid of new instruments, it had become possible to "measure and label the features of the soul," which had for so long been thought to be "ungraspable" other than by introspection.[43] Indeed, Patrizi would advance the thesis that all crimes started here, at the level of the emotional or "sentimental." It is not surprising that his research relied on inscription devices and the graphical method, which he imagined could reveal both the intensity and "sincerity" of any emotion.[44]

But I want here to call attention to Patrizi's emphasis on the leakage of the categories of normal and pathological. Patrizi proposed a continuum that ranged from the born criminal to the "emotional" criminal, that "close neighbor of the honest man."[45] The continuum embraced everyone from the moral madman, to the primitive criminal, to the habitual or occasional offender, to the epileptic. In Patrizi's view, these multiple and overlapping categories both confirmed and extended the concept of congenital criminality:

> The graphical expression of Lombroso's, which distributed the various figures of criminals, not pigeonholing them, but staggering them along a single inclined plane, with no division between them but a narrow tier, remains an accurate symbol. . . . It follows that from the first tier of guilt to normality the descent is, unfortunately, smooth. . . . [T]here is no leap from the pathological to the physiological.[46]

Patrizi, to be sure, took his distance from Lombroso, but we ought to take seriously his joking claim that, in blurring the lines between the normal and the abnormal, he was being "more monarchical than the king, more Lombrosian than Lombroso. "[47] The image of German and American criminals from the atlas of *L'uomo delinquente* is, in the end, precisely what Patrizi describes (Figure 6.1). Far from reassuring, it appears to be a montage of the citizens of the modern European city; readers could reasonably be expected to bring the scrutiny of the criminologist to their encounters on the streets of Turin, Paris, London, and New York. A generalized anxiety—that everyone was potentially dangerous, if not equally so—was only partially assuaged by the hope that the bodies of the truly dangerous would signal their difference.

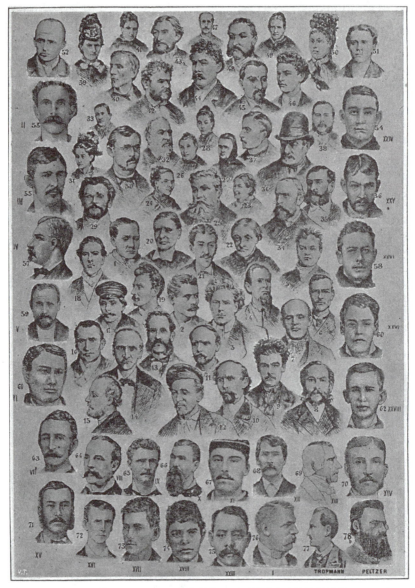

ALBUM DI DELINQUENTI TEDESCHI E AMERICANI.

Fig. 6.1 Album of German and American Criminals.

IV. History of the Present

Patrizi's work points us to the ways in which the Lombrosian faith in the testifying body would play itself out in the science of psychology, particularly in relation to psycho-physiological testing. As suggested at the end of the previous chapter, one such technology is the penile plethysmograph, a modification of Mosso's device that measures the flow of blood to the penis. Although the plethysmograph has met resistance in the courtroom, it continues to be used to identify and monitor sex offenders. Other scientists would pursue evidence of social danger at the level of the endocrine system. Giuseppe Vidoni, although cautious to guard against monocausal explanations or to reify categories of criminals, suggested it might be possible to link hormonal constitutions and particular forms of criminality. The "hypo-vegetative type" predominated among purse snatchers, the evidence suggested, while a "hyper-vegetative type" characterized violent criminals.[48]

More recently, scanning techniques have offered the hope that images of the brain might help to understand and to identify psychiatric diseases such as schizophrenia.[49] It has not taken a great leap to imagine that scans of the brains of criminals might also tell interesting stories. A group of scientists led by Adrian Raine at the University of Southern California have, for example, proposed that pictures produced by Positron Emission Tomography (PET) might help to identify patterns of brain activity characteristic of "predatory murderers," "affective murderers" (what Lombroso might have called criminals of passion), and a control population.[50]

We might also point to exegetical practices linked to other kinds of difference coded as deviance, for example the effort to read sexual orientation from the body. As we saw in Chapter 1 (Note 99), researchers have proposed that homosexuals might be identified by the distinctive patterns of their fingerprints. Other scientists have focused on the ratio of the length of the index finger to the length of ring finger,[51] on the size of the hypothalamus, and on genetic markers on the X chromosome.[52]

However, the efforts to "decode" and then "read" the human genome offer perhaps the broadest range of possibilities for identifying criminal dangers.[53] Here, the link is less with genetic "fingerprinting"—a forensic tool that is part of the genealogy of "signaletics" rather than semiological practices—than with cytogenetic tests that aim to identify chromosomal patterns (in particular, men who have an extra Y chromosome), or attempt to identify genetic markers that might indicate a propensity to violence or other forms of social danger (a predisposition to alcoholism or schizophrenia, for example).[54] As recently as 1984, law professor Lawrence Taylor found the 1960s research on men with XYY to have "disturbing" implications: "That there appears to be a genetic 'type' that is inherently disposed to criminal conduct appears to be a distinct possibility."[55] Taylor cited the work of the English psychologist H. J. Eysenck, in wondering whether Lombroso was "perhaps, not far wrong."[56] He found, in any event, that the trend of research in genetics was clear:

> Assuming that the legal system is presented with the scientific capability of "reading" DNA and the statistical ability of predicting aberrant genetic structure, some very difficult questions will be posed. How should the criminal justice system deal with a criminal offender whose conduct was caused by a genetic aberration? Does society have the right to seek out such individuals before they cause harm and remove them from the community? Can society prevent such individuals from being born in the first place?[57]

It is reassuring, perhaps, to imagine that we can dismiss this fantasy as "junk science"; Taylor is, after all, not even a geneticist. But as I suggested at the outset, it is important to avoid dismissive readings of either nineteenth-century or twentieth-century sciences of the criminal body as pseudoscience. On one hand, the work of criminal anthropologists was not without its effects: it made possible, even urgent, the production of new knowledge about bodies and populations; the development of new practices of measurement, collection, and display; and the elaboration of new forms of policing: social technologies for the prevention and management of risk. On the other hand, by attending to projects like electrical algometry, penile plethysmography, and PET scans, we may come to understand precisely how the boundaries between forms of knowledges have been drawn, how the body has come to be scrutinized as a source of evidence, and how pain, blood flows, and genetic codes have been mobilized to make sense of human differences.

Of course, we should not expect the fantasies and anxieties that drive our interest in the testifying body in the twenty-first-century United States to be the same as those that prevailed in Italy at the end of the nineteenth century. If science still seeks the body's evidence of social danger, the task of the critic is to make sense of the hold of *current* fantasies, the entailments of *current* cultural anxieties, the ongoing production of both popular wisdom and scientific common sense about the anatomies of deviance.

Notes

1. See, for example, Vinigi Grotanelli, "Ethnology and/or Cultural Anthropology in Italy: Tradition and Developments," *Current Anthropology* 18 (1977): 593–601 and Grotanelli "Italy: Cultural Anthropology Reconsidered," in *Anthropology: Ancestors and Heirs,* ed. Stanley Diamond (The Hague: Mouton, 1980), 221–42. Grotanelli, who traces the origins of the discipline back to Julius Caesar's commentaries on the Celts, finds that "even the positivistic trends of the 19th century did not succeed in blurring that classic distinction" between natural and social sciences (598). On the history of Italian cultural anthropology and its relations with ethnology, also see Francesco Remotti, "Tendenze autarchiche nell'antropologia culturale italiana," *Rassegna italiana di sociologia* 19 (1978): 183–226; George Saunders, "Contemporary Italian Cultural Anthropology," in *Annual Review of Anthropology* 13 (1984): 447–66. The exception is the work of Sandra Puccini and Massimo Squillacciotti, "Principali tappe dello sviluppo statutario delle discipline etno-antropologiche italiane (Appendice B)," in *Studi antropologici italiani e rapporti di classe, dal positivismo al dibattito attuale* (Milan: Franco Angeli, 1980), 202–12.
2. *Archivio per l'Antropologia e la Etnologia* was edited by Paolo Mantegazza and published by the Società italiana di antropologia e etnologia.
3. As Antonio Marazzi has observed, "if you say 'I am an anthropologist,' people may think that you are a follower of Malinowski or Lévi-Strauss, but certainly not of Lombroso." Comment [on Grotanelli, "Ethnology and/or Cultural Anthropology"], *Current Anthropology* 18 (1977): 605.
4. Stephen Jay Gould, *The Mismeasure of Man* (New York: Norton, 1981), 21, 139, 125. On the stakes of more recent border struggles see, for

example, Constance Penley, *NASA/TREK: Popular Science and Sex in America* (London: Verso, 1997), 1–10; Andrew Ross, "New Age—A Kinder, Gentler Science?" in *Strange Weather: Culture, Science and Technology in the Age of Limits* (London: Verso, 1991), 15–74.

5. Charles Goring, *The English Convict: A Statistical Study* (London: T. Fischer Unwin, 1913). On Goring, see David Garland, "British Criminology before 1935," *The British Journal of Criminology* 28 (1988): 140–42 and Daniel Pick, *Faces of Degeneration: A European Disorder, c. 1848–c. 1918* (Cambridge: Cambridge University Press, 1989), 186–88. As Pick observes, although Goring rejected the idea of an *anthropological* criminal type, he did find there was a physical and moral type of person who was predisposed to crime. For Pick, "the very establishment of Goring's project in the 1900s could be seen as evidence of Lombroso's lingering discursive importance, at least in framing central issues of debate" (186).

6. See especially the influential article by Robert Nye, "Heredity or Milieu: The Foundations of Modern European Criminological Theory," *Isis* 67 (1976): 335–55; much of the article is reprinted in Nye, *Crime, Madness and Politics in Modern France: The Medical Concept of National Decline* (Princeton: Princeton University Press, 1984), 97–131. Also see Ruth Harris, *Murder and Madness: Medicine, Law, and Society in the* Fin de Siècle (Oxford: Clarendon Press, 1989), 80–98.

7. The argument is perhaps stated most forcefully by Pierre Darmon, *Médecins et assassins à la belle époque: La médicalisation du crime* (Paris: Seuil, 1989), 82–113.

8. See Marc Renneville, "La réception de Lombroso en France (1880–1900)," in *Histoire de la criminologie française,* ed. Laurent Mucchielli (Paris: L'Harmattan, 1994), 107–35; Laurent Mucchielli, "Hérédité et 'Milieu social': le faux antagonisme franco-italien," in *Histoire de la criminologie française,* 189–214. On the shifting understandings of "nature" and "nurture" in the age of molecular biology, see Evelyn Fox Keller, "Nature, Nurture, and the Human Genome Project," in *The Code of Codes: Scientific and Social Issues in the Human Genome Project,* ed. Daniel J. Kevles and Leroy Hood (Cambridge: Harvard University Press, 1992), 281–99.

9. See, for example, Paolo Mantegazza, *La scienza nell'Italia nuova* (Florence: Le Monnier, 1880). The anthropologist Mantegazza complained that scientists in Milan were ignorant of what was published in Naples, and that it was more difficult to obtain a book from Palermo than from St. Petersburg. What was worse, Italy was importing professors from Germany and exporting its own students: the botanist Gasparini had given up his citizenship to go to Paris to learn how to use a microscope (6). Mantegazza shared with many of his contemporaries the conviction that sciences developed *differently* in different national contexts: "Every race, every people, every epoch brings to scientific research a certain group of energies, and the different modes of observation, induction, and conclusion in turn give the science of each country and epoch a certain physiognomy" (8).

10. The best comparative study remains Pick, *Faces of Degeneration*. On the impact of Lombroso's work in France, see Renneville, "La reception de Lombroso"; on Great Britain, see David Garland, "The Criminal and His Science: A Critical Account of the Formation of Criminology at the End of the Nineteenth Century," *The British Journal of Criminology* 25 (1985): 109–37 and Garland, "Of Crimes and Criminals: The Development of Criminology in Britain," in *The Oxford Handbook of Criminology*, ed. Mike Maguire et al. (Oxford: Clarendon Press, 1994), 1–16; on the United States, see Nicole Rafter, "Criminal Anthropology in the United States," *Criminology* 30 (1992): 525–45 and Rafter, *Creating Born Criminals* (Urbana: University of Illinois Press, 1997); on Germany, see Richard Wetzell, *Inventing the Criminal: A History of German Criminology, 1800–1945* (Chapel Hill: University of North Carolina Press, 2000).

11. When this work is recognized, it is usually characterized as a defensive response to the withering attacks of the French—an effort that comes too late to rehabilitate the theory of the born criminal. See, for example, Gould's discussion of "Lombroso's retreat." *The Mismeasure of Man*, 132–35.

12. For intellectual biographies, see Gina Lombroso-Ferrero, *Cesare Lombroso: Storia della vita e delle opere narrata dalla figlia* (Turin: Bocca, 1915); Hans Kurella, *Cesare Lombroso: A Modern Man of Science*, trans. M. Eden Paul (London: Rebman, 1911); Marvin E. Wolfgang, "Cesare Lombroso (1835–1909)," in *Pioneers in Criminology*, ed. Hermann Mannheim, 2nd ed. (Montclair: Patterson Smith, 1972), 232–91; Luigi Bulferetti, *Cesare Lombroso* (Turin: UTET, 1975). For critical studies of Lombroso, see especially Mary Gibson, *Born to Crime: Cesare Lombroso and the Origins of Biological Criminology* (Westport: Praeger, 2002) and Renzo Villa, *Il deviante e i suoi segni: Lombroso e la nascita dell'antropologia criminale* (Milan: Franco Angeli, 1985). More focused studies include Marie-Christine Leps, *Apprehending the Criminal: The Production of Deviance in Nineteenth-Century Discourse* (Durham: Duke University Press, 1992); Nancy Harrowitz, *Antisemitism, Misogyny, and the Logic of Cultural Difference: Cesare Lombroso and Matilde Serao* (Lincoln: University of Nebraska Press, 1992).

13. Lombroso published five editions of the book between 1876 and 1897: *L'uomo delinquente, studiato in rapporto all'antropologia, alla medicina legale ed alle discipline carcerarie* (Milan: Hoepli, 1876); *L'uomo delinquente, in rapporto all'antropologia, alla giurisprudenza ed alle discipline carcerarie: aggiuntavi La teoria della tutela penale del Prof. avv. F. Poletti*, 2nd ed. (Turin: Bocca, 1878); *L'uomo delinquente, in rapporto all'antropologia, alla giurisprudenza ed alle discipline carcerarie: delinquente-nato e pazzo morale*, 3rd ed. (Turin: Bocca, 1884); *L'uomo delinquente, in rapporto all'antropologia, alla giurisprudenza ed alle discipline carcerarie*, 4th ed., 2 vols. (Turin: Bocca, 1889); *L'uomo delinquente, in rapporto all'antropologia, alla giurisprudenza ed alle discipline carcerarie*, 5th ed., 3 vols. and atlas (Turin: Bocca, 1896–97). Lombroso's journal was first published in 1880, with the full title *Archivio di psichiatria, antropologia criminale e scienze*

penali per servire allo studio dell'uomo alienato e delinquente. Over the years, the order of terms in the title would change several times, and would later include neuropathology and legal medicine; it is hereafter cited as *Archivio.*

14. See Bruno Latour, *Science in Action: How to Follow Scientists and Engineers through Society* (Cambridge: Harvard University Press, 1987).

15. Even the first volume, Villa reminds us, was assembled from disparate articles that had previously appeared in regional scientific and medical journals. See *Il deviante e i suoi segni,* 149–50.

16. Latour, *Science in Action,* 21–62.

17. A similar argument could be made for criminal anthropology museums. See Giorgio Colombo, *La scienza infelice: Il museo di antropologia criminale di Cesare Lombroso* (Turin: Bollati Boringhieri, 1975).

18. On statistics and the constitution of the "social" domain, see Jacques Donzelot, "The Poverty of Political Culture," *I&C* 5 (1979): 73–86; François Ewald, *L'Etat providence* (Paris: Grasset, 1986); Ian Hacking, *The Taming of Chance* (Cambridge: Cambridge University Press, 1990); David Horn, *Social Bodies: Science, Reproduction, and Italian Modernity* (Princeton: Princeton University Press, 1994); Paul Rabinow, *French Modern: Norms and Forms of the Social Environment* (Cambridge: MIT Press, 1989); and Jacqueline Urla, "Cultural Politics in an Age of Statistics: Numbers, Nations and the Making of Basque Identity," *American Ethnologist* 20 (1993): 818–43.

19. Cesare Lombroso, *Pensiero e meteore: studii di un alienista* (Milan: Dumolard, 1878), 3.

20. Ibid., 2.

21. Cesare Lombroso, "Prefazione del traduttore," in Jacob Moleschott, *La circolazione della vita: lettere fisiologiche* (Milan: G. Brigola, 1869), x–xi.

22. Ibid.

23. Enrico Ferri, *The Positive School of Criminology: Three Lectures by Enrico Ferri,* ed. Stanley E. Grupp (Pittsburgh: University of Pittsburgh Press, 1968), 60. Ferri's lectures were originally delivered in 1901.

24. Pasquale Pasquino, "Criminology: The Birth of a Special Savoir," trans. Colin Gordon, *I&C* 7 (1980): 19–20. By Beccaria, see in particular, *Dei delitti e delle pene* [1764] (Bari: De Donato, 1983). On Beccaria, see Piers Beirne, "Inventing Criminology: The 'Science of Man' in Cesare Beccaria's *Dei Delitti e delle pene (1764), Criminology* 29 (1991): 777–820; Philip Jenkins, "Varieties of Enlightenment Criminology: Beccaria, Godwin, de Sade," *British Journal of Criminology* 24 (1984): 112–30; Graeme Newman and Pietro Marongiu, "Penological Reform and the Myth of Beccaria," *Criminology* 28 (1990): 325–45.

25. Lombroso-Ferrero, *Criminal Man,* 4. Ferri noted that "the general opinion of classic criminalists and of the people at large is that crime involves a moral guilt, because it is due to the free will of the individual who leaves the path of virtue and chooses the path of crime." *The Positive School,* 54.

26. Ibid., 71. Other contemporary histories of criminal justice added a third school, the "correctionist" school, which modified classical jurisprudence

by considering mental alienation and age as modifying personal responsibly. See, for example, Goring, *The English Convict*, 12.

27. Pasquino, "Criminology," 20. Also see Michel Foucault, "About the Concept of the 'Dangerous Individual' in 19th-Century Legal Psychiatry," *International Journal of Law and Psychiatry* 1 (1978): 1–18.

28. Ferri, *The Positive School*, 72, emphasis added. "The classical criminologists," he continued, "accept the phenomenon of criminality as an accomplished fact. They analyze it from the point of view of the technical jurist, without asking how this criminal fact may have been produced, and why it repeats itself in greater or smaller numbers from year to year, in every country."

29. Ferri, *The Positive School*, 54.

30. Ibid., 71.

31. Lombroso-Ferrero, *Criminal Man*, 5.

32. Emile Faguet, *The Dread of Responsibility*, trans. Emily James Putnam (New York: G. P. Putnam's Sons, 1914), 95.

33. Cesare Lombroso, Enrico Ferri, Raffaele Garofalo, and Giulio Fioretti, *Polemica in difesa della scuola criminale positiva* (Bologna: Zanichelli, 1886), 197.

34. Robert Fletcher, "The New School of Criminal Anthropology," *American Anthropologist* 4(3) (1891): 210. "The jurists say, without a crime there is no criminal. On the contrary, says the anthropologist, the criminal is here with the intent to commit crime; though his attempt may fail, he is as much the assassin or the thief as if the act had been completed, and he must be hanged or secluded accordingly."

35. Lombroso et al., *Polemica in difesa*, 197. In the opinion of Enrico Ferri, judges needed to "have sufficient knowledge, not of Roman or civil law, but of psychology, anthropology, and psychiatry." *The Positive School*, 36.

36. Lombroso et al., *Polemica in difesa*, 201.

37. Lombroso-Ferrero, *Criminal Man*, 212–16.

38. Cesare Lombroso, *Crime: Its Causes and Remedies*, trans. Henry Horton (Montclair, NJ: Patterson Smith, 1968[1911]), 447.

39. Lombroso et al., *Polemica in difesa*, 198.

40. Foucault, "About the Concept of the 'Dangerous Individual,'" 13.

41. George W. Stocking, Jr., "Bones, Bodies, and Behavior," in *Bones, Bodies, and Behavior: Essays on Biological Anthropology (History of Anthropology 5)*, ed. George W. Stocking, Jr. (Madison: University of Wisconsin Press, 1988), 3–17.

42. Alfredo Niceforo, *Antropologia delle classi povere* (Milan: Vallardi, 1910), 112

43. Ibid., 116.

44. Lombroso-Ferrero, *Criminal Man*, 134–35.

45. Ibid., 134. One anthropologist went beyond this relativizing of "the normal" in an effort to subvert its usual meaning. Paul Albrecht (1851–1894), in a paper read at the 1885 Congress of Criminal Anthropology, defined the modern criminal as "normal"—that is, like all other animals—and the honest, law-abiding citizen as an abnormal

being: "Abnormal men, which is to say honest men, kill and punish normal men, which is to say criminals, because the latter refuse to allow themselves to be abnormalized." Albrecht, "Sur la criminalité chez l'homme au point de vue de l'anatomie comparée," *Actes du premier congrès international d'anthropologie criminelle: Biologie et sociologie (Rome, novembre 1885)* (Turin: Bocca, 1886–1887), 111. Also see Fletcher, "The New School of Criminal Anthropology," 235.

46. See Allan Sekula, "The Body and the Archive," *October* 39 (1986): 11–12; Barbara Maria Stafford, *Body Criticism: Imaging the Unseen in Enlightenment Art and Medicine* (Cambridge: MIT Press, 1991), 84–129; Robert M. Young, *Mind, Brain and Adaptation in the Nineteenth Century: Cerebral Localization and Its Biological Context from Gall to Ferrier.* (Oxford: Clarendon Press, 1970), 9–53. While the focus on the head was in some ways "common-sensical" and continuous with popular practices of reading faces, Sekula suggests it also worked to "legitimate on organic grounds the dominion of intellectual over manual labor." "The Body and the Archive," 12.

47. Lombroso et al., *Polemica in difesa*, 5.

48. On the uses of anthropometry to manage populations in other domains, see Claude Blanckaert, "On the Origins of French Ethnology: William Edwards and the Doctrine of Race," in *Bones, Bodies, and Behavior*, 18–55. On anthropometry's relation to racist evolutionary thought, see Gould, *The Mismeasure of Man*, 73–122. On the links between anthropometry and photography, see Sekula, "The Body and the Archive," 19–23;

49. Cesare Lombroso and Guglielmo Ferrero, *The Female Offender*, ed. W. Douglas Morrison (London: T. Fisher Unwin, 1895), 1.

50. Lombroso and Ferrero reported the results of a craniometrical study by Zampa of four murderers in Ravenna that found an "exact correspondence" with the average measurements of ten normal Ravennese. However, an "anatomo-pathological" investigation of the same four crania identified thirty-three anomalies. Ibid., 2.

51. Lombroso, *L'uomo delinquente*, 5th ed., vol. 1, 136.

52. To put Lombroso's anthropometry in perspective, it is useful to know that a Hungarian anthropometrist, Aurel von Török, "enumerated for the skull alone no fewer than 5371 linear measurements and projections, together with a proportionate number of indices, and many hundreds of angles, triangles, polygons, etc." Harris H. Wilder, *A Laboratory Manual of Anthropometry* (Philadelphia: P. Blackiston's Son & Co., 1920), 5–6.

53. Lombroso, *L'uomo delinquente*, 5th ed., vol. 1, 159.

54. Ibid., 189.

55. Ibid., 334.

56. Lombroso-Ferrero, *Criminal Man*, 10.

57. Lombroso, *L'uomo delinquente*, 5th ed., vol. 1, 247.

58. Ibid., 327.

59. Ibid., 327.

60. Ibid., 327.

61. Ibid., 259, 333.

62. Ibid., 266, 268.

63. Ibid., 333. There were, Lombroso proposed, family resemblances among these offenders that preserved the criminal type.
64. Lombroso-Ferrero, *Criminal Man*, 24, emphasis added.
65. Lombroso et al., *Polemica in difesa*, 6. The degeneration of the race was due, in Lombroso's view, to the action of alcoholic beverages and "inheritance." Its effects included sterility, madness, and crime, and it manifested itself in anomalies of the ear, the skull, and the genitals.
66. Ibid., 12.
67. Ibid., 38. Compare the discussion in Lombroso-Ferrero, *Criminal Man*, 49: "Just as a musical theme is the result of a sum of notes, and not of any single note, the criminal type results from the aggregate of these anomalies, which render him strange and terrible, not only to the scientific observer, but to ordinary observers who are capable of an impartial judgment."
68. Lombroso et al., *Polemica in difesa*, 34.
69. Lombroso, *L'uomo delinquente*, 5th ed., vol. 4 (*Atlante*), iii.
70. Ibid., iv.
71. Ibid., iv. On several occasions, Lombroso noted, criminologists misread their own images. For example, Henri Joly (1839–1925), in an article on juveniles imprisoned in France, had found no evidence among them of the criminal type. But Lombroso found this evidence in the very zincographic images Joly had published: "Only a glance is required to see how great is the frequency of the criminal type. . . and we have before us only zincotypes, which provide only a weak image of the physiognomy." *L'uomo delinquente*, 5th ed., vol. 1, 320.
72. John Tagg , *The Burden of Representation: Essays on Photographies and Histories* (Amherst: University of Massachusetts Press, 1988), 78.
73. Lombroso and Ferrero, *The Female Offender*, 88–102.
74. Jennifer Terry makes a similar point for scientific photographs of lesbian bodies produced in the 1930s: "Although the images of these lesbians do not appear to be at all different from what one would expect heterosexual women to look like, the very composition of the photograph and the fact that it serves as an indicator of variant characteristics invites the viewer to look for and find pathology or difference." "Lesbians Under the Medical Gaze: Scientists Search for Remarkable Differences," *Journal of Sex Research* 27 (1990): 324–25.
75. As we will see in Chapter 3, Lombroso was prohibited from using photographs of convicted Italian criminals.
76. Sekula, "The Body and the Archive," 18. Also see David Green, "Veins of Resemblance: Photography and Eugenics," in *Photography/Politics: Two*, ed. Patricia Holland, Jo Spence, and Simon Watney (New York: Comedia, 1986), 9–21.
77. See Alphonse Bertillon, *La photographie judiciaire : avec un appendice sur la classification et l'identification anthropométriques* (Paris: Gauthier-Villars, 1890).
78. Alphonse Bertillon, *Signaletic Instructions, Including the Theory and Practice of Anthropometrical Identification* (London: Werner, 1896). Bertillon credited Emile Littré (1801–1881) with the definition of

"signalment" as "the description of one whom it is desired to identify." "In prison practice," Bertillon continued, "the signaletic notice accompanies every reception and every delivery of human individuality; it is the *muster-roll* which preserves the evidence of the real and effective presence of the person had in view by the administrative or judicial act." In or outside prison, the aim of signaletics was "always the same: to preserve a sufficient record of the personality to be able to *identify* the present description with one which may be presented at some future time" (11).

79. Giovanni Gasti and Umberto Ellero, "I connotati nel vivo e nella fotografia," *Atti della Società Romana di Antropologia* 12 (1906): 136. On the unreliability of photographs, also see Umberto Ellero, "Identità e dissomiglianza fotografica," *Archivio* 25 (1904): 534–37; Luigi Anfosso, "Il segnalamento dei delinquenti ed il nuovo antropometro popolare," *Archivio* 9 (1888): 363–74. Anfosso noted that the high cost of photographs contributed to their rarely being used in Italy.

80. See F. J. Mouat, "Notes on M. Bertillon's Discourse on the Anthropometric Measurement of Criminals," *Journal of the Anthropological Institute* 20 (1891): 182–97. Bertillon had, according to Mouat, "pointed out how a vast experience in human physiognomy is required to recognize in many of the photographs he exhibited, that they are the likeness of the same man taken at different times. Nevertheless, he adds, that those photographs were all taken in the same studio, by the same photographers, with the same apparatus, and as nearly as possible at the same hour in the morning" (187). Bertillon had therefore added several measurements of the head, foot, middle finger and forearm.

81. See Salvatore Ottolenghi, *Polizia scientifica: quadri sintetici delle lezioni tenute nella Scuola di Polizia* (Rome: Società Poligrafia, 1907) and "L'opera di Cesare Lombroso e la polizia scientifica," in *L'opera di Cesare Lombroso nella scienza e nelle sue applicazioni* (Turin: Bocca, 1908), 220–37. Also see Mary Gibson, *Born to Crime*, 127–74.

82. On new discourses on "identity" that went beyond "identification," see also Jane Caplan, "'Speaking Scars': The Tattoo in Popular Practice and Medico-Legal Debate in Nineteenth-Century Europe," *History Workshop* 44 (1997): 127.

83. On Bertillon, ears, and the reading of clues, also see Carlo Ginzburg, "Morelli, Freud and Sherlock Holmes: Clues and the Scientific Method," *History Workshop* 9 (1980): 24–26.

84. Sekula describes both Bertillon and Galton's uses of photographs as "attempting to preserve the value of an older, optical model of truth in a historical context in which abstract, statistical procedures seemed to offer the high road to social truth and social control." "The Body and the Archive," 55.

85. Green, "Veins of Resemblance," 18.

86. Francis Galton, "Composite Portraits, Made by Combining Those of Many Different Persons into a Single Resultant Figure," *Journal of the Anthropological Institute of Great Britain and Ireland* 8 (1879): 132–44. Compare the efforts to produce composites of criminals from different

historical periods in Edouard Lefort, *Le type criminel d'après les savants et les artistes* (Lyon: Storck, 1892), 13–15.

87. Galton, "Composite Portraits," 143.

88. Sekula, "The Body and the Archive," 17.

89. Ibid.

90. Cesare Lombroso and Guglielmo Ferrero, *La donna delinquente, la prostituta e la donna normale*, 3rd ed. (Turin: Bocca, 1915), 198.

91. See Franco Cagnetta, ed., *Nascita della fotografia psichiatrica* (Venice: La Biennale di Venezia, 1981), 42–43; Augusto Tebaldi, *Fisonomia ed espressione studiate nelle loro deviazioni, con una appendice sulla espressione del delirio nell'arte* (Verona: Drucker & Tedeschi, 1884).

92. On the history of fingerprinting as a means of identification, see Edward Richard Henry, *Classification and Uses of Finger Prints* (London: Routledge, 1900); William James Herschel, *The Origin of Finger-Printing* (London: Oxford University Press, 1916); Francis Galton, *Finger Prints* (London: Macmillan, 1892).

93. Giuseppe D'Abundo, "Contributo allo studio delle impronte digitali," *Archivio* 12 (1891): 517–19; "Le impronte digitali in 140 criminali," *Archivio* 16 (1895): 262.

94. D'Abundo, "Contributo," 517.

95. Ibid., 518.

96. Sante De Sanctis and P. Toscano, "Le impronte digitali dei fanciulli normali, frenastenici e sordomuti," *Atti della Società Romana di Antropologia* 8(2) (1902): 62–79. Also see H. Mutrux-Bornoz, *Les troublantes révélations de l'empreinte digitale et palmaire* (Lausanne: R. Roth, 1937).

97. Attilio Ascarelli, "Les empreintes digitales dans les prostituées," in *Comptes-rendus du VIe congrès international d'anthropologie criminelle (Turin, 28 avril–3 mai 1906)* (Turin: Bocca, 1908), 420–22.

98. Lombroso, *L'uomo delinquente*, 5th ed., vol. 1, 248. Also see Simon A. Cole, *Suspect Identities: A History of Fingerprinting and Criminal Identification* (Cambridge: Harvard University Press, 2001), 105–7.

99. Galton, *Finger Prints*, 197. Galton held out hope that studies of the general shape of the hand might yield more eugenically interesting results. On Galton's and earlier efforts to read fingerprints for signs of difference, see Colin Beavan, *Fingerprints: The Origins of Crime Detection and the Murder Case that Launched Forensic Science* (New York: Hyperion, 2001), 94–111, and Cole, *Suspect Identities*. As Cole points out, if today we think of fingerprinting solely as an identification technique, this is not an accident: "Fingerprinting examiners strengthened their authority by dissociating themselves from their colleagues who speculated about the predictive powers of fingerprints to tell, not only the past, but also the future. By turning the fingerprint into an empty signifier—a sign devoid of information about a body's race, ethnicity, heredity, character, or criminal propensity—fingerprint examiners made fingerprint identification seem less value-laden, more factual" (100). Also see Paul Rabinow, "Galton's Regret: Of Types and Individuals," in *DNA on Trial: Genetic Identification and Criminal Justice*, ed. Paul R. Billings

(Plainview, NY: Cold Spring Harbor Laboratory Press, 1991), 5–18. For more recent efforts to use fingerprints diagnostically—in this case to identify the ridge patterns characteristic of male homosexuality—see Zoe Brennan, "Prints Put the Finger on Gays," *The Sunday Times* (8 February 1998): 7. The story reports the results of a study by Richard Green, a researcher at Charing Cross Hospital in London and the Institute of Criminology at Cambridge University who examined 300 fingerprints of gay men and found that more than a third had a "female pattern," with significantly fewer ridges on their right thumbs than heterosexual males. Brennan mused that this discovery might, among other things, "enable historians to settle arguments about whether celebrities such as Cary Grant and James Dean were closet homosexuals." I am grateful to Jennifer Terry for this reference. Also see Jeff Hall and Doreen Kimara, "Dermatoglyphic asymmetry and sexual orientation in men," *Behavioral Neuroscience,* 108 (1994): 1203–6.

100. Marco Treves, "Les caractères anthropologiques des ongles," in *Congrès international d'anthropologie criminelle: Compte rendu des travaux de la cinquième session tenue à Amsterdam, du 9 au 14 settembre 1901* (Amsterdam: J. H. De Bussy, 1901), 296.

Chapter 2

1. Cesare Lombroso, "Introduction," in Lombroso-Ferrero, *Criminal Man,* xi–xii.
2. Ibid., xii.
3. Ibid., xii–xiv.
4. Ibid., xiv. Lombroso recounted similar stories of the birth of criminal anthropology in an 1895 article in the American journal *The Forum* and in an address to the sixth international congress of criminal anthropology, held in Turin in 1906. See Cesare Lombroso, "Criminal Anthropology: Its Origin and Application," *The Forum* 20 (1895): 35 and "Discours d'ouverture," in *Comptes-rendus du VIe Congrès international d'anthropologie criminelle,* xxxii. The date of the examination of Villella's skull varies from one account to the next (1864 and 1870, respectively).
5. Lombroso, "Discours d'ouverture," xxxii.
6. Lombroso, "Introduction," xiv. Lombroso reported elsewhere that "the weather and the place did not permit [him] to make a thorough autopsy." "Criminal Anthropology," 35. Other accounts suggest Lombroso had access only to Villella's skeletized skull.
7. The discovery of this structure was first reported in Cesare Lombroso, "Esistenza di una fossa occipitale mediana nel cranio di un delinquente nato," *Rendiconti (Reale Istituto lombardo di scienze e lettere)* 4 (1871): 37–41. Also see Cesare Lombroso, "Della fossetta cerebellare mediana in un criminale," *Rendiconti (Reale Istituto lombardo di scienze e lettere)* 5 (1872): 1058–65 and "Deformità cranica congenita in un vecchio delinquente," *Annali universali di medicina* 1874.

8. Lombroso, "Introduction," xxiv–xxv. Though these last lines certainly could not have characterized Villella, Lombroso wrote elsewhere that his reading of Villella's skull was "perfected a few days later" when he was called in as an expert witness in the trial of Vincenzo Verzeni (b. 1849), a "young peasant, with cross eyes and enormous jaws, [who] was possessed with a desire to disembowel, chew, and eat morsels of women, young and old, who happened to cross his path." "Criminal Anthropology," 35. For a discussion of Verzeni, see also Richard von Krafft-Ebing, *Psychopathia Sexualis: A Medico-Forensic Study*, trans. Harry E. Wedeck (New York: Physicians and Surgeons Book Company, 1965), 99–101.

9. On the reinvention of Villella, see Renzo Villa, *Il deviante e i suoi segni*, 148; Baima Bollone, *Cesare Lombroso ovvero il principio dell'irresponsabilità* (Turin, 1992), 14–16; Delia Frigessi, "Introduzione," in Cesare Lombroso, *Delitto, genio, folia: scritti scelti*, ed. Delia Frigessi, Ferruccio Giacanelli, and Luisa Mangoni (Turin: Bollati Boringhieri, 1995), 344–45. Also see Gina Lombroso-Ferrero, *Cesare Lombroso*, 130–31. For a particularly close reading of the story of Villella see Marc Renneville, "Lumière sur un crâne? Une lecture spéculaire de la découverte de l'atavisme criminel," in *La découverte et ses récits en sciences humaines: Champollion, Freud et les autres*, ed. Jacqueline Carroy and Nathalie Richard, (Paris: L'Harmattan, 1998), 15–36.

10. Lombroso, "Esistenza di una fossa," 37.

11. Lombroso, "Introduction," xiv.

12. Lombroso-Ferrero, *Criminal Man*, 6. Lombroso-Ferrero evidently confused Villella and Verzeni, to whom her father had applied this nickname. Historian Pierre Darmon refers to Villella as a "famous assassin." See *Médecins et assassins*, 14.

13. Renneville, by contrast, finds no evidence of any discovery in the original text. "Lumière sur un crâne," 17.

14. Lombroso, "Esistenza di una fossa," 37, 41.

15. Ibid., 40–41. On Canestrini, Darwin, and Lombroso, see Giuliano Pancaldi, *Darwin in Italy: Science across Cultural Frontiers*, trans. Ruey Brodine Morelli (Bloomington: Indiana University Press, 1991), 145–46.

16. Lombroso, "Esistenza di una fossa," 39.

17. Ibid., 37. Critics and historians would, however, cite the article as proof that Lombroso too slavishly followed the phrenologists' associations of cranial structures with the shape of the soft tissue of the brain.

18. Lombroso, "Esistenza di una fossa," 41.

19. Cesare Lombroso, "Deformità cranica congenita," in *Delitto, genio, follia*, 238. Also see Cesare Lombroso and Gaspare Bergonzoli, "La fossetta occipitale mediana e il vermis cerebellare studiati in 181 alienati," *Il Morgagni* 16 (1874): 801–25.

20. Lombroso, "Criminal Anthropology," 35.

21. Pancaldi, *Darwin in Italy*, 147.

22. Lombroso-Ferrero, *Cesare Lombroso*, 130. Lombroso-Ferrero quotes from a letter her father had written to his fiancée in January 1870 (135).

23. On this last point, see Pick, *Faces of Degeneration*, 128: "[Lombroso] desired to unify the dangers, to hold them within a single conceptual

model, in order to hold them outside the state, outside the fragile coherence of 'Italy.' "

24. See Sandra Puccini, "Les manuels italiens pour l'observation, la description et la collecte des données: entre l'ethnographie, l'anthropologie et les enquêtes sociales (XIXe siècle)," in *Le terrain des sciences humaines: instructions et enquêtes (XVIIIe-XXe siècle)*, ed. Claude Blanckaert (Paris: L'Harmattan, 1996), 301.

25. Cesare Lombroso, *Delitti vecchi e delitti nuovi* (Turin: Bocca, 1902), vii–viii.

26. Ibid., 3.

27. Ibid., 274. As Lombroso put it, "Savage ethics is moral madness." Lombroso et al., *Polemica in difesa*, 36.

28. Lombroso, *Delitti vecchi e delitti nuovi*, 274.

29. Ibid.

30. Ibid., 290.

31. In *Delitti vecchi e delitti nuovi*, Lombroso devoted an entire chapter to bicycle crimes. The roles of bicycles as objects of theft, means to commit crimes, and causes of madness were, in the author's view, offset by the bicycle's physical benefits.

32. For Lombroso, early twentieth-century Australia offered the best model for the rational management of social dangers. From Australia "radiated, as if from an immense lamp, that happy state of civilization that our grandchildren will enjoy." Ibid., 29.

33. Ibid., 11.

34. Ibid., 12.

35. Cesare Lombroso, *Sull'incremento del delitto in Italia e sui mezzi per arrestarlo* (Turin: Bocca, 1879), 3.

36. Ibid., 4.

37. Ibid., 5–6.

38. Ibid., 6.

39. On the anthropology of northern and southern Italy, also see the work of Alfredo Niceforo (1876–1960), especially *L'Italia barbara contemporanea: studi ed appunti* (Milan: Remo Sandron, 1898) and *Italiani del nord e Italiani del sud* (Turin: Bocca, 1901). On Niceforo's role in constructing a paradigm of "two Italies," see Silvana Patriarca, "How Many Italies? Representing the South in Official Statistics," in *Italy's "Southern Question": Orientalism in One Country*, ed. Jane Schneider (Oxford: Berg, 1998), 88–90. Also see Mary Gibson, *Born to Crime*, 109–11.

40. Lombroso, *Sull'incremento del delitto*, 40.

41. Ibid., 135. Also see Cesare Lombroso, *Troppo presto: appunti al nuovo progetto di codice penale* (Turin: Bocca, 1888).

42. Lombroso, *Sull'incremento del delitto*, 138.

43. Cesare Lombroso, "L'Italia è unita, non unificata," *Archivio* 9 (1888): 147.

44. On the deviant nature of genius, see Cesare Lombroso, *L'uomo di genio, in rapporto alla psichiatria, alla storia ed all'estetica*, 6th ed. (Turin: Bocca, 1894).

45. See, for example, Pancaldi, *Darwin in Italy*, 139–52. On Darwinism in Italy, also see Giovanni Landucci, "Darwinisme italien," in *Dictionnaire*

du Darwinisme et de l'évolution, ed. Patrick Tort (Paris: Presses Universitaires de France, 1996), vol. 1, 954–1041; on Darwin's understanding of atavism, see Patrick Tort, "Atavisme (Théorie darwinienne de l')," in *Dictionnaire du Darwinisme,* vol. 1, 147–57.

46. Villa, *Il deviante e i suoi segni,* 87-104. On the influence of Marzolo on Lombroso, also see Lombroso-Ferrero, *Cesare Lombroso,* Chapter 2.

47. Pancaldi, *Darwinism in Italy,* 145. Referring to Lombroso's study of Villella's skull, Pancaldi notes that "the reversions admitted by Darwin hypothesized far more limited backward leaps in evolution than that hypothesized by Lombroso when he compared the criminal's skull to the lemur's" (146).

48. Nancy Stepan, "Race and Gender: The Role of Analogy in Science," in *Anatomy of Racism* (Minneapolis: University of Minnesota Press, 1990), ed. David Theo Goldberg, 40. On the role of metaphor and analogy in structuring nineteenth-century scientific seeing and explanation, also see Laura Otis, *Organic Memory: History and the Body in the Late Nineteenth and Early Twentieth Centuries* (Lincoln: University of Nebraska Press, 1994), especially 27–34.

49. This section is omitted in the second edition of the book, which opens instead with the examination of 101 crania of Italian criminals. *L'uomo delinquente,* 2nd ed., 1.

50. Lombroso, *L'uomo delinquente,* 5th ed., vol. 1, 1. Also see Cesare Lombroso, "Criminalità negli animali," *Archivio* 14 (1893); Miguel Bombarda, "La criminalité chez les animaux," in *Congrès international d'anthropologie criminelle,* 211–14; Alessandro Muccioli, "Degenerazione e criminalità nei columbi," *Archivio* 14 (1893): 39–42; Pio Mingazzini, "Il collezionismo negli animali," *Archivio* 16 (1895): 70–89; G. Mingazzini, "Sul collezionismo nelle diverse forme psicopatiche," *Rivista sperimentale di freniatria,* 1891. Even Lombroso's critic Aléxandre Lacassagne suggested the study of crimes among animals could help scientists better to appreciate those committed by humans: "The morality of the wolf can clarify that of man." Lacassagne, "De la criminalité chez les animaux," *Revue scientifique,* 3rd ser., 2 (1882): 42.

51. Lombroso, *L'uomo delinquente,* 5th ed., vol. 1, 2.

52. Charles Darwin, *Insectivorous Plants* (New York: Appleton, 1884).

53. Lombroso, *L'uomo delinquente,* 5th ed., vol. 1, 3.

54. Ibid., 4.

55. Ibid., 7. Lombroso may have been responding to the gentle critique offered by his collaborator and son-in-law, Guglielmo Ferrero: "Prof. Lombroso has quoted, as examples of crimes among animals, certain actions which cannot be regarded as real crimes, as they are solely the result of the struggle for existence." William Ferrero, "Crime among Animals," *The Forum* 20 (1895–1896): 492.

56. Stephen Jay Gould, for example, counts Lombroso's discussion of animal criminality as "the most ludicrous excursion into anthropomorphism ever published." *The Mismeasure of Man,* 125.

57. Lombroso, *L'uomo delinquente,* 5th ed., vol. 1, 9.

58. Ibid., 22.

59. Compare the remarks of Lacassagne, for whom the "animal criminal" exhibited passions, desires, and instincts that were "not those of its race" and were "transmissible and hereditary." "De la criminalité chez les animaux," 42.

60. Lombroso, *L'uomo delinquente*, 5th ed., vol. 1, 27. Ferrero found animals to be "in a certain sense less criminal than men. When we wish to convey the idea that a man is extremely cruel, we say that he is like a wild beast; but this is an insult to animals which the latter do not deserve, for they never attain the hideous monstrosities of man." "Crime among Animals," 498.

61. Lombroso, *L'uomo delinquente*, 5th ed., vol. 1, 28.

62. Ibid., 98. Also see Cesare Lombroso, "Criminal Anthropology Applied to Pedagogy," *The Monist* 6 (1895): 50–59.

63. Lombroso, *L'uomo delinquente*, 5th ed., vol. 1, 99. See Bernard Perez, *La psychologie de l'enfant (les trois premières années)*, 2nd ed. (Paris, G. Baillière: 1882) and *L'enfant de trois à sept ans*, 3rd ed. (Paris: Alcan, 1894).

64. Lombroso, *L'uomo delinquente*, 5th ed., vol. 1, 101–2.

65. Ibid., 107–8.

66. Ibid., 107.

67. Arthur MacDonald, *Criminology* (New York: Funk & Wagnalls, 1893), 30.

68. Ibid., 33.

69. E. De Silvestri, "Osservazioni di antropologia criminale nei bambini," *Archivio* 16 (1895):179.

70. Havelock Ellis, *The Criminal*, 5th ed. (Montclair: Patterson Smith, 1973[1914]), 258.

71. Ibid., 258–59.

72. Ibid., 260.

73. Lombroso, "Criminal Anthropology Applied to Pedagogy," 56.

74. Ibid., 58–59.

75. Lombroso's most sustained treatment of the anthropology of non-Western peoples can be found in *L'uomo bianco e l'uomo di colore: letture sull'origine e le varietà delle razze umane* (Padua: Sacchetto, 1871).

76. Lombroso cited in Dario Melossi, "Changing Representations of the Criminal," *British Journal of Criminology* 40 (2000): 301. As Melossi notes, many of the physical characteristics identified by Lombroso were also ascribed to southern Italians in the nineteenth century.

77. Lombroso, "L'uomo primitivo e l'atavismo," *Archivio* 17 (1896): 164. Lombroso wrote that he was responding to an objection raised by Elisée Reclus (1830–1905), Petr Kropotkin (1842–1921), and Edward Westermarck (1862–1939) that crime and prostitution were not as common among savages as among "barbarous" (or "semi-savage") peoples. Also see S. R. Steinmetz, "L'ethnologie et l'anthropologie criminelle," *Congrès international d'anthropologie criminelle*, 99–105.

78. Lombroso, *L'uomo delinquente*, 5th ed., vol. 1, 469.

79. Ibid., 69.

80. Ibid., 330–31. Also see Giulio Fano, *Criminali e prostitute in oriente* (Turin: Bocca, 1894). Lombroso notes that in India the physiologist Fano found no lower-caste criminals with the criminal type; only a few Brahmins showed signs of degeneration. *L'uomo delinquente,* 5th ed., vol. 1, 330.

81. Ibid.

82. Ibid., 149.

83. Ibid., 231–34. Also see Salvatore Ottolenghi and Mario Carrara, "Il piede prensile negli alienati e nei delinquenti," *Archivio* 13 (1892): 373–81.

84. Lombroso, *L'uomo delinquente,* 5th ed., vol. 1, 231–32.

85. Ibid., 232.

86. Ibid., 234. Lombroso also found that the ability to wiggle one's ears was a regression to a stage of development in which it was important to prick up the ears to sense distant dangers. Lombroso, *L'uomo bianco,* 150.

87. Ibid., 61. The language of Hottentots, argued Lombroso, was particularly "deficient," lacking cases, declination of adjectives, relative pronouns, and abstract words (65).

88. See Ellis, *The Criminal,* 201. Ellis treated slang as a series of survivals and borrowings (especially from gypsies). Also see Alfredo Niceforo, *Il gergo nei normali, nei degenerati e nei criminali* (Turin: Bocca, 1897); Vincenzo Giuffrida-Ruggeri, "Una spiegazione del gergo dei criminali al lume dell'etnografia comparata," *Archivio* 25 (1904): 26–33.

89. Lombroso, *L'uomo delinquente,* 5th ed., vol. 1, 550–51. Niceforo made similar claims for the Italian poor. See Niceforo, *Antropologia delle classi povere,* 139.

90. C. Toselli and Cesare Lombroso, "Scrittura ideografica in un monomaniaco con sintomi iniziali di demenza," *Archivio* 1 (1880): 8. Also see Enrico Morselli, "Intagli ideografici di un alienato," *Archivio* 2 (1881): 421–25. On the medical and criminological attention to writing, especially in France, see Philippe Artières, *Clinique de l'écriture: Une histoire du regard médical sur l'écriture* (Le Plessis-Robinson: Institut Synthélabo, 1998).

91. Lombroso, *L'uomo bianco,* 66.

92. Ibid., 66.

93. Ibid., 67.

94. Ibid., 71.

95. Ibid., 75. Also see Andrea Cristiani, "Atavismo dell'arte in un paranoico originario con delirio fastoso-persecutorio a colorito artistico," *Archivio* 18 (1897): 559–66; G. C. Ferrari, "Manifestazioni artistiche accessuali in una bambina," *Archivio* 19 (1898): 238–56.

96. Lombroso, *L'uomo delinquente,* 5th ed., vol. 1, 553–55. The Lombrosian Hans Kurella (1858–1916) remarked, "The astonishing vividness and speech-forming power often recognizable in such jargon is really somewhat atavistic when compared with the wearisome newspaper jargon ('journalese') of our modern books among civilized peoples." *Cesare Lombroso,* 92.

97. See Cesare Lombroso, *I palimsesti del carcere* (Turin: Bocca, 1888).

98. Lombroso, *L'uomo delinquente*, 5th ed., vol. 1, 555–59. Havelock Ellis argued that the hieroglyphs and ideograms of criminals were indeed remarkably consistent from nation to nation. *The Criminal*, 210. Also see Cesare Lombroso, "Geroglifici criminali in Germania, in Inghilterra ed in Italia," *Archivio* 7 (1886): 193–95.

99. Lombroso, *L'uomo delinquente*, 5th ed., vol. 1, 558. Lombroso anticipated that many of his readers would be skeptical of the notion that an individual's handwriting or signature could indicate something about his "psychic conditions." Indeed, earlier research on handwriting had sought only to "satisfy a puerile curiosity," and even when serious had mixed science with phrenological and chiromantic superstitions." But if, as he suggested, "everyone acknowledged" that the gestures, voice, accent and gait of a person *could* be revealing, they needed only to recognize that writing was—like these—simply a result of the movement of muscles. Writing was, however, a far more precious resource for the criminal scientist, as it remained fixed for centuries (559–60). For Lombroso's more detailed treatment of the topic see *Grafologia* (Milan: Hoepli, 1896).

100. Lombroso-Ferrero, *Criminal Man*, 135.

101. On the scientific fascination with and debates surrounding tattoos in the nineteenth century, see Jane Caplan, " 'National Tattooing': Traditions of Tattooing in Nineteenth-century Europe," in *Written on the Body: The Tattoo in European and American History*, ed. Jane Caplan (Princeton: Princeton University Press, 2000), 156–73. As Caplan notes, the conceptual association of tattoos and criminality "drew powerfully on the prior stigmatization of irreversible body alteration in dominant European cultures." Caplan, " 'Speaking Scars,' " 113.

102. Cesare Lombroso, "The Savage Origin of Tattooing," *Popular Science Monthly* 48 (1896): 793–803. Also see Cesare Lombroso, "Sul tatuaggio in Italia, in inspecie fra i delinquenti," *Archivio per l'antropologia e la etnologia* 4 (1874): 389–403.

103. Lombroso, "The Savage Origin of Tattooing," 793. "Simplicity in ornamentation and clothing is an advance gained during these last centuries by the virile sex, by man, and constitutes a superiority in him over woman, who has to spend for dress an enormous amount of time and money, without gaining any real advantage, even to her beauty." Lombroso ended his article with an exhortation to his American audience: "O Fashion! You are very frivolous; you have caused many complaints against the most beautiful half of the human race! But you have not come to this, and I believe you will not be permitted to come to it" (803).

104. Ibid., 793.

105. See Pierpaolo Leschiutta, "Le pergamene viventi: Interpretazioni del tatuaggio nell'antropologia positiva italiana," *La ricerca folklorica* 27 (1993): 129–38.

106. Of 141 tattooed persons he had examined, only three had stopped a tattoo midway because they could not tolerate the pain. Lombroso, *Sulla medicina legale del cadavere secondo gli ultimi studi di Germania ed*

Italia: Tecnica-identità fisiologia del cadavere (Turin: Baglione, 1877), 82.

107. Lombroso, "The Savage Origin of Tattooing," 800. Kurella argued that "aesthetically, in fact, a criminal who has his skin tattooed stands nearer to the savage than he does to the European decorative taste of the common people, as displayed in the shops of the working-class quarters in which chimney 'ornaments' are sold." *Cesare Lombroso,* 93.

108. Lombroso, "The Savage Origin of Tattooing," 801–2.

109. Ibid., 802.

110. Lombroso, *Sulla medicina legale del cadavere,* 79.

111. Ibid., 71.

112. Lombroso, "The Savage Origin of Tattooing," 803. Lombroso-Ferrero reports that in some cases tattoos were relied upon to make more specific determinations of social danger—or even guilt—as when pederasts bore "portraits of those with whom they [had] unnatural commerce," or a rapist was "covered with pictorial representations of his obscene adventures." *Criminal Man,* 232.

113. Lombroso, "Sul tatuaggio in Italia," 402–3. Compare Ellis's discussion in *The Criminal,* 194–199. For Ellis, the tattoo was not atavistic, but a survival. While it had "little psychological significance," the tattoo did serve "as an indication of mental abnormality, of indiscipline, of tendency to vice" (199).

114. It is worth noting that *La donna delinquente* was the first of Lombroso's books on criminals to be partially translated into English, and after only two years. *L'uomo delinquente* was not made available (also in a greatly abbreviated form) until 1911. However, in his introduction to *The Female Offender* W. Douglas Morrison made no mention of the sex of the book's object; he simply described the volume as "an example of the method in which [Lombroso's] inquiries are conducted." "Introduction," in Lombroso and Ferrero, *The Female Offender,* xv.

115. Lombroso and Ferrero cited studies of a total of 1,033 criminal women, 685 prostitutes, and 225 normal women in hospitals, as well as studies of 176 crania of deceased criminal women and 30 of normal women. Lombroso and Ferrero, *La donna delinquente,* 164. Also see, for examples of research on women, F. Puglia, "La donna delinquente," *Archivio* 7 (1886): 88–89; G. Salsotto, "Sulla donna delinquente," *Archivio* 10 (1889): 262–71; Antonio Marro, "Sui caratteri della donna criminale," *Archivio* 10 (1889): 576–80; Cesare Lombroso, "Tatto e tipo degenerativo nelle donne," *Archivio* 12 (1891): 1–6; and Guglielmo Ferrero, "La crudeltà e la pietà nella femmina e nella donna," *Archivio* 12 (1891): 393–434.

116. These problems had been identified by Gabriel Tarde, the French crowd psychologist and a persistent critic of the atavistic elements of Italian anthropology. See Gabriel Tarde, *La criminalité comparée* (Paris: Alcan, 1886). Also see Paolo Mantegazza, "L'uomo nel sesso: differenze morali [1870]" in *Lezioni di antropologia (1870–1910)* (Florence: Società Italiana di Antropologia e Etnologia, n.d.), 15–19. Mantegazza found

that criminal statistics confirmed the moral superiority of women to men (16).

117. The detailed discussion of the normal woman was based almost exclusively on the writings and research of others. The entire discussion of the normal woman was omitted in the abridged English translation, which also deleted virtually every reference to sexuality, fertility, and menstruation. Lombroso complained in the preface to the French translation that these editorial decisions were "absurd." Cesare Lombroso and Guglielmo Ferrero, *La femme criminelle et la prostituée,* trans. Louise Meille (Paris: Alcan, 1896), xiii.

118. In the various editions of *L'uomo delinquente,* occasional reference was made to "normal" and "honest" man, but neither was marked as an object of urgent scientific scrutiny. Compare Lombroso and Ferrero, *La donna delinquente,* 3.

119. Ibid. 4, 98. For a contemporary critique (published in Lombroso's own journal) of the "infantilization" of women see Vincenzo Giuffrida-Ruggeri, "Sulla pretesa inferiorità somatica della donna," *Archivio* 21 (1900): 353–60. Giuffrida-Ruggeri cited embryological evidence that males fail to become fully female as much as females fail to become fully male. Also see Henri Thulié, *La femme: essai de sociologie physiologique* (Paris: A. Delahaye et É. Lecrosnier, 1885), 189.

120. Lombroso and Ferrero, *La donna delinquente,* 95–98.

121. Ibid., 112.

122. Tarde, *Criminalité comparée,* 48. Tarde went on to note that improvidence, vanity, a lack of inventiveness, and a tendency to imitate others were all shared by women and criminals.

123. Lombroso and Ferrero, *The Female Offender,* 27.

124. Lombroso and Ferrero, *The Female Offender,* 104; *La donna delinquente,* 208.

125. Ibid., 29.

126. Lombroso and Ferrero, *The Female Offender,* 108–9; *La donna delinquente,* 210.

127. Ibid., 31. The reduced variability of females could be further explained, the authors argued, by the operation of sexual selection. In "savage" societies, "Man not only refused to marry a deformed female, but ate her, while, on the other hand, preserving for his enjoyment the handsome woman who gratified his peculiar instincts." Lombroso and Ferrero, *The Female Offender,* 109. Sexual selection operated differently, however, in the Italian countryside, where women were chosen for their strength, and among the rich, who selected wives on the basis of wealth. Lombroso, "Donna criminale e prostituta," *Archivio* 10 (1889): 381–82.

128. Lombroso and Ferrero, *The Female Offender,* 122.

129. Lombroso and Ferrero, *La donna delinquente,* 1.

130. Ibid., 2.

131. Lombroso and Ferrero, *The Female Offender,* 111.

132. Lombroso and Ferrero, *La femme criminelle,* 212–14.

133. Ibid., 214–15, 238.

134. See, for example, Abele De Blasio, "Steatopigia in prostitute," *Archivio* 26 (1905): 257–63. In an editor's note, Lombroso expressed his delight at being able finally to publish an image of a prostitute with steatopygia, the accumulation of fat on the buttocks more commonly associated with Sarah Bartmann, the "Hottentot Venus" (later editions of *L'uomo delinquente* and *La donna delinquente* included images of a Hottentot woman taken from a volume by Hermann Ploss). The condition was rare among European women, Lombroso reasoned, because they were "less exposed" to anomalies than were European men. On the scientific interest in the female Hottentot body, see Sander Gilman, "Black Bodies, White Bodies: Toward an Iconography of Female Sexuality in Late Nineteenth-Century Art, Medicine, and Literature," *Critical Inquiry* 12 (1985): 204–42; Anne Fausto-Sterling, "Gender, Race, and Nation: The Comparative Anatomy of 'Hottentot' Women in Europe, 1815–1817," in *Deviant Bodies*, ed. Jennifer Terry and Jacqueline Urla (Bloomington: Indiana University Press, 1995), 19–48; Claude Rawson, *God, Gulliver, and Genocide: Barbarism and the European Imagination, 1492–1945* (Oxford: Oxford University Press, 2001), 108–38.
135. Lombroso and Ferrero, *The Female Offender*, 32, 113–14.
136. Ibid., 107. If this seemed to credit criminal women with more deviance than was their due, Lombroso was quick to observe that "it is incontestable that female offenders seem almost normal when compared to the male criminal, with his wealth of anomalous features."
137. Lombroso and Ferrero, *La donna delinquente*, 195.
138. Lombroso and Ferrero, *The Female Offender*, 94.
139. Ibid., 85.
140. Ibid., 97.
141. Ibid., 101–2.
142. Ibid., 102. G. B. Moraglia found that prostitutes also exhibited atavistic facial expressions at the moment of orgasm. See Mary Gibson, *Born to Crime*, 72.

Chapter 3

1. Lombroso et al., *Polemica in difesa*.
2. Among Lombroso's fiercest critics on this point was Gabriel Tarde. See, for example, *Criminalité comparée*.
3. Lombroso et al., *Polemica in difesa*, 39. Lombroso argued that although the ninety-five other Italians exhibited "only fractions" of the type, these fractions stood out in any comparisons with foreigners.
4. Lombroso, "L'Italia è unita," 146.
5. Lombroso et al., *Polemica in difesa*, 42. Twenty years later, Lombroso could more confidently assert that the old proverb, "there is nothing new under the sun," applied well to criminal anthropology: "Its most important conclusions, indeed those that seemed the most paradoxical, had been divined by savants over many centuries; they were on the lips of the people. We know that since the most remote times people remarked that vicious men or criminals have abnormal wrinkles,

asymmetries of the face or the body, leftsidedness, strabismus."
Lombroso, "Discours d'ouverture," xxxi.

6. Compare Guarnieri's discussion of asylum doctors' efforts to distance
   themselves from popular and previous medical understandings of
   madness. Patrizia Guarnieri, "Misurare le diversità," in *Misura d'uomo:
   Strumenti, teorie e pratiche dell'antropometria e della psicologia sperimentale
   tra '800 e '900*, ed. Giulio Barsanti et al. (Florence: Istituto e Museo di
   Storia della Scienza, 1986), 136.

7. For a discussion of the growing authority of medicine and physicians in
   nineteenth-century Italian culture see Guido Panseri, "Il medico: note su
   un intellettuale scientifico italiano nell'Ottocento," in *Storia d'Italia:
   Annali*, ed. Ruggero Romano and Corrado Vivanti (Turin: Einaudi,
   1978–1998), vol. 4, 1133–55.

8. Sandra Puccini and Massimo Squillacciotti, "Principali tappe dello
   sviluppo statutario," 202–12.

9. On criminological museums as sites of knowledge production,
   see Susanne Regener, "Criminological Museums and the Visualization of
   Evil," in *Criminals and Their Scientists: Essays on the International History
   of Criminology*, ed. Richard Wetzell and Peter Becker (Cambridge:
   Cambridge University Press, forthcoming), as well as Giorgio Colombo,
   La scienza infelice: Il museo di antropologia criminale di Cesare Lombroso
   (Turin, 1975). For a discussion of the importance of criminological
   conferences, see Martine Kaluszynski, "The International Congresses
   of Criminal Anthropology: Structuration of the French and International
   Criminological Movement (1886–1914)," in *Criminals and Their Scientists*.

10. Patrizia Guarnieri, "Misurare le diversità," 126.

11. Lombroso et al., *Polemica in difesa*, 42.

12. Ibid., 43

13. Giuseppe Antonini, *I precursori di Lombroso* (Turin: Bocca, 1900). Also
    see Bulferetti, *Cesare Lombroso*, 286–93. A similar historiographical
    strategy was adopted by the psychiatrist Enrico Morselli (1852–1929) in
    an article on eighteenth-century physiognomy. Critics, Morselli
    complained, had accused criminal anthropology of exaggerating the
    importance of somatic characteristics in order to give "an organic
    foundation to psychic tendencies. If instead they had searched the history
    of physiognomy (as has already been done for popular proverbs) they
    would have found more advanced and complete intuitions about the
    relations of the physical and the moral." Enrico Morselli, "Dalla storia
    della fisiognomonia," *Archivio* 9 (1888): 104.

    Morselli offered as an example the work of the Girolamo Bocalosi,
    *Della fisonomia: principii derivati dall'anatomia, dalla fisiologia, e dinamica
    del corpo umano per mezzo de' quali si distinguono gli aristocratici, e i realisti
    dai democratici*, 5th ed. (Milan: Francesco Pogliani, 1797). The claims
    made by Bocalosi, wrote Morselli, were even bolder than those of the
    criminal anthropologists. Bocalosi had argued that "the passions reside in
    the organs of man, and not in the spirit"; the spirit "only acted as a
    consequence of the nature and texture [*testura*] of the organ." This and
    similar passages demonstrated for Morselli "that the idea of reducing

psychic phenomena to organic phenomena is not as new as many would claim" (104).

14. Antonini, *I precursori di Lombroso,* 169.
15. Ibid., 2.
16. Ibid., 3.
17. On history of physiognomy, see Christopher Rivers, *Face Value: Physiognomical Thought and the Legible Body in Marivaux, Lavater, Balzac, Gautier, and Zola* (Madison: University of Wisconsin Press, 1994); Lucy Hartley, *Physiognomy and the Meaning of Expression in Nineteenth-Century Culture* (Cambridge: Cambridge University Press, 2001); Julio Caro Baroja, *Historia de la fisiognomica: El rostro y el carácter* (Madrid: ISTMO, 1988); Elena Agazzi and Manfred Beller, *Evidenze e ambiguità della fisionomia umana: Studi sul XVII e XIX Secolo* (Viareggio: Mauro Baroni, 1998); Judith Wechsler, *A Human Comedy: Physiognomy and Caricature in 19th Century Paris* (London: Thames and Hudson, 1982); Stafford, *Body Criticism.*
18. Antonini, *I precursori di Lombroso,* 40. The treatise on "physiognomics" attributed by Antonini to Aristotle is now considered to have been authored by others. See, for example, Elizabeth C. Evans, "Physiognomics in the Ancient World," *Transactions of the American Philosophical Society* 59 (1969): 7. On the Greek and Roman roots of criminal anthropology, also see Cesare Lombroso, "Le nozioni dell'antropologia criminale nei pensatori antichi," *Archivio* 21 (1900): 85–89; Guglielmo Ferrero, "Positivismo degli antichi," *Archivio* 18 (1897): 110; Alessandro Levi, "La criminalità negli scrittori della grecia antica," *Archivio* 24 (1903): 207–13; and Lombroso, *L'uomo delinquente,* 5th ed., vol. 1, 309–10.
19. Antonini, *I precursori di Lombroso,* 46.
20. Ibid., 55.
21. Ibid., 56.
22. Giambattista della Porta, *Della fisonomia dell' hvomo* (Naples: Giacomo Carlino and Costantino Vitale, 1610). The first edition of the volume appeared in 1586.
23. Antonini, *I precursori di Lombroso,* 62, 67, 69–70.
24. Ibid., 156. Also see Cesare Lombroso, "Il delinquente e il pazzo nel dramma e nel romanzo moderno," *Archivio* 22 (1901): 107–17; Giuseppe Ziino, *Shakespeare e la scienza moderna: studio medico-psicologico e giuridico* (Messina: Amico, 1897); Enrico Ferri, *I delinquenti nell'arte* (Genoa: Ligure, 1896); and Edouard Lefort, *Le type criminel d'après les savants.* At same time, anthropologists had proposed that their science could aid in the study of artistic genius. Antonini and a number of colleagues had undertaken studies of literary figures such as Leopardi, Poe, and Alfieri, but had been accused of "invading the territory" of other scholars. However, for Antonini, all they had done had been to "bring to light the relations that link the [physical] constitution of the writer, the environment [*ambiente*] and the works or art, and had lifted the veils that had covered the faces of men of genius, bringing them back into reality and nature." For this, they had been made to suffer the accusation that

they were "artificially applying the theories of the master—at all costs and with no regard for the facts." *I precursori di Lombroso,* 160.

25. Lombroso-Ferrero, *Criminal Man,* 49.
26. Lombroso, "Il delinquente e il pazzo nel dramma," 117.
27. Antonini, *I precursori di Lombroso,* 130.
28. On the links between Camper and Lavater, see Miriam Claude Meijer, *Race and Aesthetics in the Anthropology of Petrus Camper (1722–1789)* (Amsterdam: Rodopi, 1999), 115–23. On Lavater as developing a "science of physiognomical perception," see Michael Shortland, "The Power of a Thousand Eyes: Johann Caspar Lavater's Science of Physiognomical Perception," *Criticism* 28 (1986): 379–408.
29. Antonini, *I precursori di Lombroso,* 134.
30. Ibid., 138–39.
31. Ibid., 132.
32. Augusto Tebaldi, "La fisionomia nella scienza e nell'arte dopo I recenti studii," *Archivio per l'antropologia e la etnologia* 6 (1876): 184–97.
33. Paolo Mantegazza, *Physiognomy and Expression* (New York: Scribner & Welford, 1890).
34. Paolo Mantegazza, [Review of Darwin, *The Expression of the Emotions*], *Archivio per l'Antropologia e la Etnologia* 1 (1871): 32. Mantegazza's genealogy of physiognomy included Le Brun, Charles Bell, Lemoine, Thomas Burgess, Guillaume-Benjamin Duchenne, and Pierre Gratiolet.
35. Ibid., 32–33. This alternation between negations and affirmations of Lavater, Mantegazza found, was proof that the study of human expression was still in a chaotic state, a situation that was best remedied by the development of a physiology of emotion. He followed Darwin in affirming that all humans express the same emotions in the same manner (38). For more on Mantegazza's physiology of emotion, see Chapter 4.
36. On the history of phrenology, see Roger Cooter, *The Cultural Meaning of Popular Science: Phrenology and the Organization of Consent in Nineteenth-Century Britain* (Cambridge: Cambridge University Press, 1984); David De Giustino, *Conquest of Mind: Phrenology and Victorian Social Thought* (London: Croom Helm, 1975); Charles Colbert, *A Measure of Perfection: Phrenology and the Fine Arts in America* (Chapel Hill: University of North Carolina Press, 1997); Marc Renneville, *Le langage des crânes: histoire de la phrénologie* (Paris: Sanofi-Synthélabo, 2000); Georges Lantéri-Laura, *Histoire de la phrénologie: l'homme et son cerveau selon F. J. Gall* (Paris: Presses Universitaires de France, 1970); and Robert M. Young, *Mind, Brain and Adaptation in the Nineteenth Century: Cerebral Localization and Its Biological Context from Gall to Ferrier* (Oxford: Clarendon Press, 1970), esp. 9–53.
37. Stafford, *Body Criticism,* 117–18; Renville, *Le langage des crânes,* 20–22.
38. For a similar argument about French psychiatry see Lantéri-Laura, *Histoire de la phrénologie.*
39. Hubert Lauvergne, *Les forçats considérés sous le rapport physiologique, moral et intellectuel, observés au bagne de Toulon* (Grenoble: Jérome Millon 1991[1841]).
40. Villa, *Il deviante e i suoi segni,* 60–68.

41. Lantéri-Laura, *Histoire de la phrénologie,* 172. At the same time, argues Lantéri-Laura, Lombroso distanced himself from Gall by simplifying the problem of responsibility and diminishing the role of prevention in favor of social defense.

42. As Robert M. Young points out for England, "Even in the 1840s phrenology was in such bad repute that Professor Adam Sedgwick felt that he could best indicate his low opinion of Robert Chambers' *Vestiges* be stressing its links with 'phrenology (that sink-hole of human folly and prating coxcombry).'" *Mind, Brain and Adaptation,* 10.

43. Renneville, *Le langage des crânes,* 287.

44. See Lantéri-Laura, *Histoire de la phrénologie,* 192–9, 201.

45. On this point see Bruno Latour, *Science in Action,* especially 21–62.

46. For a rare (and patriotic) defense of the important contributions of Gall to criminology, see the remarks of Lacassagne reported in "Congrès d'anthropologie criminelle de Rome," *Archives de l'anthropologie criminelle* 1 (1886): 169. Lacassagne resisted the equation of Gall's contributions with the bizarrely-labeled plaster heads available for sale in scientific supply shops: "By designating Gall's body of work a 'system of bumps,' [critics] have wanted to heap ridicule on one of the most remarkable conceptions of our century." Comparing Gall to Galileo, Lacassagne found he had had the "incomparable merit of having shown that sentiments, acts, intelligence—all of moral man, finally—is localized within the brain." For a more recent appraisal of phrenology's importance for criminology, see Leonard Savitz, Stanley H. Turner, and Toby Dickman, "The Origin of Scientific Criminology: Franz Joseph Gall as the First Criminologist," in *Theory in Criminology: Contemporary Views,* ed. Robert F. Meier (London: Sage, 1977), 41–56.

47. Léonce Manouvrier, "Existe-t-il des caractères anatomiques propres aux criminels? Les criminels présent-ils en moyenne certains caractères anatomiques particuliers? Comment doit-on interpréter ces caractères?" [Report presented at session of 13 August, Deuxième congrès international d'anthropologie criminelle], *Archives de l'anthropologie criminelle* 4 (1889): 591.

48. Paolo Mantegazza, [Review of Léonce Manouvrier, *La genèse normale du crime*], *Archivio per l'antropologia e la etnologia* 23 (1893): 466. Also see Mantegazza's editor's note to Raffalele Zampa, "Della comparazione dei caratteri fisici dei delinquenti e dei non delinquenti," *Archivio per l'antropologia e la etnologia* 20 (1900): 111. There Mantegazza predicted that in future years "posterity will relegate [criminal anthropology] along with astrology, chiromancy, and phrenology among the false sciences which, born of a marriage of fanaticism and impatience, glitter like a rocket and then disappear, leaving a few ashes." Mantegazza went on to call Lombroso the "founder of a new religion" and a "false prophet."

49. Giovanni Mingazzini, "'Etude anthropométrique sur les prostituées et les voleuses,' della Dott.ssa Pauline Tarnowski," *Archivio* 12 (1891): 146–48.

50. Lombroso, "Sulla medicina legale delle alienazioni studiata col metodo sperimentale," *Gazzetta medica italiana, provincie venete* 9 (1866): 22–23; reprinted in *Delitto, genio, follia,* 56.

51. Lombroso et al., *Polemica in difesa*, 5.

52. Ibid., 6.

53. Cesare Lombroso, "Sul cranio di Volta," *Rendiconti (Reale Istituto lombardo di scienze e lettere)* 11 (1878): 341.

54. *L'uomo delinquente*, 5th ed., vol. 1, 311. Lombroso offered a similar explanation for the gestures that accompanied prayer, movements that had been inherited from barbarous times in which they signaled submission and saved the lives of defeated combatants.

55. Ibid., 311–12.

56. Lombroso, "Il delitto nella coscienza popolare," in *Pazzi ed anomali: saggi*, 2nd ed. (Citta di Castello: S. Lapi, 1890), 26. The article had originally been published eight years earlier: "Il delitto nella coscienza popolare," *Archivio* 3 (1882): 451–56.

57. As we will see in Chapter 6, this tension would also play itself out in the courtroom.

58. Lombroso, "Il delitto nella coscienza popolare," 26. On proverbs also see A. Balladoro, "L'antropologia criminale nei proverbi veneti," *Archivio* 18 (1897): 157–62; A. Castelli, "Delitti e pene nei proverbi," *Archivio* 11 (1890): 558–59.

59. Lombroso, "Il delitto nella coscienza popolare, 26. Also see Lombroso-Ferrero, *Criminal Man*, 50. Lombroso does not comment on the fact that many of these sayings are examples of gender transgression.

60. Lombroso, "Il delitto nella coscienza popolare, 28.

61. Ibid., 28–29.

62. Pitrè and Lombroso had, however, a pointed exchange in *Rivista Europea* about the songs and poems written by criminals and prisoners. See Cesare Lombroso, "La poesia ed il crimine," *Rivista Europea* 7(1) (1876): 475–90; Giuseppe Pitrè, "Sui canti popolari italiani di carcere" [letter to the editor, Angelo De Gubernatis] *Rivista Europea* 7(2) (1876): 320–26; and Cesare Lombroso, "Sui canti carcerari e criminali in Italia: lettera al Prof. G. Pitrè," *Rivista Europea* 7 (1876): 155–60. Pitrè, a specialist on southern Italian songs, objected to Lombroso's transcriptions and interpretations of Sicilian passages, as well as his claim that criminal songs were confined to the south.

   Lombroso's original article, which argued that prison songs were a real and spontaneous "criminal literature," was premised on the notion that great poets, artists, and even scientists, had something in common with criminals. Although scientists were, on the whole, able to manage their extraordinary passions, the same could not be said for poets and artists. Thus, it was no surprise that many poets were criminals, and many criminals were poets. "La poesia ed il crimine," 476.

63. Giuseppe Pitrè, *Medicina popolare siciliana* (Bologna: Forni, 1969[1896]), 147.

64. Ibid., 148. Michele Pasquarelli also invoked Pitrè to argue that modern psychiatry, in its "somatomania," take its cues from popular wisdom. "Il Folk-lore nell'antropologia criminale," *Archivio* 17 (1896): 507–18.

65. Lombroso, "Il delitto nella coscienza popolare," 33.

66. Elsewhere *mancino* was contrasted with *manritto* or *mandiritto*. See, for example, Giovanni Faralli, "Sulla preeminenza del lato destro del corpo: studj dell Dott. Ogle, del Dott. Savory, e del. Prof. Iacini Filipo," *Archivio per l'antropologia e la etnologia* 2 (1872): 67.

67. Cesare Lombroso, "Left-Handedness and Left-sidedness," *North American Review* 562 (1903): 441. On the handedness of animals, also see E. Audenino, "L'homme droit, l'homme gauche et l'homme ambidextre," in *Comptes-rendus du VIe Congrès international d'anthropologie criminelle*, 211–12; Daniel Wilson, *The Right Hand: Left-Handedness* (London: Macmillan, 1891), 198–201.

68. Carmelo Andronico, "Il mancinismo in rapporto alla delinquenza," *Archivio* 5 (1884): 481. Also see Salvatore Ottolenghi, "Il mancinismo anatomico nei criminali," *Archivio* 10 (1889): 332–38. Lombroso pointed out that Polemon's (88–145) writings on physiognomy had anticipated his claims about the left-handedness of criminals. Lombroso et al., *Polemica in difesa*, 42.

69. Lombroso, "Left-Handedness," 442. Also see Cesare Lombroso, "Il mancinismo," *Rivista di discipline carcerarie* 14 (1884):128.

70. Ibid., 126.

71. Lombroso, "Left-Handedness," 444. Also see Lombroso, "Il mancinismo," 130.

72. Lombroso, "Il mancinismo sensorio ed il tatto nei delinquenti e nei pazzi," *Archivio* 4 (1883): 445.

73. Faralli, "Sulla preeminenza del lato destro," 75. On the (failed) attempt to link left-sidedness with blood pressure asymmetries, see Cesare Lombroso and E. Audenino, "Contribution à l'étude de l'asymétrie de pression du sang chez les épileptiques, les prostituées et les criminels," in *Congrès international d'anthropologie criminelle*, 282–85.

74. Lombroso, "Il mancinismo sensorio," 446

75. Lombroso, "Il mancinismo," 126.

76. Lombroso, *L'uomo delinquente*, 5th ed., vol. 1, 407. In a similar experiment, Lombroso suggested to a hypnotized young boy "of honest habits" that he was the brigand La-Gala; the boy in this case reproduced the handwriting typical of criminals, abandoning his own "refined" and "feminine" hand in favor of "crude" letters. Ibid., 564. For a more general discussion of hypnotism and criminology see Cesare Lombroso, *Studi sull'ipnotismo*, 3rd ed. (Turin: Bocca, 1887).

77. Lombroso, "Il mancinismo sensorio," 447.

78. Lombroso, *L'uomo delinquente*, 5th ed., vol. 1, 311.

79. Ibid., 310.

80. Ibid., 311.

81. Lombroso et al., *Polemica in difesa*, 7.

82. Ibid., emphasis added.

83. Lombroso, *L'uomo delinquente*, 5th ed., vol. 1, 311.

84. Cesare Lombroso, "Un esperimento nuovo sulla Fisionomia criminale," in *Pazzi ed anomali*, 247. The book chapter is identified as a response to attacks on earlier article on folklore, proverbs, and criminal physiognomy that had appeared in *Domenica del Fracassa*, a Sunday news magazine.

85. Ibid.
86. Ibid., 248.
87. See, for example, Morselli, "Dalla storia della fisiognonomia," 103–4.
88. Lombroso et al., *Polemica in difesa*, 11.
89. Aristide Gabelli, "La nuova scuola di diritto penale in Italia," *Nuova Antologia* 82 (1885): 580.
90. Ibid., 581.
91. Ibid.
92. Lombroso et al., *Polemica in difesa*, 11.
93. See the discussion in Lombroso, "Il delitto nella coscienza popolare."
94. Lombroso et al., *Polemica in difesa*, 8.
95. Antonio Marro, *I carcerati: studio psicologico del vero* (Turin: Roux e Favale, 1885), 94.
96. Lombroso, *L'uomo delinquente*, 5th ed., vol. 1, 276.
97. Ibid., 282.
98. Gould, *The Mismeasure of Man*, 73–74. On the authority of numbers and practices of quantification, also see Theodore Porter, *Trust in Numbers: The Pursuit of Objectivity in Science and Public Life* (Princeton: Princeton University Press, 1995) and, for Italy, Silvana Patriarca, *Numbers and Nationhood: Writing Statistics in Nineteenth-Century Italy* (Cambridge: Cambridge University Press, 1996), especially 238–39.
99. Paolo Mantegazza, [Review of Cesare Lombroso, *Pensiero e Meteore*], *Archivio per l'antropologia e la etnologia* 9 (1879): 326.
100. For insightful discussions of the history of anthropometrical instruments and techniques, see Barsanti et al., eds., *Misura d'uomo*, and especially the essays by Pogliano and Guarnieri.
101. Villa, *Il deviante e i suoi segni*, 31.
102. Ibid., 32.
103. On the role of the prison physician, see Joe Sim, *Medical Power in Prisons: The Prison Medical Service in England 1774–1989* (Philadelphia: Open University Press, 1990).
104. Villa, *Il deviante e i suoi segni*, 33.
105. Luigi Ferrio, "La vita di Cesare Lombroso," in *Antologia Lombrosiana* (Pavia: Società Editrice Pavese, 1962), 20–21. For a description of the Turin laboratory, see Gina Lombroso-Ferrero, *Cesare Lombroso*, 195–98.
106. Ibid., 197.
107. Ibid., 198.
108. Bulferetti, *Cesare Lombroso*, 256–57.
109. Lombroso, *L'uomo delinquente*, 5th ed., vol. 1, 221. Lombroso observed that the difficulties were doubled in the case of female offenders and prostitutes: "We might have offended the sense of shame of these chaste virgins." Lombroso and Ferrero, *La donna delinquente*, 195.
110. Ibid.
111. Lombroso, *L'uomo delinquente*, 5th ed., vol. 1, 331.
112. Ezio Sciamanna, "Guida nelle ricerche anatomiche e antropologiche sui cadaveri dei condannati," *Rivista di discipline carcerarie* 14 (1884): 234–71. Circular n. 42948-36-1-a (14 September 1883) from the Direzione Generale delle Carceri placed cadavers of inmates who died

while in prison infirmaries at the disposal of universities. See *Bullettino ufficiale della Direzione Generale delle Carceri* 12 (1883): 189–93.

113. Sciamanna, "Guida nelle ricerche anatomiche," 243.

114. Augusto Tamburini and Giulio Benelli, "L'antropologia nelle carceri," *Rivista di discipline carcerarie* 15 (1885):136. Beltrani-Scalia was also the editor of the journal.

115. Ibid., 137.

116. Lombroso, "Criminal Anthropology," 47.

117. Cesare Lombroso, *La perizia psichiatrico-legale coi metodi per eseguirla e la casuistica penale classificata antropologicamente* (Turin: Bocca, 1905), 490–544. Also see Francis Galton, "On the Anthropometric Laboratory at the Late International Health Exhibition," *The Journal of the Anthropological Institute of Great Britain and Ireland* 14 (1885): 205–21.

118. On the relations between the refinement of instrumentation, the construction of models, and the evolution of conceptual frameworks see Timothy Lenoir, "Models and Instruments in the Development of Electrophysiology, 1845–1912," *Historical Studies in the Physical and Biological Sciences* 17 (1986): 1–54.

119. A. Severi and Cesare Lombroso, "Prima esposizione internationale d'antropologia criminale a Roma," *Archivio* 7 (1886): 27. Evidently, no one had thought to invite instrument makers from Italy or abroad. Compare with Galton, "On the Anthropometric Laboratory."

120. Giuseppe Sergi, "Craniforo di Benedikt," *Archivio* 14 (1893): 143–45.

121. Carlo Gaudenzi, "Un nuovo strumento per le misure angolari del capo," *Archivio* 12 (1891): 305–22. Also see A. Mariani and G. Prati, "Nuovo goniometro per misurare l'angolo facciale, il prognatismo e tutti gli altri elementi del triangolo facciale," *Archivio* 23 (1902): 43–48.

122. Paolo Mantegazza, "Una nota sull'indice cefalospinale," *Archivio per l'antropologia e la etnologia* 1 (1871): 61.

123. *L'uomo delinquente,* 5th ed., vol. 3, 648. Also see Cesare Belloni, "Il compasso indice," *Archivio* 23 (1902): 133–38; the index-compass automatically calculated the cephalic index.

124. On the graphical method in the physiological sciences, see Robert G. Frank, "The Tell-Tale Heart: Physiological Instruments, Graphic Methods, and Clinical Hopes, 1854–1914," in *The Investigative Enterprise: Experimental Physiology in Nineteenth-Century Medicine,* ed. William Coleman and Frederic L. Holmes (Berkeley: University of California Press, 1988), 211–90; Otniel E. Dror, "Creating the Emotional Body: Confusion, Possibilities, and Knowledge," in *An Emotional History of the United States,* ed. Peter Stearns and Jan Lewis (New York: New York University Press, 1998), 173–94; and Robert Brain, "Representation on the Line: Graphic Recording Instruments and Scientific Modernism," in *From Energy to Information: Representation in Science and Technology, Art, and Literature,* ed. Bruce Clarke and Linda Dalrymple Henderson (Stanford: Stanford University Press, 2002), 155–77.

125. Frank, "The Tell-Tale Heart," 213.

126. Etienne-Jules Marey, cited in Marta Braun, *Picturing Time: The Work of Etienne-Jules Marey (1830–1904)* (Chicago: University of Chicago Press, 1992), 40.

127. Brain, "Representation on the Line," 156. Also see Latour, *Science in Action,* 65–69.

128. Brain, "Representation on the Line," 156.

129. Frank, "The Tell-Tale Heart," 212.

130. Claude Bernard, "Sur la physiologie du coeur at ses rapport avec le cerveau," *Leçons sur les propriétés des tissus vivants* (Paris: Germer Ballière, 1866), 437.

Chapter 4

1. Lombroso identifies his assistants as the future Nobel laureate Camillo Golgi (1843–1926) and two "young friends" named Bettoni and Pisa. Cesare Lombroso, "Algometria elettrica nell'uomo sano ed alienato," *Annali universali di medicina* (1867): 104.

2. Lombroso-Ferrero, *Cesare Lombroso,* 102. The presence of the induction coil in Lombroso's medical office points us both toward a nineteenth-century fascination with electricity and its potential medical uses, and toward a competitive international traffic in induction coils. Heinrich Daniel Ruhmkorff (1803–1877), an instrument maker in France, had begun producing his more efficient version of the coil (a modification of earlier apparatuses developed by Masson and Breguet, Neef, Wagner, and others) in 1851; his coils were of such a level of refinement, and manufactured on such a large scale, that Ruhmkorff's name was for a time applied to induction coils generally. See Frederick Collins, *The Design and Construction of Induction Coils* (New York: Munn, 1909), 1–12; Herbert W. Meyer, *A History of Electricity and Magnetism* (Norwalk: Burnly, 1972), 180.

In later research, however, Lombroso (and many of his contemporaries) would rely on an inductorium developed by the German physiologist Emil DuBois-Reymond (1818–1896), which added a separate current interrupter to the circuit. And although earlier studies of sensibility to electricity had been performed by the German physiologist Ernst von Leyden, Lombroso would later give his own name to the algometrical apparatus he had assembled in Pavia. See L. A. Geddes, "A Short History of the Electrical Stimulation of Excitable Tissue Including Electrotherapeutic Applications," *The Physiologist* (Supplement) 27:1 (February 1984): S-18; Cesare Lombroso, "Algometria ed estesiometria elettrica: rettificazione di priorità," *Annali universali di medicina* (1867): 654–56. For a discussion of the further development of the electrical algometer, see Luigi Roncoroni and Giovanni Albertotti, "Le sensibilità elettrica generale e dolorifica esaminate col Faradireometro in pazzi e normali," *Archivio* 14 (1893): 423–29; Cesare Lombroso, "Algometro e Faradireometro," *Archivio* 16 (1895): 262–63.

3. Lombroso, "Algometria elettrica," 102.

4. Ibid., 106.

5. On autoexperiment, also see Marco Treves, "Intorno alla sensibilità termica delle varie mucose," *Archivio* 22 (1901): 459–62. Treves had developed a thermoesthesiometer to test the body's sensibility to even small variations in temperature, and conducted a series of experiments to determine the "extreme limits" that were tolerable in the various mucous membranes of the body and on various regions of the skin. Treves recounted an experiment on his own urethra that went badly wrong: after leaving the device in for half an hour, "the extraction of the catheter was painful beyond words." Treves became alarmed when a citrine fluid came out of his urethra, and when he discovered the catheter was almost scalding when he touched it with his finger. Treves however repeated the experiment, "naturally guided by a prudence suggested by the experiment I have described," on the genitals, rectums, mouths and noses of male and female volunteers (461).

6. Neither the "recruitment" of subjects for these unusual procedures nor the experimental protocol is discussed in Lombroso's article. Another study by two of Lombroso's associates reports experiments on forty girls from a Bologna orphanage, sixty prostitutes examined in a "dermo-syphilitic" clinic, and fifteen women "of good standing" who consented to be examined "after much difficulty." Measurements of sensibility among the orphan girls were limited to the hands, forehead, tongue, and cheek, whereas prostitutes were tested in eleven places. "Naturally," we are told, "all of the exams performed on prostitutes could not be extended to all the normal women." Still, twelve of fourteen "normal" women apparently agreed to have shocks applied to their clitorises. See Raffaele Gurrieri and Ettore Fornasari, *I sensi e le anomalie somatiche nella donna normale e nella prostituta* (Turin: Bocca, 1893), 5–6. In addition, prostitutes were subjected to a thorough physical exam and asked about their medical and sexual history, whereas normal women had only their age and visible "degenerative characteristics" recorded (18–24). On recruitment, also see Raffaele Gurrieri, "La sensibilità nella donna normale e la prostituta," *Archivio* 14 (1893): 185–90, in which the author thanks the directors of the Cliniche di Sant'Orsola and the Ospedale Maggiore in Bologna for allowing him to investigate the sensibility of fifty patients there.

7. Lombroso, "Algometria elettrica," 103.

8. Ibid., 120. In addition, many mentally ill persons seemed to be more sensitive on the forehead than were normal persons.

9. See Martin Pernick, *A Calculus of Suffering: Pain, Professionalism and Anesthesia in Nineteenth-Century America* (New York: Columbia University Press, 1985). On the "modernity" of the scientific understanding of pain see René Fülöp-Miller, *Triumph Over Pain*, trans. Eden and Cedar Paul (New York: Literary Guild, 1938), 392.

10. See, for example, Edward James Swift, "Sensibility to Pain," *The American Journal of Psychology* 11 (3) (1900): 312–17; Ada Carman, "Pain and Strength Measurements of 1,507 School Children in Saginaw, Michigan," *The American Journal of Psychology* 10 (3) (1899): 392–98; Gurrieri and Fornasari, *I sensi e le anomalie somatiche;* Salvatore

Ottolenghi, *La sensibilità dei sordomuti* (Rome: Tip. Dell'Unione Cooperative Editrice, 1895); Roncoroni and Albertotti, "Le sensibilità elettrica."

11. See, for example, Lombroso, *La perizia;* Cesare Lombroso, *Lezioni di medicina legale,* 2nd ed. (Turin: Bocca, 1900); Salvatore Ottolenghi, *Polizia scientifica: identificazione fisica e psichica; investigazioni giudiziarie* (Rome: Società Poligrafica Editrice, 1907). On the rise of legal medicine in Europe and the United States see Michael Clark and Catherine Crawford, eds., *Legal Medicine in History* (Cambridge: Cambridge University Press, 1994). For Italy in particular, see Patrizia Guarnieri, *A Case of Child Murder: Law and Science in Nineteenth-Century Tuscany,* trans. Claudia Miéville (London: Polity Press, 1993) and Angelo Zuccarelli, "L'evoluzione odierna della medicina legale e l'antropologia criminale," *Psichiatria: Gazzetta Trimestrale* 5 (1887):149–64.

12. Augusto Tamburini, "L'applicazione del metodo sperimentale nella semeiotica psichiatrica," in *L'opera di Cesare Lombroso,* 61.

13. See Ernst Heinrich Weber, *De Tactu* (1834), reprinted in *The Sense of Touch,* trans. H. E. Ross (New York: Academic Press, 1978).

14. Lombroso, "Algometria ed estesiometria elettrica," 655.

15. Lombroso, "Algometria elettrica," 104. Augusto Tamburini (1848–1919) and Enrico Morselli (1852–1929) found that "idiots" did not, in fact, pay adequate attention; these researchers relied on subjects' reflexes and (following Foà and Moritz Schiff's work on animals) on the dilation of the pupils as an indication of painful sensation. "Delle degenerazioni fisiche e morali dell'uomo: idioti," *Rivista sperimentale di freniatria e di medicina legale* 2 (1876): 552–67.

16. Ottolenghi, *La sensibilità dei sordomuti,* 16. Ottolenghi, asserting a professional competence, reassured his readers that his "familiarity with this kind of research, and attentive observation of the individual and of his expression during the exam, permitted [him] to ensure that [he] was always successful at catching the moment at which the stimulus used provoked real pain."

17. Roncoroni and Albertotti, "Le sensibilità elettrica," 428. Richard Behan found that susceptibility to pain depended chiefly on the build of individuals ("those of a thin and neurotic build suffer much more severely than do the heavier and more robust") and on the "degree of mentality": "the higher the development and the more vivid the imagination, the greater is the susceptibility." *Pain: Its Origin, Conduction, Perception, and Diagnostic Significance* (New York: Appleton, 1916), 115.

18. See the remarks of Tamburini, who found algometrical results were difficult to compare because researchers used apparatuses and batteries of differing sizes, intensities, and quality. "L'applicazione del metodo sperimentale," 62. Tamburini suggested this inconvenience had been remedied by the introduction of the Faradimeter.

19. For a survey of algometrical methods see Franz Geotzl, Daniel Burrill, and Andrew Ivy, "A Critical Analysis of Algesimetric Methods with Suggestions for a Useful Procedure," *Quarterly Bulletin of Northwestern University Medical School* 17(4)(1943): 280–91. For discussion of a more

recent device, see Barnard Tursky, Peter D. Watson, and D. N. O'Connell, "A Concentric Shock Electrode for Pain Stimulation," *Psychophysiology* 1(3) (1965): 296–98.

20. Paolo Mantegazza, *Fisiologia del dolore,* new edition, (Florence: Bemporad, 1930), 323–24.

21. For discussions of the feud, see Bulferetti, *Cesare Lombroso,* 160; Lombroso-Ferrero, *Cesare Lombroso,* 101–3; Renzo Villa, *Il deviante e i suoi segni,* 124–25.

22. Lombroso, "Algometria elettrica," 113–14.

23. For earlier discussions, see, for example, Montesquieu's (1689–1755) reflections "On the laws in their relation to the nature of the climate." Montesquieu sought to link degrees of sensibility to both pain and pleasure to degrees of latitude: "It is evident that the large bodies and coarse fibers of the northern peoples are less capable of falling into disorder than the delicate fibers of the peoples of hot countries; therefore, the soul is less sensitive to pain. A Muscovite has to be flayed before he feels anything." *The Spirit of the Laws,* trans. Anne Cohler, Basia Miller, and Harold Stone (Cambridge: Cambridge University Press, 1989), 233.

24. Pernick, *A Calculus of Suffering,* 157. For a general discussion of the problem of pain and its management in the nineteenth century, see Roselyne Rey, *The History of Pain,* trans. Louise Wallace, J. A. Cadden, and S. W. Cadden (Cambridge: Harvard University Press, 1993), 132–260.

25. Fülöp-Miller, *Triumph Over Pain,* 397. Other researchers were more inclined to be wary of claims that, for example, "the Hebrew stands pain less easily than any other race." See Behan, *Pain,* 112. On animals and humans, see George Mivart, *On the Genesis of Species* (New York: D. Appleton, 1871), 277: "The momentary pang, the present pain, which beasts endure, though real enough, is yet, doubtless, not to be compared with the suffering which is produced in man through his high prerogative of self-consciousness."

26. Fülöp-Miller, *Triumph Over Pain,* 397.

27. See, for example, discussions among physicians of women's suffering during menstruation: sensibility was found to be highest among upper-class women, and lowest among peasants and savages. Although some advocated the further development of the sensibility of national populations (see M. Maurice Wolff, *L'education nationale* (Paris: Giard et Brière, 1867)), others such as the physiologist Angelo Mosso called for measures to *reduce* the sensibility of women and men in civilized society. *Les exercises physiques et le dévelopment intellectuel* (Paris: Félix Alcan, 1904), 210–13. Mosso relies on the studies made by George Engelmann of menstrual discomfort among women in the United States: "The American Girl of To-day: Modern Education and Functional Health," *American Physical Education Review* 6 (1) (1901):49.

28. Francis Galton, *Inquiries into Human Faculty and Its Development* (London: Macmillan, 1883), 27.

29. Ibid., 32.

30. Cesare Lombroso, "Sull'algometria elettrica,"*Rendiconti (Reale istituto lombardo di scienze e lettere)* 1 (1868): 395.
31. Mantegazza, *Fisiologia del dolore,* 313. As he put it, "a clock can only become a chronograph by becoming more expensive and delicate" (158).
32. Ibid., 313.
33. Salvatore Ottolenghi, "La sensibilità e l'età," *Archivio* 16 (1895): 546, 551.
34. Ottolenghi, "La sensibilità e la condizione sociale," *Archivio* 19 (1898): 101–4. However, Ottolenghi found that some 25 percent of the lower classes possessed an upper class sensibility, whereas 28 percent of the upper classes had the diminished sensibility of the poor, suggesting anthropological and physiological inequalities were less "fatalistic" than had been supposed (103).
35. R. W. Felkin, "The Differences of Sensibility between Europeans and Negroes, and the Effect of Education in Increasing the Sensibility of Negroes," *Report of the Fifty-Ninth Meeting (1889) of the British Association for the Advancement of Science* (London: 1890), 787–88. On the education of the senses also see Jean-Marc-Gaspard Itard, *The Wild Boy of Aveyron,* trans. George and Muriel Humphrey (New York: Century, 1932 [1801]), 16–17, 48–49.
36. The Dinka men and women may well have been part of a traveling show. On Virchow's reliance on such exhibitions for his anthropometrical work, see Erwin Ackerknecht, *Rudolf Virchow: Doctor, Statesman, Anthropologist* (Madison: University of Wisconsin Press, 1953), 217.
37. Cesare Lombroso and Maria Carrara, "Contributo all'antropologia dei Dinka," *Archivio* 17 (1896): 349–63.
38. See W. McDougall, "Cutaneous Sensitivity," *Reports of the Cambridge Expedition to the Torres Straits, vol. II: Physiology and Psychology* (Cambridge: Cambridge University Press, 1901), 189–95. "In view of the oft-repeated statement that savages are less susceptible to pain than white men," wrote McDougall," it seemed a matter of some interest to obtain a measure of the threshold of sensibility to pain" (194). McDougall's experiments, under the supervision of W. H. R. Rivers, found that Murray Islander men had a sense of touch "twice as delicate" as English men (chiefly "inmates" of the Cheadle Convalescent Hospital) and a sensitivity to pain "hardly half as great" (195). The Cambridge expedition also addressed visual acuity, color vision, hearing, smell, taste, "muscular sense," variations in blood-pressure, and "reaction times." For a contemporary critique, see E. B. Titchener, "On Ethnological Tests of Sensation and Perception with Special Reference to Tests of Color Vision and Tactile Discrimination Described in the Reports of the Cambridge Expedition to Torres Straits," *Proceedings of the American Philosophical Society* 55 (1916): 204–36.
39. Paul Hyades and Joseph Deniker, eds., *Mission scientifique du Cap Horn, 1882–1883, vol. VII: Anthropologie, ethnographie* (Paris: Gauthier-Villars et fils, 1891).
40. MacDonald, *Criminology,* 70. For MacDonald, analgesia helped to explain the remarkable "hardiness" of criminals.
41. Ellis, *The Criminal,* 123. However, Paul Brouardel (1837–1906)

suggested that the analgesia of inmates was an effect of imprisonment. See Lombroso, *Le più recenti scoperti ed applicazioni della psichiatria ed antropologia criminale* (Turin: Bocca, 1893), 163.

42. Raffaele Garofalo, *Criminology*, trans. Robert Millar (Montclair, NJ: Patterson Smith, 1968[1914]), 92.

43. Ellis, *The Criminal*, 123.

44. Lombroso, *L'uomo delinquente*, 2nd ed., 89. Other researchers had mistaken the cowardice of criminals facing surgical procedures for signs of physical sensibility. See Lombroso, *Le più recenti scoperti*, 164.

45. Lombroso, *L'uomo delinquente*, 2nd ed., 90.

46. Lombroso, *L'uomo delinquente*, 5th ed., vol. 1, 388.

47. Lombroso, "Il mancinismo sensorio," 441–47 (the experiments cited had been performed by Antonio Marro). Compare G. Amadei and S. Tonnini, "La sensibilità laterale nei pazzi," *Archivio* 4 (1883): 511–12; Cesare Lombroso, "Sul mancinismo e destrismo tattile nei sani, nei pazzi, nei ciechi e nei sordomuti," *Archivio* 5 (1884): 187–97. Lombroso dismissed the popular notion that the blind and the deaf developed an exquisite sense of touch; the frequent obtuseness and lateralism of this sense instead showed that both conditions were more commonly due to degeneration than people supposed (197).

48. See, for some examples, Salvatore Ottolenghi, "L'olfatto nei criminali," *Archivio* 9 (1888): 495–99; "L'occhio del delinquente," *Archivio* 7 (1886): 543–54; "Il gusto nei criminali in rapporto coi normali," *Archivio* 10 (1889): 332–38; and Giuseppe Gradenigo, "L'udito nei delinquenti," *Archivio* 10 (1889): 325–31.

49. Ottolenghi, "L'olfatto nei criminali," 499. Ottolenghi had expected to find heightened olfactory abilities in criminals, as among savages and animals (495). Also see Lombroso-Ferrero, *Criminal Man*, 26.

50. Ibid., 251.

51. Ibid., 26.

52. Ibid., 248. "My father once detected simulation in a *soi-disant* hysterical patient by means of a piece of wood shaped and colored to represent a magnet. On application of either magnet, the real or sham one, the patient's sensations were identical, whereas hysterical persons experience very diverse sensations and are able to distinguish very sharply between the contact, not only of wood and metal, but of the different kinds of metal, and are particularly sensitive to the magnet" (248–49).

53. Ibid., 26. Also see Ottolenghi, "L'occhio del delinquente," 544–45, which cites a comparative study by Carl Seggel (b. 1837) of German soldiers and African "savages." Havelock Ellis, citing the work of Charles Oliver, suggested the "healthiness of eye in criminals" could be compared to a similar condition in imbeciles. Ellis, *The Criminal*, 128–29.

54. For a detailed discussion of experiments designed to test the sensibility of women, see Mary Gibson, "On the Insensitivity of Women: Science and the Woman Question in Liberal Italy, 1890–1910," *Journal of Women's History* 2 (2) (1990): 11–41. Also see David Horn, "This Norm Which Is Not One: Reading the Female Body in Lombroso's Anthropology," in *Deviant Bodies*, 109–28.

55. Cesare Lombroso, "The Physical Insensibility of Woman," *The Fortnightly Review* 51 (1892): 354–57. When a version of Lombroso's paper was read aloud by Charles Richet (1850–1935) at the International Congress of Experimental Psychology, some in the audience remained unpersuaded on this point. Psychologist Alexander Bain (1818–1903) warned that the paper's conclusions would likely be "tested by the critical judgment and experience of educated women," whereupon a Miss Foley observed that Lombroso, "in relying on the experience of surgeons and dentists, did not seem to have taken sufficiently into account the extent to which woman's superior power of enduring pain might be due, not to a less [sic] degree of sensibility, but to a greater degree of self-control." "La sensibilité de la femme," *International Congress of Experimental Psychology* (London: Williams & Northgate, 1892), 43–44.

56. Lombroso, *La donna delinquente*, 43–48.

57. Ibid., 44. Lombroso cites Campbell's *Differences in the Nervous Organization of Man and Woman: Physiological and Pathological* (London: Lewis, 1891).

58. For Ellis' own (skeptical) discussion of female frigidity, see *Studies in the Psychology of Sex* (New York: Random House, 1942), vol. 1, part 2, 203–27. Ellis rejected the suggestion that working-class women were naturally frigid (217n), and found more broadly that there was, in scientific circles, "a tendency to unduly minimize the sexual impulse in women" (227).

59. Lombroso, *La donna delinquente*, 48.

60. Ibid., 46–47.

61. Giuseppe Sergi, "Sensibilità femminile," *Archivio* 13 (1892): 5–6. Also see his *Dolore e piacere: storia naturale dei sentimenti* (Milan: Dumolard, 1894).

62. Lombroso, "The Physical Insensibility of Woman," 355. Here, as with criminals and savages, the insensibility of women appeared to be accompanied by a kind of "disvulnerability," enabling them to recover from surgery and injury. Also see Ellis, *Man and Woman: A Study of Human Secondary Sexual Characteristics*, 6th ed., (London: A. & C. Black, 1930), 151–54.

63. Lombroso, "The Physical Insensibility of Woman," 355.

64. Lombroso and Ferrero, *La donna delinquente*, 52.

65. Roncoroni and Albertotti, "Le sensibilità elettrica," 428.

66. Sergi, "Sensibilità femminile," 3–4. Though more interested in emotional than organic sensibility, Sergi found the two to be "indissolubly linked."

67. Galton, *Inquiries into Human Faculty*, 29.

68. Ibid., 29–30.

69. Francis Galton, "The Relative Sensitivity of Men and Women at the Nape of the Neck," *Nature* 50 (1894): 40–41.

70. Ibid., 41. Galton also reminded readers, citing Tennyson for support, of the greater moral variability of women. Galton's conclusions about the sensitivity of women were also arrived at by Mantegazza and a variety of British and American researchers. Much of this research is summarized in Ellis, *Man and Woman*, 144–54.

71. Salvatore Ottolenghi, "La sensibilité de la femme," *Revue scientifique,* 4th ser., 5 (13) (1896): 395–98.
72. Ibid., 396. Compare Charles Féré's distinction between "emotivity" and "sensibility." Féré (1852–1907), a psychiatrist and physician at Bicêtre, cautioned: "Because women more frequently present emotional troubles of a pathological sort, it is not necessary therefrom to conclude that they have a higher emotivity; *they have a defective emotivity in relation to their sensibility.* General and special sensibility is less in the feminine sex." *The Pathology of Emotions: Physiological and Clinical Studies,* trans. Robert Park (London: The University Press, 1899), 431. Also see G. T. W. Patrick, "The Psychology of Woman," *Popular Science Monthly* 47 (1895): 217.
73. Ottolenghi, "La sensibilité de la femme," 397–98.
74. Ibid., 398. Ottolenghi disputed Sergi's claim that women's excitability corresponded to a primitive degree of sensibility; in children, Ottolenghi countered, insensibility was the norm. Instead, excitability was a "sign of weakness, an exaggerated psycho-sensorial reaction that can mask true sensibility" (398).
75. Ibid. Also see Patrick, "The Psychology of Woman," 211.
76. Lombroso, "The Physical Insensibility of Woman," 356. "Inferior sensory irritability" also helped to explain the relatively low number of cases of sexual psychopathology among women, the association of chastity and femininity, and woman's acceptance, with "equal facility," of both polygamy and monogamy: "a certain physical obtuseness or indifference is at the root of her readiness to put up, according to circumstances, with either system" (357).
77. Gibson, "On the Insensitivity of Women."
78. An exception seemed to be that prostitutes tested more sensitive on the hands than normal women did, but the authors explained that prostitutes were diffident, egoistic and irritable, and because the hand was the first part of the body tested, they were likely to react too quickly and overestimate their sensibility. Gurrieri and Fornasari, *I sensi e le anomalie somatiche,* 17.
79. Ibid., 6. The breasts of women who had nursed were, however, found to be less sensitive than those of childless women (10). Experiments performed by the Russian anthropologist Pauline Tarnowsky [Praskov'ia Tarnovskaia] on the sensory capacities of 100 women criminals, fifty prostitutes, and fifty honest peasants offered no support for the "opinion that there is a notably reduced sensibility to pain among criminal women." "Sur les organes de sens des femmes criminelles et des prostituées," *Archivio* 14 (1893): 31. On Tarnowsky's studies of Russian prostitutes see Laurie Bernstein, *Sonia's Daughters: Prostitutes and Their Regulation in Imperial Russia* (Berkeley: University of California Press, 1995), 126–28.
80. Lombroso and Ferrero, *La donna delinquente,* 138–39.
81. Ibid., 140.
82. G. B. Verga, *Cenni storici e considerazioni intorno alla pazzia morale,* cited in Lombroso, *L'uomo delinquente,* 5th ed., vol. 2, 8–9. "Emotivity," Verga explained, could be understood as a late evolutionary development:

"latent in inferior organisms, it becomes active and moral in superior organisms" (9).

83. Salvatore Ottolenghi, while affirming the links between what he called "pain sensibility" and "psychic sensibility," used algometrical studies to expand the boundaries of the normal, arguing that deaf-mutes were "unfortunate" rather than "degenerate" (and hence should be accorded the juridical status of adults) because they proved themselves to have a normal sensibility to pain. *La sensibilità dei sordomuti.*

84. Garofalo, *Criminology,* 115. "It must be admitted," Garofalo encouraged his readers, "that this lack of vulnerability, very frequent in other races, as, for example, the Chinese, is seldom found among Europeans, and is especially rare in the city population, where even the lower social strata have acquired a certain degree of refinement."

85. Moriz Benedikt, "La disvulnerabilité des criminels," *Archivio* 7 (1886): 187.

86. Lombroso, *L'uomo delinquente,* 5th ed., vol. 1, 425.

87. Ellis, *The Criminal,* 125n. Also see J. Delboeuf, *Théorie générale de la sensibilité* (Brussels: F. Hayez, 1876).

88. Edward Tregear, "The Maoris of New Zealand," *Journal of the Anthropological Institute of Great Britain and Ireland* 19 (1890): 104. Frazer's questions had been published the previous year: J. G. Frazer and T. V. Holmes, "Questions on the Manners, Customs, Religion, Superstitions, &c. of Uncivilized or Semi-Civilized Peoples," *Journal of the Anthropological Institute of Great Britain and Ireland* 18 (1989): 431–40.

89. Benedikt, "La disvulnerabilité," 188.

90. For example, Ellis extracted a brief parenthetical remark made by surgeon T. H. Parke in his massive *Experiences in Equatorial Africa.* Commenting on the treatment of a Zanzibar man with a gunshot wound, Parke noted "Had this man been a European I would have preferred amputation under the circumstances: but the Zanzibaris have such wonderful power of repair of wounds, that I hoped he would recover fair use of the limb; and the event justified the anticipation." Thomas Heazle Parke, *My Personal Experiences in Equatorial Africa as Medical Officer of the Emin Pasha Relief Expedition* (London: Sampson Low, Marston & Co., 1891), 435.

91. George Harley, "Comparison between the Recuperative Bodily Power of Man in a Rude and in a Highly Civilised State; Illustrative of the Probable Recuperative Capacity of Men of the Stone-Age in Europe," *Journal of the Anthropological Institute of Great Britain and Ireland* 17 (1888): 108. Compare Victor Horsley, "Trephining in the Neolithic Period," *Journal of the Anthropological Institute of Great Britain and Ireland* 17 (1888): 100–102.

92. Harley, "Comparison," 108.

93. Ibid., 109.

94. Ibid., 111.

95. Ibid., 112.

96. Ibid. Harley cited as further evidence of a general degeneration the deleterious effects of animal breeding, which made, for example, the

Italian greyhound unable to survive a surgical operation that a mongrel cur would scarcely even notice.

97. Ibid., 113.
98. H. Ling Roth, "On the Signification of Couvade," *Journal of the Anthropological Institute of Great Britain and Ireland* 22 (1893): 204. For a contrasting discussion, see George Engelmann, *Labor among Primitive Peoples* (St. Louis: J. H. Chambers, 1882). For Engelmann, what was remarkable was the knowledge about labor positions found among primitive peoples. Modern birthing practices were by contrast marked as anomalous: "Does the great number of natural labors not point to a law greatly at variance with the teachings of modern obstetrics?" (xvi).
99. Roth, "On the Signification of Couvade," 205.
100. Ibid.
101. Lombroso, "Il delitto nella coscienza popolare," 30.
102. Pateri and Lombroso, "Sull'analgesia e anestesia dei criminali e dei pazzi morali," *Archivio* 4 (1883): 228.

Chapter 5

1. Lombroso, *L'uomo delinquente*, 5th ed., vol. 1, 411.
2. For a discussion of "affective sensibility" and "aberrations of the sentiments" see ibid., 428–34, as well as the following discussion.
3. Criminologists also undertook research on a variety of other reflexes. See, for example, Gina Lombroso, "Sur les réflexes cutanés chez les criminels et chez les normaux," *Congrès international d'anthropologie criminelle*, 294–95.
4. Lombroso, *L'uomo delinquente*, 5th ed., vol. 1, 411.
5. Ibid. On pathologies of the blush also see Charles Féré, *The Pathology of Emotions;* Harry Campbell, *Flushing and Morbid Blushing: Their Pathology and Treatment* (London: H. K. Lewis, 1890).
6. This conventional wisdom was ratified by a number of scientists in the late nineteenth and early twentieth centuries. See, for some examples, Charles Darwin, *The Expression of the Emotions in Man and Animals*, 3rd ed., ed. Paul Ekman (New York: Oxford University Press, 1998), 311; Arthur Mitchell, *About Dreaming, Laughing and Blushing* (Edinburgh: William Green, 1905); Charles Féré, *Dégénérescence et criminalité: essai physiologique*, 2nd ed. (Paris: Félix Alcan, 1895), 76–77; G. E. Partridge, "Blushing," *Pedagogical Seminary* 4 (April 1897) (3): 394; Havelock Ellis, *Man and Woman*, 399–425.

   Women's facility at blushing was not usually taken as evidence of a greater modesty or capacity for shame, but was instead often read as a sign of a greater susceptibility to emotional disturbances, or of a retarded evolutionary development. On the evolution of modesty, see Havelock Ellis, *Studies in the Psychology of Sex*, vol. 1, part 1, 1–84. Ellis's survey of the available research convinced him that reflex action generally was more developed in women and "less under the control of the higher centers." Broadly speaking, he concluded, women are "more ticklish." Ellis, *Man and Woman*, 405. Also see Lombroso, "Sur les réflexes cutanés." Some criminologists argued that women had, as a rule, less modesty than men. The proof, Giuseppe Sergi suggested, was that women were "always showing off as much of their chests, arms, and back as possible." Sergi, "Sensibilità femminile," 6. Lombroso, for his part, traced the origin of the Italian word for sexual modesty [*pudore*] to the Latin *putere*, to stink, suggesting that shame had its cultural origins in woman's need to hide the smells associated with menstruation. Such practices, he further suggested, habituated women to lying. Lombroso and Ferrero, *La donna delinquente*, 96.

7. Lombroso, *L'uomo delinquente*, 5th ed., vol. 1, 412.
8. Ibid., 413.
9. Ibid.
10. Bartolomeo Bergesio, "Sull'arrossimento nelle pazze," *Archivio* 5 (1884): 112–13.
11. G. Amadei and S. Tonnini, "Dell'arrossimento nei pazzi," *Archivio* 5 (1884): 113–14.
12. Lombroso, *L'uomo delinquente*, 5th ed., vol. 1, 427.
13. Ibid. On the history of the problem of sensibility and sensation among the mad, see Michel Foucault, *Madness and Civilization: A History of Insanity in the Age of Reason*, trans. Richard Howard, (New York: Random House, 1965), 156–58.
14. As we will see, Darwin relied on the writings of Alexander von Humboldt and James Cowles Prichard, among others.
15. See, for example, the discussions in Mary Ann O'Farrell, *Telling Complexions: The Nineteenth-Century English Novel and the Blush* (Durham: Duke University Press, 1997) and Christopher Ricks, *Keats and Embarrassment* (Oxford: Clarendon Press, 1974). For the influence of Darwin on Lombroso, see Pancaldi, *Darwin in Italy*, 139–51; Renzo Villa, "Cesare Lombroso," in *Dictionnaire du darwinisme*, vol. 2, 2677–80.
16. Janet Browne, "Darwin and the Expression of the Emotions," in *The Darwinian Heritage*, ed. David Kohn (Princeton: Princeton University Press, 1985), 317.
17. Thomas Burgess, *The Physiology or Mechanism of Blushing: Illustrative of the Influence of the Mental Emotion on the Capillary Circulation, with a General View of the Sympathies, and the Organic Relations of Those Structures with Which They Seem to be Connected* (London: John Churchill, 1839).
18. Ibid., iii.
19. Burgess cited in Darwin, *The Expression of the Emotions*, 335.
20. Burgess, *The Physiology or Mechanism of Blushing*, 22.
21. Ibid., 23. Also see Campbell, *Flushing and Morbid Blushing*, 36: "Blushing from shame is normal and legitimate, while blushing from shyness, except in the young and inexperienced, can scarcely be regarded as such, certainly not in its exaggerated forms." Campbell found that the shameful (legitimate) blush accounted for only ten percent of all cases.
22. Burgess, *The Physiology or Mechanism of Blushing*, 47.
23. Ibid., 26, emphasis in the original.

24. Ibid., 70.
25. Ibid., 33.
26. Alexander de Humboldt and Aimé Bonpland, *Personal Narrative of Travels to the Equinoctial Regions of the New Continent, during the Years 1799–1804,* trans. Helen Maria Williams, vol. 3 (London: Longman, 1818), 229–30. On Humboldt's writing about the Americas see Mary Louise Pratt, *Imperial Eyes: Travel Writing and Transculturation* (London: Routledge, 1992), 111–43.
27. Burgess, *Physiology or Mechanism of Blushing,* 30–31.
28. Ibid., 31.
29. The legibility of scars was also discussed by the physician and physiognomist Charles Bell (1774–1842), a contemporary of Burgess's who authored the influential *Anatomy and Philosophy of Expression as Connected with the Fine Arts,* 3rd ed. (London: John Murray, 1844). (An earlier version of Bell's argument is contained in *Essays on the Anatomy of Expression in Painting* (London: Hurst, Rees and Orme, 1806).) Bell's interest in the blush formed part of an argument about the "extensive influence of the corporeal on the intellectual part of man." *Anatomy and Philosophy of Expression,* 83. For Bell, blushing was a "suffusion" that "serves no purpose of the economy, whilst we must acknowledge the interest which it excites as an indication of mind" (95). Bell was, like Burgess, convinced that humans had a range of feeling unique to the species, and that particular muscles and mechanisms had been provided by God for rendering these visible. On this account, blushing was "a provision for expression" that "is not acquired; it is from the beginning." Blushing was also imagined to be an "advantage possessed by the fair family of mankind, and which must be lost to the dark; for I can hardly believe that a blush may be seen in the Negro." But Bell did allow that the white scars of blacks might redden with passion. "If the black blushes unseen, it only shews [sic] that the incidental colour does not affect the general structure and processes." Bell offered readers an analogy from the comparative anatomy of animals, which had revealed structures in some that were "apparently useless or superfluous," but which in other animals achieve "full developement [sic] and appropriate functions" (95–96).

    On Bell and his influence on Darwin, see Janet Browne, "Darwin and the Face of Madness," in *The Anatomy of Madness: Essays in the History of Psychiatry,* ed. W.F. Bynum, Roy Porter, and Michael Shepherd, vol. 1 (London: Tavistock, 1985), 151–65.
30. Compare Buffon's account of a "white Negresse," an albino Dominican woman who showed a "light shade of carnation on the cheeks when she approached a fire, or when she was overcome by the shame she felt at being seen naked." James Cowles Prichard, *Researches into the Physical History of Mankind,* 4th ed., vol. 1 (London: Houlston and Stoneman, 1851), 225. Also see O'Farrell, *Telling Complexions,* 84–85.
31. Burgess, *The Physiology or Mechanism of Blushing,* 47.
32. Browne, "Darwin and the Expression of the Emotions," 307. Darwin's sources were varied, including observations of children, the insane, and

the "commoner animals"; responses to questionnaires sent to missionaries and others; a study of masterpieces of painting and sculpture; and the research of Duchenne.

33. Darwin, *The Expression of the Emotions*, 17.
34. Browne, "Darwin and the Expression of the Emotions," 308–9.
35. Darwin, *The Expression of the Emotions*, 310.
36. Ibid.
37. Ibid.
38. Ibid., 336–40. See, for example, Henry Holland, *Medical Notes and Reflections* (London: Longman, 1839); Henry Maudsley, *Body and Mind: An Inquiry into Their Connection and Mutual Influence, Specially in Reference to Mental Disorders* (London: Macmillan, 1870); Pierre Gratiolet, *De la physiognomie et des mouvements d'expression* (Paris: J. Hetzel, 1865).
39. Darwin, *The Expression of the Emotions*, 324. For a contrasting view see Camille Mélinand, "Pourquoi rougit-on?" *Revue des Deux Mondes* 63 (119) (1893): 631–46. For Mélinand, blushing was always due to a single moral state: the feeling that another sees what one wishes to hide (637).
40. Darwin, *The Expression of the Emotions*, 324.
41. Ibid., 326.
42. Ibid.
43. Ibid., 313.
44. Ibid., 331.
45. Ibid.
46. Ibid., 343.
47. Ibid., 20. Also see Browne, "Darwin and the Face of Madness," 153.
48. For a discussion of the relations and correspondence of Darwin and Crichton-Browne, see Sander Gilman, "Darwin Sees the Insane," *Journal of the History of the Behavioral Sciences* 15 (1979): 253–62; Browne, "Darwin and the Face of Madness."
49. Darwin, *The Expression of the Emotions*, 311.
50. Browne, "Darwin and the Expression of the Emotions," 321.
51. Darwin, *The Expression of the Emotions*, 22.
52. Ibid.
53. O'Farrell, *Telling Complexions*, 85.
54. Ibid.
55. Darwin, *The Expression of the Emotions*, 317. The observation is part of a lengthy citation Darwin finds in Prichard, *Researches into the Physical History of Mankind*, 271: "The Indian, properly speaking, cannot blush, and the '*Erubescit, salva res est*,' cannot be applied to this unpolished race."
56. Prichard cited in Darwin, *The Expression of the Emotions*, 317.
57. Darwin, *The Expression of the Emotions*, 317.
58. Ibid., 318.
59. Ibid., 319.
60. Ibid., 335.
61. Dror, "Creating the Emotional Body," 173. On the physiology of emotion, also see Otniel Dror, "The Scientific Image Of Emotion:

Experience and Technologies of Inscription," *Configurations* 7 (1999): 355–401; "The Affect of Experiment: The Turn to Emotions in Anglo-American Physiology, 1900–1940," *Isis* 90 (1999): 205–37.

62. On Mosso's materialism (and its limits) and his relations to Schiff and Ludwig, see Claudio Pogliano, "Inquietudini della scienza positiva," *Giornale critico della filosofia italiana* 2(2) (1982): 207–21. Also see the entry on Mosso by Patrizia Guarnieri in *Dictionnaire du darwinisme*, vol. 2, 3103–4.

63. Angelo Mosso, *Fear*, 5th ed., trans. E. Lough and F. Kiesow (London: Longmans, Green, and Co., 1896), 14.

64. Ibid., 15.

65. Ibid., 16.

66. Ibid., 10.

67. Ibid., 10–11.

68. Ibid., 89.

69. Ibid., 90.

70. Paraphrasing Mosso, Havelock Ellis wrote that "the heart, the whole circulatory system, and all the viscera and glands form, as it has been said, a kind of sounding-board, against which every change in consciousness, however slight, at once reverberates." Ellis, *Man and Woman*, 401.

71. Darwin, *The Expression of the Emotions*, 323. Darwin relied in part on the results of Crichton-Browne's experiments with amyl nitrite.

72. Partridge, "Blushing," 391. Also see Campbell, for the whom "the blush is the external sign of an inward working of the mind; it betrays that which one would be at great pains to conceal; the strongest effort at self-control is powerless to hide this glaring testimony to the inner thought." *Flushing and Morbid Blushing*, 134.

73. Ibid., 389; cf. Ellis, *Man and Woman*, 404–5; *Studies in the Psychology of Sex*, vol. 1 (New York: Random House, 1942), 72–73.

74. Patrizi, *Dopo Lombroso: nuove correnti nello studio della genialità e del delitto* (Milan: Società Editrice Libraria, 1916), 83, emphasis added. This would allow scientists to measure, among other things, the "sincerity" or "intensity" of an emotion.

75. Mosso, *Fear*, 82.

76. Bertino was one of several subjects with openings in the skull that allowed researchers to investigate reactions of the brain to varied stimuli. For studies of an "epileptic idiot" confined to an asylum in Turin, and suffering from a temporoparietal lesion, see Giovanni Albertotti and Angelo Mosso, "Osservazioni sui movimenti del cervello di un idiota epilettico," *Giornale della R. Accademia di medicina di Torino* (1878). Also see Enrico Morselli and Guido Bordoni-Uffreduzzi, "Sui cangiamenti della circolazione cerebrale prodotti dalle diverse percezioni semplici," *Archivio* 5 (1884): 111–12. The authors conducted 112 experiments with tactile, electrical, olfactory and other stimuli on a man who suffered from osteosarcoma and was missing a large portion of his skull, allowing them to measure the "cerebral pulse." Also see Pogliano, "Inquietudini della scienza positiva," 211.

77. Mosso, *Fear,* 79–80. In another experiment, Mosso found he could make Bertino lose consciousness by applying pressure to his carotid artery; for Eugène Gley, this was further proof of the link between psychological and material phenomena. Gley, *Etudes de psychologie physiologique et pathologique* (Paris: Alcan, 1903), 90.
78. Mosso, *Fear,* 77.
79. Patrizi, *Dopo Lombroso,* 79.
80. According to Marta Braun, the device was based on the kymograph, developed by the German physiologist Carl Ludwig (1816–1895), the "first application of graphing instruments to physiology." Braun, *Picturing Time,* 18. On the work of Marey, also see François Dagognet, *Etienne-Jules Marey : A Passion for the Trace,* trans. Robert Galeta with Jeanine Herman (New York : Zone Books, 1992); Anson Rabinbach, *The Human Motor: Energy, Fatigue, and the Origins of Modernity* (Berkeley: University of California Press, 1990), especially 84–119. On the history of the sphygmograph also see Robert G. Frank, "American Physiologists in German Laboratories, 1865–1914," in *Physiology in the American Context (1850–1940),* ed. Gerald Geison (Bethesda: American Physiological Society, 1987), 34–35.
81. Braun, *Picturing Time,* 18.
82. Gley, *Etudes de psychologie physiologique;* Alfred Binet and J. Courtier, "Influence de la vie émotionelle sur la coeur, la respiration et la circulation capillaire," *L'Année psychologique* 3 (1897): 65–126; Alfred Binet and Nicolas Vaschide, "Influence du travail intellectuel, des émotions, et du travail physique sur la pression du sang," *L'Année psychologique* 3 (1897): 127–83.
83. Gley, *Etudes de psychologie physiologique,* 23–25. On the work required to established a state ostensibly free of emotion in physiological experiments also see Otniel Dror, "The Scientific Image of Emotion," 382.
84. Mosso, *Fear,* 93. For a more detailed discussion of the plethysmograph's history and construction, see Angelo Mosso, "Sopra un nuovo metodo per scrivere i movimenti dei vasi sanguini nell'uomo," *Atti della R. Accademia delle scienze di Torino* 11 (1875–1876): 21–81.
85. Mosso, *Fear,* 94.
86. Mosso, "Sopra un nuovo metodo," 37.
87. Mosso, *Fear,* 94.
88. Mosso, "Sopra un nuovo metodo," 37–38.
89. Havelock Ellis, "Urinary Bladder, Influence of the Mind on the," *A Dictionary of Physiological Medicine,* ed. Hack Tuke, vol. 2 (Philadelphia: Blakiston, 1892), 1340. See Angelo Mosso and Paolo Pellacani, "Sur les fonctions de la vessie," *Archives italiennes de biologie* 1 (1892): 97–128; 291–324.
90. Ibid., 107.
91. Ellis, "Urinary Bladder," 1340.
92. Ellis, *Studies in the Psychology of Sex,* 73. Ellis followed Féré and Partridge in seeing the blush as a vestige of the "general erethism of sex,

in which shame originated." The blush was once widely diffused, and still was among women of the lower races, while in more civilized peoples it had become confined to the face as a result of sexual selection. Also see Partridge, "Blushing," 394.

93. Féré, *Dégénérescence et criminalité*, 20.
94. Angelo Mosso, "A l'étude de la circulation du sang chez l'homme," *Archives italiennes de biologie* 5 (1884): 130–43. Also see Havelock Ellis, "Plethysmograph and Balance," *A Dictionary of Physiological Medicine*, ed. Hack Tuke (Philadelphia: Blakiston, 1892), vol. 2, 964–66.
95. Frank, "The Tell-Tale Heart," 212.
96. Dror, "Creating the Emotional Body," 183.
97. Among Lombroso's least successful experiments was an attempt to characterize varied kinds of dangerous persons based on asymmetries of blood pressure in the right and left arms. See Lombroso and Audenino, "Contribution à l'étude de l'asymétrie de pression du sang," 282–85.
98. Filippo Cougnet and Cesare Lombroso, "Sfigmografia di delinquenti ed alienati (communicazione preventiva)," *Archivio* 2 (1881): 234–35; "La reazione vasale nei delinquenti e nei pazzi," *Archivio* 5 (1884): 1–16.
99. Lombroso-Ferrero, *Criminal Man*, 203.
100. Ibid.
101. Lombroso, *L'uomo delinquente*, 5th ed., vol. 1, 413.
102. Ibid., 414.
103. Ibid., 415.
104. Ibid., 416–17.
105. Cesare Lombroso, "La polizia scientifica," *Archivio* 7 (1886): 611.
106. Lombroso, *Le più recenti scoperti*, 274.
107. Lombroso, *L'uomo delinquente*, 5th ed., vol. 1, 421.
108. Ibid., 422.
109. Ibid.
110. Ottolenghi, "L'opera di Cesare Lombroso e la polizia scientifica," 227. Ottolenghi reports that he had never missed an opportunity to use the sphygmograph in those cases where it was necessary to "scrutinize the psyche for evidence of guilt or simulation."
111. Cougnet and Lombroso, "Sfigmografia di delinquenti ed alienati," 234–35.
112. Augusto Tamburini, Review of Mosso, "D'un nuovo metodo per scrivere i movimenti dei vasi sanguini nell'uomo," *Rivista di freniatria sperimentale* 3 (1877): 55–56.
113. Augusto Tamburini, Review of Wolff, "Del metodo clinico in psichiatria," *Rivista di freniatria sperimentale* 3 (1877): 433–47. Ottolenghi and Carrara proposed in 1895 that the handwriting of criminals and lunatics also could reveal signs of emotional states produced by particular stimuli. See Salvatore Ottolenghi and Mario Carrara, "Un nuovo carattere rilevato nella scrittura dei criminali e degli alienati colla pena elettrica Edison," *Archivio* 15 (1894): 290–91.
114. Lombroso-Ferrero, *Criminal Man*, 225.
115. Ibid., 262–65. A few months later, there was a similar assault on another girl living in the same house. "In this case, however, the victim survived

and was able to point out the criminal—an imbecile, afflicted with goitre, stammering, strabismus, hydrocephaly, trochocephaly, and plagiocephaly, with arms of disproportionate length, the son and grandson of drunkards, who confessed the double crime and entreated pardon for the 'trifling offence' since he had always done his duty and swept the staircase, even on the day he committed the crime."

116. On Lombroso's place in the (contested) history of the lie detector see, for example, Ken Alder, "To Tell the Truth: The Polygraph Exam and the Marketing of American Expertise," *Historical Reflections/Reflexions Historiques* 24 (1998): 494; Eugene Block, *Lie Detectors: Their History and Use* (New York: David McKay, 1977), 11–12; John A. Larson, *Lying and Its Detection: A Study of Deception and Deception Tests* (Chicago: University of Chicago Press, 1932), 171–74; and William Moulton Marston, *The Lie Detector Test* (New York: Richard Smith, 1938), 19–20. Marston, who took credit for the discovery in 1915 of "the only workable lie detection test," complained that "there are almost as many men who claim to be the 'inventor of the Lie Detector' as there were monks, in the old days, who claimed to posses a piece of the true cross" (18). On Marston, who could also say (without controversy) that he had invented the female superhero Wonder Woman, see Geoffrey Bunn, "The Lie Detector, *Wonder Woman* and Liberty: The Life and Work of William Moulton Marston," *History of the Human Sciences* 10 (1997): 91–119.

117. Lombroso-Ferrero, *Criminal Man*, 224–25.

118. On the "honesty" of the body, see Alder, "To Tell the Truth," 4878. On the problem of "transparency," see Vittorio Benussi (1878–1927), "The Respiratory Symptoms of Lying," *Polygraph* 4 (1975[1914]): 52.

119. Münsterberg, *On the Witness Stand: Essays on Psychology and Crime* (New York: Clark Boardman, 1923), 114.

120. Benussi, "The Respiratory Symptoms of Lying," 52. Benussi is credited with the development of pneumograph, which recorded changes in breathing patterns associated with deception. On the skin galvanometer as a "betrayal of the inmost mind," see Münsterberg, *On the Witness Stand*, 130. Dror quotes Otto Veraguth on the psychogalvanic response: "We cannot prevent the electric confession of our skins." Dror, "Creating the Emotional Body," 183.

121. Compare Münsterberg, *On the Witness Stand*, 76; Lombroso, "La polizia scientifica," 611.

122. Münsterberg, *On the Witness Stand*, 76.

123. See Alan Hyde, *Bodies of Law* (Princeton: Princeton University Press, 1997), 173–86.

Chapter 6

1. Of course, as Patrizia Guarnieri notes for psychiatric records, these forms were not always completed by admitting physicians. "Misurare le diversità," 139.

2. Cesare Lombroso, "Il piacere e il dolore: teoria scientifica della sensibilità," in *Antologia lombrosiana,* ed. Luigi Ferrio (Pavia: Società Editrice Pavese, 1963), 89.

3. Lombroso, "Prolusione al corso di medicina legale," in *Antologia lombrosiana,* 83.

4. Garofalo, "Le perizie psichiatriche," *La scuola positiva* 1 (1891): 577.

5. Ibid., 577. For a brilliant microhistorical account of expert testimony see Guarnieri, *A Case of Child Murder.*

6. Foucault, "About the Concept of the 'Dangerous Individual,'" 13.

7. Lombroso, "Prolusione," 84.

8. Antonio Raffaele, "Della dignità del medico nelle questioni di giustizia e delle relative riforme all'attuale legislazione," *Rivista di freniatria sperimentale* 3 (1877): 73–74.

9. Guarnieri, "Misurare le diversità," 129. Also see *A Case of Child Murder.*

10. Lombroso, "Prolusione," 84.

11. Raffaele, "Della dignità del medico," 74.

12. Lombroso's daughter informs us the author took no pleasure in authoring this text, and others like it, because he "hated anything that smacked of the scholastic." Lombroso-Ferrero, *Cesare Lombroso,* 399. In *Lezioni di medicina legale,* Lombroso notes gruffly that the book is written out of a "professional duty" rather than a "deeply felt desire." He reports he has been "disgusted to see what was spoken from the professor's chair interpreted carelessly, and at times turned on its head, by impatient listeners and imitators." Cesare Lombroso, *Lezioni di medicina legale,* 2nd ed. (Turin: Bocca, 1900), v.

13. Lombroso, *La perizia,* viii.

14. Ibid., ix.

15. Ibid., 486.

16. Ibid., 487.

17. Ibid.

18. Ibid. "No naturalist," argues Lombroso by way of comparison, "would refuse to analyze, tissue by tissue, insofar as this were possible, an unknown animal before fixing its taxonomic position."

19. Lombroso, "Criminal Anthropology," 45–46.

20. Ibid., 46.

21. Ibid., 47.

22. Ibid., 48. For more on the Elmira Reformatory, see Rafter, *Creating the Born Criminal,* 93–109.

23. See Horn, *Social Bodies,* 31–34; also see Gibson, *Born to Crime,* 234–41.

24. Ibid., 127–74.

25. Foucault, "About the Concept of the '"Dangerous Individual,'" 14.

26. Ibid., 15.

27. See, for example, Malcolm Feeley and Jonathan Simon, "Actuarial Justice: The Emerging New Criminal Law," in *The Futures of Criminology,* ed. David Nelken (London: Sage, 1994), 173–201.

28. Patrizia Guarnieri and Claudio Pogliano, "Il positivismo," in *La storia: I grandi problemi dal Medioevo all'Età Contemporanea* (Turin: UTET, 1988), vol. 7, part 2, 305.

29. See Franca Pieroni Bortolotti, *Alle origini del movimento femminile in Italia, 1848–1892* (Turin: Einaudi, 1963).

30. In fact, Lombroso and Ferrero multiplied the objects of scientific and social technical concern to include hysterical offenders, suicides, criminal lunatics, occasional criminals, epileptic delinquents, and those guilty of crimes of passion.

31. Maternity, Lombroso and Ferrero suggested, was the antithesis of criminality, and had never been "the motive power of crime in a woman." Lombroso and Ferrero, *The Female Offender,* 154.

32. Ibid., 216.

33. Ibid., 151.

34. The discussion of "therapies" was added by Lombroso's daughter to later editions of the volume, on the basis of Lombroso's notes. See Lombroso and Ferrero, *La donna delinquente,* 449.

35. Ibid., 3; Lombroso-Ferrero, *Criminal Man,* 181.

36. Ibid. For a discussion of proposals for male criminals, see Lombroso, *Crime: Its Causes and Remedies,* 245–451.

37. Lombroso-Ferrero, *Criminal Man,* 181.

38. Lombroso and Ferrero, *La donna delinquente,* 453–54.

39. Lombroso and Ferrero, *The Female Offender,* 154. At the same time, Lombroso and Ferrero recommended relaxing the punishments for abortion and infanticide. *La donna delinquente,* 453–56.

40. Horn, *Social Bodies,* 10–13. Also see Denise Riley, *"Am I that Name?" Feminism and the Category of "Women" in History* (Minneapolis: University of Minnesota Press, 1988).

41. Maria Sinatra, *L'aurora della psicotecnica* (Bari: Laterza, 1999), 19. Much of Patrizi's early work focused on relations of cerebral activity and muscular force, but he was also interested in applying criminology to art and literature. His book *Dopo Lombroso,* in fact, consists of two parts, the first devoted to the anthropological and bio-psychological study of figurative art, and the second to criminological thought and practice.

42. Patrizi, *Dopo Lombroso,* 79.

43. Ibid.

44. Ibid., 88.

45. Ibid., 89.

46. Ibid., 91.

47. For a contrasting reading, see Gibson, *Born to Crime,* 216.

48. Giuseppe Vidoni, *Valore e limiti dell'endocrinologia nello studio del delinquente* (Turin: Bocca, 1923), 100–1. Also see Gibson, *Born to Crime,* 217–23. Gibson finds that criminal anthropology reached its "theoretical culmination" (220) in 1943 with the publication of the *Dizionario di criminologia,* ed. Eugenio Florian, Alfredo Niceforo, and Nicola Pende, 2 vols. (Milan: Vallardi, 1943).

49. Berman et al., "Regional Cerebral Blood Flow in Monozygotic Twins Discordant and Concordant for Schizophrenia," *Archives of General Psychiatry* 49 (1992): 927–34.

50. Adrian Raine et al., "Reduced Prefrontal and Increased Subcortical Brain Functioning Assessed Using Positron Emission Tomography in

Predatory and Affective Murderers," *Behavioral Sciences and the Law* 16 (1998): 319–32. Also see Adrian Raine, Monet Buchsbaum, and Lori LaCasse, "Brain Abnormalities in Murderers Indicated by Positron Emission Tomography," *Biological Psychiatry* 42 (1997): 495–508. On PET scans and the fashioning of identities, see Joseph Dumit, "A Digital Image of the Category of the Person: PET Scanning and Objective Self-Fashioning," in *Cyborgs and Citadels: Anthropological Interventions in Emerging Sciences and Technologies*, ed. Gary Downey and Joseph Dumit (Santa Fe: SRA Press, 1997), 83–102.

51. See Terrance J. Williams et al., "Finger-Length Ratios and Sexual Orientation," *Nature* 404 (2000): 455–56. The study measured the hands of 720 men and women at public streets fairs in San Francisco, who were asked about their sexual orientation, handedness, and birth order. The authors also cite research purporting to link male homosexuality with higher levels of circulating androgens, larger genitalia, and "more 'masculine' auditory evoked potentials" than heterosexual men (455). For a history of scientific constructions of the homosexual body, see Jennifer Terry, *An American Obsession: Science, Medicine, and Homosexuality in America* (Chicago: University of Chicago Press, 1999).

52. See, for example, Simon LeVay, "Evidence for Anatomical Differences in the Brains of Homosexual Men," *Science* 253 (1991): 1034–37; Dean Hamer et al., "A Linkage between DNA Markers on the X Chromosome and Male Sexual Orientation," *Science* 361 (1993): 321–27.

53. See Jeffrey Botkin, William McMahon, and Leslie Francis, eds., *Genetics and Criminality: The Potential Misuse of Scientific Information in Court* (Washington: American Psychological Association, 1999), especially Mary Coombs, "A Brave New Crime—Free World?" 227–42.

54. For an example of the research purporting to link XYY and violence, see P. A. Jacobs et al., "Aggressive Behaviour, Mental Subnormality and the XYY Male," *Nature* 208 (1965): 1351–52. For critical reviews of this research, see Jonathan Kaplan, *The Limits and Lies of Human Genetic Research: Dangers for Social Policy* (New York: Routledge, 2000), 89–103.

55. Lawrence Taylor, *Born to Crime: The Genetic Causes of Criminal Behavior* (Westport: Greenwood Press, 1984), 81.

56. Ibid., 20. Eysenck suggested in 1964 that there could be "some kind of gene, chromosome or other structure which could be the physiological or neurological basis for differences between the criminal and non-criminal kind of person." Cited in Taylor, *Born to Crime*, 20.

57. Ibid., 161.

Name Index

Subject Index